John Taylor is the bass player and a founding member of Duran Duran. To date, the band has sold over 80 million records worldwide and been awarded six prestigious Lifetime Achievement awards, including the BRITs and MTV. Their most recent album *All You Need is Now*, debuted at number one in fifteen countries. John has also recorded and toured with members of Chic, The Sex Pistols and Guns N' Roses. *In the Pleasure Groove* was an international bestseller in hardback and was on both the *New York Times* and *Sunday Times* bestseller lists.

Born in Birmingham, John now lives between Wiltshire and Los Angeles. He is married with three children.

IN THE PLEASURE GROOVE
LOVE, DEATH & DURAN DURAN

JOHN TAYLOR
with TOM SYKES

sphere

SPHERE

First published in Great Britain in 2012 by Sphere
This paperback edition published in 2013 by Sphere

A CIP catalogue record for this book
is available from the British Library.

ISBN 978-0-7515-4903-4

Designed by Patty Palazzo

Typeset in Bembo by M Rules
Printed and bound in Great Britain by
Clays Ltd, St Ives plc

Papers used by Sphere are from well-managed forests
and other responsible sources.

MIX
Paper from
responsible sources
FSC
www.fsc.org FSC® C104740

Sphere
An imprint of
Little, Brown Book Group
100 Victoria Embankment
London EC4Y 0DY

An Hachette UK Company
www.hachette.co.uk

www.littlebrown.co.uk

To look backward for a while is to refresh the eye,
to restore it, and to render it the more fit
for its prime function of looking forward.

MARGARET FAIRLESS BARBER

And I won't cry for yesterday, there's an
ordinary world somehow I have to find
And as I try to make my way to the ordinary world
I will learn to survive.

DURAN DURAN, 'ORDINARY WORLD'

CRISIS=OPPORTUNITY

CHINESE PROVERB

IN THE PLEASURE GROOVE
LOVE, DEATH & DURAN DURAN

Brighton, 29 June 1981

It's a Monday night at the Brighton Dome, two weeks before our third single, 'Girls on Film', is due out. It's a week after my twenty-first birthday.

The lights go down and 'Tel Aviv' strikes up. We have chosen the haunting, Middle Eastern-inspired instrumental track from our new album to function as a curtain-raiser, to let the audience know the show is about to begin.

But something strange is happening. None of us can hear the music. What is going on out there? The sound of an audience. Getting louder. Larger. Chanting.

Screaming.

And then, out onto the stage, behind the safety curtain, we go. A frisson of fear. We look to each other with nervous glances. Faces are made. *'Is that for real?'*

We plug in; bass working, drums beating, keyboards and guitars in tune.

Ready.

'Tel Aviv' reaches its coda. Here we go.

And the curtain rises on our new life.

The power of our instruments, amplified and magnified by PA stacks that reach to the roof, is no match for the overwhelming force of teenage sexual energy that comes surging at us in unstoppable waves from the auditorium.

The power of it is palpable. I can feel it take control of my arms, my legs, my fingers, for the duration of the opening song. It is unrelenting, waves of it crashing onstage.

There is no way we can be heard, but that doesn't matter. No one is listening to us anyway. They have come to hear themselves. To be heard. And what they have to say is this: 'Take me, ME! I am the one for you! John! Simon! Nick! Andy! Roger!'

As our first song grinds to a hiccupping halt, we turn to each other for support. But the next song has already somehow begun without us. We are not in control any more. Seats are smashed. Clothes torn. Stretcher cases. Breakdowns. It is a scene out of Bosch. Every female teenager in Britain is having her own teenage crisis, simultaneously as one, *right now*, vaguely in time to our music. The frenzy is contagious. We are the catalyst for their explosions, one by one, by the thousands.

We have become idols, icons. Subjects of worship.

PART 1
ANALOGUE YOUTH

1 Hey Jude

I am four years old. Confident and shy. Hair blonder than it would be in my teen years. In shorts and sandals, a young prince of the neighbourhood, the south Birmingham suburb of Hollywood. How perfect.

Ten o'clock in the morning on any given weekday in 1964, and I have stepped down off the porch and wait, kicking at the grooved concrete driveway, watching as Mum pulls the front door closed, locks it up, and puts the key in her handbag; she puts the handbag in the shopping bag, and off we go. Left off the drive and up the hill that is the street on which we live, Simon Road. Our house is number 34, one up from where the road ends.

We walk together along the pavement, counting down: 32, 30, 28. On the left side of the street are all the even-numbered semi-detached houses, single buildings designed to function as two separate homes (ours is twinned with number 36). Across the street, the odd-numbered houses are detached, each building a single dwelling, all much larger than ours, and so are the back gardens, which are long and tree-filled and bordered at the bottom by a stream. The driveways are slicker too, with space for more than one car.

Later on, when I started to become a little status-aware, I would ask my parents, 'Why didn't you pay the extra six hundred quid that would have got us a stream at the back?'

I hold Mum's hand, remembering the Beatles song that is so often on the radio, as the incline gets steeper. We reach the crest of the hill, where Simon Road meets Douglas Road, and turn right.

We pass a twelve-foot-high holly bush, the only evidence I have found that suggests where the estate got its name. We march on, crossing Hollywood Lane in front of Gay Hill Golf Club, an establishment that will assume mythical proportions in my imagination as a venue for wife-swapping parties, not that anyone in my family ever set foot in the place. There was no truth in the rumour.

Cars flash by, at twenty or even thirty miles an hour. We make it to Highter's Heath Lane, another main artery of the neighbourhood, which must be taken if you're visiting the old Birmingham of nans and aunts and uncles, recreational parks and bowling greens. It gets traversed a lot by the Taylor family at weekends. It must also be used by mother and son if we are to reach our destination today – St Jude's parish church.

All this walking. We've been doing it together for as long as I can remember. Mum doesn't drive and never will. At first, I'd be in my pushchair, but now I'm old enough, we walk side by side, which must have come as relief to Mum. There's no complaining from me, it just is and ever shall be. Amen.

She's sweating now in her woollen skirt and raincoat, keen to get there. We walk past the Esso filling station where, in 1970, I will complete my set of commemorative football World Cup coins. One last left turn and we are on the paved forecourt, upon which sits, in breeze-block splendour, St Jude's parish church.

I would go to many beautiful, awe-inspiring churches when I was older – St Patrick's on Fifth Avenue, St Peter's in Rome, Notre-Dame de Paris – but St Jude's on Glenavon Road was the most pragmatic people's church anywhere in the First World. Built in the post-World War II years, St Jude's was intended as a temporary structure, not meant to last more than a few years. It's coming up on twenty now and yawning with cold air and aching joints. Single storey, with windows every six feet along its length, and a roof of corrugated iron.

Its crude purity enhanced the idea the St Jude's faithful had about being the chosen ones. Why else would we gather together in this cold, ugly place unless it was an absolute certainty that we would benefit from it?

Father Cassidy's great fundraising scheme of the seventies eventually resulted in a new St Jude's church. This was no small achievement. None of the congregants could be considered rich or even well-off. Everyone had to count their pennies. Getting the money to build a new church from his parishioners took a great deal of persuading.

Fortunately, he had God on his side.

A communal sense of readiness sends us through the small lobby where, on raw wooden tables, literature is offered; some for sale, some for free. Textbooks, Bibles, songbooks and other merchandise, including rosaries, crucifixes, and pendants of St Jude (the patron saint of hopeless cases, really).

On into the nave, where there is a smell of sweat and yesterday's incense. It's usually cool in here, sometimes warm but never hot. A tall redheaded man plays a rickety-looking organ, quietly piping sweet music that is barely there. Eno would call it ambient. Candles burn lazily with a holy scent.

On the strike of eleven the service begins. The priest enters smartly, followed by a pair of young men in white robes – the priest's team, his posse – one of whom swings a silver chalice from which more incense issues. The air in the church needs a good cleansing before the good father can breathe it.

He wears elaborate clothing, a robe of green-and-gold silk with a red cross on his back. Beneath the cloak, ankle-length turned-up trousers reveal the black socks and black brogues of any other working man.

The music surges in volume and we all stand. The red-haired man leads us in a song we know well, 'The Lord Is My Shepherd'. I open the hymnal to read the words. I like this one but, like Mum, I'm too embarrassed to sing out loud. I wish I could, I just don't, but I like the feeling of togetherness that comes from every-one in the room singing the same words.

Once the song is over, the priest walks to the dais. He glances down at his Bible, opens his hands wide and says, 'Let us pray.'

2 Jack, Jean and Nigel

Church just was. Like electricity, heat or black-and-white TV – something that just existed. I assumed everyone went five times a week. I didn't know I was one of a subset, a species. A Roman Catholic.

You don't question things like that when you're little. I never questioned why Mum and I went to church almost every day or why, when Dad drove us on Sundays, he just dropped us off and picked us up afterwards.

My parents grew up in Birmingham's inner city. Mum had been born in Liverpool, but when she was a toddler, her family, the Harts, moved to Birmingham, to Colemeadow Road, where they occupied a large detached family house on a corner. They needed the space: Mum was one of five, until her sister Nora gave birth to Trevor, who the family raised, which made six. Mum's dad, Joseph, who died before my birth, spent his working life in labour relations; he worked for the shipbuilding union in Liverpool originally, but

moved to Birmingham for a better job. The Lord Mayor of Birmingham would go to his funeral. Up the street from the Harts, the dwellings were smaller; tight Victorian terraced houses that were well built, small but proud, with the toilet out back.

The Taylors lived in one of these, at number 10.

My Dad, Jack, was born John in 1920, which made him – aged nineteen in 1939 – prime meat for the Second World War. He was shipped out to Egypt, where he was given an administrative posting; clerking and driving trucks and officers around the base. One weekend, he was due to be on leave in Cairo but he traded his time off with another soldier. This good deed would not go unpunished. That weekend, the German army seized the base on which Dad was stationed and he, along with many others, was captured. The British prisoners were then transported up through Italy to Germany, where they were interned in Stalag 344.

Dad would spend the remaining three years of the war there. He was forced to live off raw potatoes, watery soups and the occasional Red Cross food parcel. At least he didn't smoke, so he could trade in his tobacco ration for a few extra spuds.

Mum used to say to me confidentially, 'Your father had a terrible time in the war, but he'll never talk about it.' Dad's wartime experiences were the khaki elephant in our living room. No one could talk about it, but we were all living with it, still, twenty years later.

It's clear to me now that Dad had post-traumatic stress disorder and what he really needed was some therapy – which he would get these days. The most anyone could ever get out of him on the subject, if he was pushed into a corner, would be: 'I had it easy compared to George.'

George was Dad's brother. Their father had died when Dad was five and George was ten, so George became like a surrogate parent. Dad idolised him. George did his soldiering in Burma and had been taken prisoner by the Japanese. George had been in a mine near Nagasaki, mere miles from the site of the atomic bomb, and felt the explosion.

When Dad got back to Birmingham after his war, amid the celebrations of VE Day, his mother, Frances, and his elder sister, Elsie, were of course overjoyed to see him. But anxiety still ran high in the household, as no one had heard from George or even knew if he had survived, and this cast a shadow over Dad's return.

Almost a year later, in a scene that could have been directed by Steven Spielberg, Dad was waiting for a bus to take him to work, when he vaguely recognised a figure coming down the street towards him out of the morning mist. It was his brother George, free since VJ Day, but emaciated and exhausted not just by his captivity but also by his long journey home by way of the Pacific, then across the United States by train.

I'm sure Dad looked different to George too. But they were stoic, each with his overdeveloped sense of responsibility, and no tears would have been shed between these men. A handshake for sure, possibly a hug. Dad might have let a few buses go by, but I doubt very much that he took the day off work. Any tears shed would have been female tears.

This story was so hard for my father to tell that he didn't share it with me until he was in his eighties and I was in my forties.

The Second World War was omnipresent growing up in England in the 1960s. It was this enormous event that had affected everybody. In spite of Dad's reluctance to go there, nobody else could stop talking about it. It dominated TV and the movies.

Mum Jean, born Eugenie, had wartime experiences of her own, working on the Austin automobile assembly lines at Longbridge, which had been converted to manufacture parts for the massive

Avro Lancaster bomber planes. Also in her twenties during the 1940s, Mum enjoyed the society and fellowship on the swing shift.

In 1946, the processes of life that had been interrupted by the war began again, and thoughts returned to the normal: jobs, marriage and starting families. Hope returned. Being neighbours, Mum and Dad had been aware of each other for years, but only on shyly passing acquaintance terms. Dad was good pals with Mum's brothers, Sid and Alf, and one night, at the Billesley Arms, a plan was hatched by the three of them.

The following bright November Saturday morning, Dad strode down the block to the Harts' house and knocked on the front door. Familiar as he was to the family there, he was immediately invited in. But he was not there this time to ask Sid if he fancied going fishing tomorrow, or to ask Alf if he had a game of bowls lined up later on up at the Billesley. He was there to ask old Joe Hart if he could take his younger daughter, Eugenie, out on a date.

I don't think either of my parents had great expectations about love and marriage. They were both practical people. They each wanted a family and to not grow old alone. They would have both felt enormous gratitude to have been wanted and accepted by the other but would never have expressed it in quite that way.

From the first date, they knew they were a good fit, and all their friends and family knew it too. In their community, their partnership was a symbol of survival in the aftermath of the war: two working-class families giving up their youngest to each other. Their marriage would be a source of great pride to many.

The forty-two guests at the wedding all lived within a few miles of each other. When I was ten they were almost all of them in my life; they were the fabric that formed me. They were good, honest and loving folk. I was raised to love them as they loved me – non-judgementally and unconditionally. There is something about my parents' wedding that represents the apogee of English working-class family life.

There was a shortage of new, affordable homes in the 1950s, another legacy of the war, so after Mum and Dad married, they moved in temporarily with Mum's parents.

They would soon become part of the working-class diaspora that was moving out of the inner cities into the new housing estates and 'garden cities' that were being built to replace the bombed-out town centres and to accommodate the exploding population. The story would be told many times about how Dad had shown up at the site office of one new development in Hollywood at 7.00 a.m. on a Monday morning in 1954, demanding to be allowed to buy the last house available.

The new house was perfect. It was a two-up, two-down, with a pebbledash relief between the ground floor and upstairs bow windows. The living room, where we would eat, watch TV, sit, do just about everything, was 8 by 12 feet. The other room downstairs was known as the 'front room', and it was where the wedding gifts and the alcohol were stored. The three of us would have lunch in there every Sunday, and it's where the Christmas tree was put up every year. Other than that, it went unused.

Number 34 Simon Road had its own garage, where my father would spend weekends tinkering with his car. There was a small garden at the front and a slightly larger one at the back.

In June of 1960, Mum gave birth to me at Sorrento Maternity Hospital in Solihull after an easy labour. I was never any trouble, she would tell me. I was soon brought back from the hospital, by which point the house was well lived-in and comfortable, perfectly snug for a newborn.

My parents named me Nigel. It was quite an unconventional choice. My second name was John.

3 Sounds for the Suburbs

Living in the suburbs was fine for Dad. More than fine. He jumped into his Ford every morning at eight, drove himself to his job in export sales at Wilmot-Breeden, an engineering and manufacturing firm that made car parts, and was back home around six. He even got to make trips abroad, primarily to Sweden, handling the firm's accounts with Volvo and Saab. Those trips were infused with romance and glamour for me. He would return home smelling of cigars, airport lounges and expensive alcohol, with gifts of perfume for Mum and toys for me. In the 1960s, Dad loved his work and loved his life. He was living the dream.

For Mum, who didn't drive, Hollywood was isolating. She was stuck out there in the suburbs, away from her family and friends, and had stopped working the day she found out she was pregnant. Alone with me, the only child.

There were few local shops, and she made friends slowly. But

Mum was a churchgoer, had been all her life, and that became her social life, which is why the daily journey to St Jude's had to be made, regardless of distance or weather.

Of course, I went along with her to church too.

I still remember the music. St Jude's was where I would get a handle on the Catholic songbook; 'All Things Bright and Beautiful', 'The Lord Is My Shepherd', 'Faith of Our Fathers' formed the daily fare. But they saved the real megahits for Christmas: 'We Three Kings', for example – not even I could resist singing along with that one; it was a real 'manthem', a manly anthem, proud and forceful – or 'O Come, All Ye Faithful', which could be sung in Latin as 'Adeste Fideles' if the priest was feeling confident.

Some of those hymns, like 'Away in a Manger', they have to be amazing. They've been written to grab the imagination of people aged from five to ninety-five. Some of the arrangements had been appropriated from titans like J. S. Bach so, without even knowing it, I was being exposed to some of the greatest music ever written. The organ would be cruising those major-to-minor moves, and the hairs would be standing up on the back of my neck.

Most European pop music is based on Christian church music, in the same way that so much American pop is based on gospel church music, which is more call-and-response. Le Bon turned me on to that idea. The experience of church music in my childhood has never gone away and continues to be a deep influence on any songwriting I am involved in.

Mum's other saviour from her suburban exile came by way of technology and her transistor radio, which was always on, tuned to the BBC Light Programme. My waking memory of any new day was the sound of that radio. I would hear the radio before I saw or heard any parent.

Mum adored popular music. She had been a fan as a teenager, a stage-door Jeannie, idolising the bandleaders of her day: Harry James, Artie Shaw. I found a little black book of hers recently in which she had transcribed, in her always elegant handwriting, about sixty hit songs of the day, with titles like 'My Foolish Heart', 'Come with Me My Honey' and 'Boy of My Dreams'.

All of this passion built to a crescendo for her – and almost everyone else in the country – when the Beatles came along in 1962, when I was two. They were, in equal measure, romantic, cheeky and adventurous. And they were from Liverpool.

All those new mothers in love with the mop-tops – while we were learning to walk, some of us still in our cots – would be singing to us, '*Love, love me do*', '*All my loving*' or '*She loves you, yeah, yeah, yeah . . .*'

Oedipus, kick up your heels.

4 The Catholic Caveat

When I reached the age of four, church was replaced by school. I was happy to go. If I had known what was in store for me, they would have had to drag me there.

I now look back, somewhat wryly, on those preschool years as idyllic. It was my first experience of being at the exclusive centre of a woman's attention.

Mum and Dad had signed me up for a Catholic primary school, Our Lady of the Wayside. Despite Dad's agnosticism, he was all for it. The theory was there was a better quality of education to be had there than at the local school.

The first morning, Mum dressed me in my new school uniform – yellow-and-grey tie, grey flannel shorts and a tiny blazer – fed me and walked me up the hill to join the other half-dozen victims waiting for the bus.

I was perfectly relaxed about all of this. Confident, excited, keen. Mum and Dad had done a good job of preparing me for this

day. I must have exuded a certain calmness, as the boy who was causing the most trouble in the classroom, screaming and shouting, was sat next to me.

The best aspects of the primary-school classroom were the sandbox and the 'tuck trolley' that delivered Jammie Dodgers at eleven o'clock sharp. My clearest memory of first-year infants is of the Monday I showed up wearing my new National Health standard-issue thick-rimmed glasses, at age five. The teacher suggested I stand on the desk so everyone could get a good look at the new me. It was like, 'Hey, just call me four-eyes, guys!' I'm sure Mrs Gilmore hadn't meant it to be humiliating but, for a five-year-old, it was.

Jammie Dodgers were not the only religion handed out at Our Lady of the Wayside. Catholic dogma was high up on the curriculum, with religious knowledge – or 'RK' – nestled cosily next to maths, history and geography. Two plus two equals four, the Battle of Hastings was in 1066, the capital of France is Paris and Jesus turned water into wine at the wedding in Cana.

Despite all the hours I had spent at church, all that ceremony, all those readings, the music, the incense, I still didn't get it. Intellectually, it never made sense to me.

Like a member of the crowd at the feeding of the five thousand, I sat there, scratching my head, trying to figure out how on earth Jesus could have made all that food out of five loaves and two small fish. How? Why? Because he was Jesus? Because he was The Man? What was I missing?

But one thing you learn early on is that asking how or why is frowned upon in the Catholic Church. Not for us the intellectual rigour of the Jewish religious people. Or the spiritual curiosity of the Buddhists.

For us, ignorance is a matter of pride.

It's what I call 'the Catholic Caveat', and it's a minor stroke of ecclesiastical genius, because what it says is this: if you have to ask, then you don't have faith, and if you don't have faith, you are totally fucked, because lightning will come searing through your bedroom window that very night and BLOW YOU OFF THE FACE OF THE EARTH!

It can be a scary and confusing world to grow up in.

5 A Hollywood Education

Dad smuggled in some coded messages that there may be life outside St Jude's and Our Lady of the Wayside.

At Christmas 1966, when I was six-and-a-half, he brought home the Wilmot-Breeden works calendar. It was not to be hung in the kitchen, this calendar, or any of the other 'public spaces' in 34 Simon Road. What Dad did was take the scissors to the thick, shiny pages and separate them, creating twelve images from around the world: Red Square in Russia, Sydney Harbour Bridge, an ancient village of red brick and tile sitting on an unimaginably blue sea and another, of the most gorgeous raven-haired temptress, dressed in red, atop a black horse that matched her hair.

Dad mixed up some wallpaper paste and glued the pages to my bedroom walls, alongside and over my bed. Above my pillows there already was the ubiquitous Jesus on the cross, the crucifix that no self-respecting Catholic is ever far away from. Now he had some competition for my imagination.

Jesus: tortured; blood dripping from the nails that had been so brutally hammered home through his hands; the crown of thorns. It was a nightmare vision, and the intention was to give Catholics a conscience. All it gave me was guilt.

Dad's presentation of beauty and adventure, of what could be found across the seas and oceans, seemed to be saying to me, in a whisper, 'There's more to life than this, lad. It's not just about Hollywood, *Him* and school.'

Gazing up at those pictures, illuminated only by the streetlight that filtered in through the curtains long after my lights had been turned out, night after night, was where all my dreams of romance, travel and escape began.

The next step in the home education that Father introduced was to begin drilling me on geography; capital cities, rivers and flags became favourite subjects of mine, and I fast became an expert. It's a useful interest to have when you are on the road six months a year.

I would beg, plead to be quizzed on my geographical knowledge on weekend mornings, when I would climb into bed with Mum and Dad.

'Ask me some rivers,' I would say excitedly, eyes popping out of my head.

Dad would fold up his *Daily Sketch*, saying, 'Can't you ask him, Jean?'

'I don't know them, Jack, no good asking me,' Mum would say.

Dad would smile resignedly and say, 'Amazon?'

'Brazil!' I would snap back like a piranha. And we were off.

It's a pretty cosy life, the life of an only child, especially when both parents are present and love is not in short supply. I had a good thing going.

We had three neighbours in the adjoining house, number 36,

over the years. The worst of them were police officers. I knew the seventies had arrived when I saw that pale blue police car roll up onto the drive.

They were fascists, man – that was clear from the uniforms.

They didn't have kids so they were like, 'Turn the music down!', 'Turn the TV down!' and 'No, you are not going to get your ball back if you keep kicking it over the fence!' I thought the husband was a real blockhead and the sight of him shouting at Dad, eyes popping out of his head – 'If you don't sort that son of yours out, I will!' – terrified me.

All I was doing was being a kid. As I got older and music took over, I wanted to listen to music all the time, ideally when no one else was in the house so I could turn it up really loud. To be fair, I had no idea what it must have been like for them on the other side of those paper-thin walls.

My parents hated these confrontations with the neighbours. Mum was very timid and Dad wasn't up for another fight. Given that he was a soldier, a hero, I couldn't understand why he wouldn't just weigh in there with his fists flying. It was an early lesson in the limitations of my parents' power.

6 In Between and Out of Sight

I enjoyed learning and acquiring knowledge, but it was a habit rarely manifested in the classroom. Only in the privacy of home, in the snug, close-fitting world of Mum, Dad and me, did I have the confidence to let fly.

Intelligence needs training, and training includes making mistakes. I never felt judged in my parents' world; at school I felt nothing but judgement. At school, being an only child had its drawbacks; I have never liked sharing my toys.

And I didn't like the rating, the constant comparative system that was going on. Who is good at this, who is the best at that? The best and the worst. Always.

'Games', that ironic synonym for sports, was the worst. In contest after contest, you could find me and my four eyes faring not too well on the playing fields of Our Lady of the Wayside. Never once was I to get the call-up: your school needs you.

Not once would I represent my school at sports. I would develop some nagging self-doubt about that.

Is there anything worse than being laughed at? I'll take surgery every time. I couldn't stand it – still can't. Thank God my friends and family know me well enough today to do it out of earshot, but back then, coming last meant getting laughed at. That had to be avoided. I began to take myself out of the race.

I didn't like coming first either – what was a boy to do? – because that meant walking to the front of class or, worse, the assembly hall, to receive a prize and maybe even having to say, 'Thank you, sir,' out loud in front of all those hooligans. Stepping forward to receive my Bobby Moore gift token from Mr Lahive for my work on 'The Lives of the Saints' was the most humiliating moment to date. All those eyes burning into my back, the sniggers of reproach. No thanks, I'll pass on the prizes too. I set my sights on being in between and out of sight.

By the age of ten, in 1970, I had become a less frequent visitor to Mum and Dad's bed (although I still remember crawling in between the two of them to read about the breakup of the Beatles. It was as unbelievable to us as the sinking of the *Titanic*), so I needed to find other ways to get their approval.

Particularly Dad's.

Military model-making was the hobby *du jour*, supremely popular with boys of my generation and a terrific father/son bonding pursuit to boot. More sons and their fathers of the late sixties bonded over Airfix models of Centurion tanks, Spitfire planes and *Victory* ships ('featuring life-like Nelson with amputated arm') than anything other than a leather football.

Dad set the bar for me when he constructed my eighth birthday present, the Short Sunderland flying boat, to such a degree of perfection that I knew I had to get up to speed pretty quick.

Which I did. I became addicted to making models. Maybe there was something in the glue, the 'construction cement' and the enamel paint?

Planes, boats, trucks, cars; I built 'em, painted 'em and stuck them in little landscape surroundings known in the modelling fraternity as 'dioramas'.

Every week my pocket money would go on something new to add to my collection. By Saturday afternoon I would be disturbing Dad in the garage. 'Look, Dad, what do you think? It's Monty on the road to Alamein.'

'That's very good, lad,' he would say. 'Fancy a trip to the off-licence to get some pop?'

Victory!

My tastes in model-making had no nationalistic allegiance. I was as happy building a Japanese Zero fighter or a Panzer tank as I was General Montgomery's Humber staff car. The *Graf Spee* or the *Ark Royal*, Grummans or Messerschmitts, I didn't care, it was all of a piece, all part of the great game: war, a battle of uniforms and battledress, crosses versus roundels. The Airfix catalogue was an astounding education, and gave my generation a great primer in industrial design, as well as developing our hand–eye skills. It was as good as anything I got taught in a classroom, and it cannot be done on a Game Boy.

It was an almost exclusively masculine world. Airfix's only concession to the female form was their Joan of Arc, which did not interest me. The only human models I built and painted were of men. Manly men doing manly things. Like killing each other.

Around about now, I had a first thought about a future career, a pilot in the Royal Air Force. I wondered to myself after lights out, did the RAF still fly Spitfires?

The relentless construction of RAF fighter planes and Panzer tanks and ships of the Royal Navy was also a way of scratching at the surface of the great unspoken subject: Dad's war years. We couldn't communicate about the subject directly, so I just kept building. Shit, we English kids had it easy; what were the German kids of my generation talking to *their* dads about? Not a lot, I would find out later, but it did provide impetus for all the great and profound German art and music of the seventies and eighties.

My obsession moved up a notch when I began collecting and painting models from Napoleon's vast *Grande Armée*. I particularly coveted bona fide rock stars such as Marshal Murat who, arm outstretched and sabre poised, rode into battle on his leopard-skin-bedecked steed.

I needed more cash to feed my habit because these figures and their smaller-scale cousins cast in lead and imported from France cost a lot more than the Airfix guys. Dad inadvertently gave me another life skill; I became the neighbourhood car washer.

Painting all those uniforms in intricate detail on three-inch figurines left its mark on my aesthetic sensibility – the epaulettes, the braids, the sashes and the boots. You can still see an Airfix influence onstage with Duran Duran today. I just can't seem to shake it off.

I was also crazy about cars, another passion I inherited from Dad. No one took greater pride in car ownership than Dad, and his relationship with his various cars was almost erotic. Every spare hour he had, he spent it alone in the garage with the car, tweaking, messing, customising. And if, while driving, the car developed the slightest rattle or vibration, he would go nuts, and as soon as we got home would disappear, taking the car apart until he found the cause of the noise and silenced it. He invested his entire working life in the British car industry, and any sign of imperfection he considered a personal affront.

Over twenty years, Dad had earned the reputation as the family's designated driving instructor, having taught many uncles and aunts, nieces and nephews how to become drivers. Ironically, his most famous failure was his own wife, Jean, my mum.

One evening after school, Dad decided it was time to teach Mum to drive. Mum wasn't sure that was a good idea, and she was nervous about getting behind the wheel of Dad's prize bull. She knew how attached Dad was to his car and how easily he could get mad. However, we all climbed into the maroon Ford, Dad behind the wheel for now, and drove to a designated lay-by spot out in the country, a few miles from home.

Dad pulled the car over onto the roadside. In front of and behind us were ten-foot piles of gravel. The space between was maybe two hundred yards. Mum and Dad switched seats.

They are both edgy, and I must be picking up on that energy because I am bouncing around in the backseat restlessly, squeezing my body between the two front seats, as I always do, to really get an idea of what is involved in the 'lesson'.

First thing Mum does is to push the gear stick into first, not taking into account the use of the clutch (these are the days before automatic transmission arrived in the UK), and the sound of screeching fills the cockpit.

'Christ, Jean! Don't crash the gears!'

Mum looks terrified.

'Oh Jack . . . I don't know, what am I supposed to do? Nigel!' – that is me – 'Sit back!'

'You have to push the clutch in, Jean, before you go into gear. Use your left foot,' says Dad.

Once again, Mum tries to engage the gear, but not only do we get the screeching again, this time the car leaps forward in clumsy bounds, bumpa bumpa THUD!

The engine stalls.

'Christ, Jean, what *is* the matter with you?' Mum's on the verge of tears, her face beet red.

'Forget it,' she says stubbornly. 'I don't *want* to drive, let me out.'

She can't get the door open, and Dad now has his dangerous, furious look on, fit to burst. Then he's out of the passenger seat, stomping around the front of the car, opening the driver door for Mum to get out. She climbs back into the passenger seat, Dad gets back behind the wheel.

'And *you*! Sit back! Sit back in that bloody seat!' he says to me. The car exits the lay-by with an uncharacteristic wheel spin.

And that's it. Mum's one and only driving lesson is over. Every time it gets mentioned in the future, my role is slowly but surely magnified until I have become the principal cause of the disaster.

'With you jumping around in the back, how was I supposed to concentrate?'

7 Junior Choice

On Saturday mornings, the three of us – Mum, Dad and Nigel – would gather at the kitchen table for breakfast. On the radio at eight would be Ed 'Stewpot' Stewart's *Junior Choice*, another terrific bonding opportunity for kids and their parents.

From up and down the country, folk would write in. Ed would begin, 'We've a letter from Edith Baker in Accrington: "Dear Ed, it's our Jimmy's eighth birthday on Saturday, and for his party he has asked for a cake with a picture of you on it!"'

Chuckling to himself, Ed would continue: 'I can't imagine anyone wanting to eat that cake, Edith, are you sure it's a good idea? She goes on, "We never miss the show. Could you please play him something from *Jungle Book*?" I would be most happy to oblige,' Ed would say in his friendly, nasal tone.

And off we would go, with 'I Wanna Be Like You'. Keith West's 'Excerpt from a Teenage Opera' was a popular selection on

Junior Choice, as was 'Puff, the Magic Dragon' and anything from *Mary Poppins*. We were all putty in Ed's hands whenever he played 'Supercalifragilisticexpialidocious'.

At 10.00 a.m., the show was over and we would dress for the weekend shopping trip. On Sunday, we would dress for church. Strangely, even though Dad was not working Sunday, he still did not come into St Jude's with us, preferring to sit in the car and read the paper. Would this mean Dad would not be accompanying Mum and me to heaven?

Back home, it was the afternoon radio broadcasts that really caught the family's ear. Dad had broken down and joined the hi-fi set in the early 1970s, which was a necessary development, in my view, like adding a vinyl roof to the Ford or buying nylon shirts. This meant we could now play music and listen to the radio in the TV room.

The hi-fi, or *stereo*, for this system had two speakers, had been put on a purpose-built shelf to the left of Dad's easy chair, so it was clearly meant to be his domain. He started buying albums: *Dvorak's Greatest Hits* and the great Rimsky-Korsakov's *Scheherazade*. Mum and he would get together on some purchases, like the Max Bygraves *Sing-Along-A-Max* series – Max doing then what Rod Stewart would do later with *The Great American Songbook*. This was great party music for when my aunts and uncles visited and drinks were being served.

But the truth was, the Taylor household was a radio household, and we were a radio family.

After the boredom of Dad's Sunday cricket had been suffered and slept through by all, including him, the Radio 1 'Top 30 Chart Show' would begin at 5.00 p.m. Dad and I – and visiting Nan – would gather around the living room table as Mum brought in our tea of sandwiches, cake and, if we were lucky, her unequalled trifle. There wasn't another event in the entire week that brought the three generations together with quite as much enthusiasm as the Top 30 show.

Let me qualify that. It was actually Mum's and my enthusiasm that really got the party started; Dad and Nan could have taken it or left it. But they went with the flow, and it felt, at least, as if we were all as excited by the ups and downs of the pop world as each other. It was one of our few family pastimes.

The highlight came at five minutes before seven o'clock when 'the nation's number 1 hit song' was played in full, unless it was a song as popular as George Harrison's 'My Sweet Lord', which sat at the top spot for seemingly months, in which case they just played a few bars of the song. After weeks and weeks of overexposure, this was a blessed relief.

I was beginning to notice that the songs I really liked rarely made it to 'the top spot'. Mostly the number 1s were a little too cheesy for my developing taste: 'Chirpy Chirpy Cheep Cheep', 'Welcome Home' or 'I'd Like to Teach the World to Sing'. Talent-show winners or songs from TV ads. The cooler songs seemed to sit a little outside the Top 10. After the number 1 song had been played, Radio 1 switched off and it would be time for the *Shipping Forecast* – that curiously interesting lesson in weather and European geography. What *was* Dogger Bite? – and after that, the airwaves were back in the hands of the controllers at BBC Light Entertainment for 'Your Hundred Best Tunes', all that maudlin stuff like 'In a Monastery Garden' and 'Songs My Mother Taught Me'. Dad would settle down in his seat, maybe with a drink of something from the front room, and Nan would doze off again, maybe singing along gently after a glass or two.

Number 34 Simon Road *was* a musical house, but not in the von Trapp family sense. Nobody could play a note and there were no instruments to be found anywhere. And other than Dad in his cups, no one had the nerve to sing out loud.

In addition to Mum's transistor radio and Dad's stereo, there was the trusty oak-panelled gramophone player, which had been sitting on the floor in the front room for as long as I could remember. It was an heirloom, something from my nan's house, and rarely used by Mum or Dad other than as a tabletop for a drinks decanter and some whisky glasses. Stuffed into the shelves beside the turntable was a selection of scruffy 78s, remnants of the 'dancing years' – Connie Francis, Frank Sinatra, Peggy Lee – parent toys that had been discarded long before I came along.

Two aspects of this old piece of furniture fascinated me. The first, since I was a toddler, was the turntable itself. It had been fun using it as a test site for my Matchbox cars, holding the tiny toys over the spinning felt, lowering them until the wheels bit into the madly spinning surface. I would duck down to get a close-up view of the tiny tyres, accompanying the visual with some voice-activated sound effects: gears changing, engines growling.

The second element of the 'radiogram' that would fascinate me in later years, as a boy, was the wireless radio, powered by tubes that took over a minute to warm up. It picked up signals from all across Europe, places on the 'wave band' such as Hilversum and Luxembourg that had an exotic allure, places I vaguely knew of from my home-school geography class. Sounds would come in spurts, sometimes consistent and soothing, sometimes loud and barking, stuttering in and out of reach. Was that a spy network? I loved the sounds of the out-of-tunedness almost as much as the broadcasts. The crackles, pops and fizzles were sounds from other planets.

I would press my ear to the single speaker and turn the dial slowly, like a safe-cracker, hoping to make a stronger connection.

Music of all sorts; some pop, but more often soaring symphonies and brittle, rhythmic music I would come to understand as jazz. Foreign languages spilled into the room, weather reports of storms, floods, and blazing heatwaves.

It was as if the entire universe was being funnelled into the front living room of our house, which was exciting, and it went on twenty-four hours a day, every day of the week. A room that measured 8 by 12 feet had become a space of infinite size, like Doctor Who's Tardis. This room was no longer going to be used only on Sundays and at Christmas. I needed to stay close to this thing.

Sunday evenings would always end with Dad saying, 'You better get ready for school tomorrow, lad. Get in the bath.'

'Right, Dad, will do,' I would respond, but instead of going upstairs straight away for the compulsory cleaning of the body parts, I would quietly sneak into the front room, leaving the lights off, and click on the old radio, the low light that emanated from it not enough to give me away. 'Now where is that Radio Luxembourg on the dial?' I would ask myself as the tubes began to warm.

8 My Moon Landing

At the age of eleven I took the compulsory eleven-plus exam, which would determine whether I would go to a 'grammar school' or a 'secondary modern'. The grammar school, traditionally, was where it was at. My dad, in an unusual show of educational insight, made me sit a special exam for King Edward's, Birmingham's finest grammar school (where they had taught J. R. R. Tolkien), but I failed that after mucking around on the playing fields between the two tests left me covered in mud, which caused Dad to have such a fit that I never quite relaxed enough during Round 2 to make any sense of the paper.

Despite not being the most diligent student, I did, however, pass the regular eleven-plus exam and left the Catholic confines of Our Lady of the Wayside for the greener pastures of the County High School in Redditch, a sixty-minute bus ride from our home in Hollywood. I never really settled down there. Again, it was a highly competitive system, and the classes were larger, so getting the attention I would have liked or needed was impossible. After a few years of questionable successes ('Worst second-year class of all time: 2F3'; 'Worst third-year class in the history of the school: 3F2'), I started skiving off.

It began with me just skipping sports, and then whatever class came after that. As time went on, it just got harder and harder to stay interested in what school had to offer. I wasn't a star on the playing fields, I wasn't getting the work done, I wasn't in the orchestra and I wasn't connecting in any of the classrooms. Mostly, I spent my time obsessing about Julie McCoy, whom I would spend at least an hour with on the telephone every night. The fact she had a boyfriend didn't stop me phoning, but it did stop us from going any further.

The school gave up on me in the end. I thought I was being so clever and getting away with it, but really the teachers probably thought, 'Why should we bother with him when we have all these other kids who want what we have on offer?'

My parents had no idea what was going on. They were even less engaged in my schooling than I was. If ever a letter from school was written to them to tell on me, I could smell it in my hands and it never made it home. I became an accomplished forger. I could do a perfect imitation of both of my parents' signatures, and it was easy to change a report card 'E' into a 'B+', which was odd if you considered the accompanying comment: 'He has had a very poor year and continues to disappoint, B+'.

As school became less important, music became a bigger and bigger force in my life.

At the age of twelve my cousin Eddie, who was five years older than me and was the neighbourhood newspaper boy, took over from Dad as my primary male role model. Right on target, according to all the books on raising boys. He had three sisters,

which may have added to the appeal that sent me on my bike to his house every chance I got.

Eddie also had a burgeoning record collection. Not just a record collection, an *album* collection. Pretty much every artist worth their salt in the early seventies, I heard them first in the company of cousin Eddie: Bowie, Rod Stewart, Elton John, Cat Stevens, James Taylor, Melanie . . . okay, maybe not every artist was all that significant, but boy, he loved his music. And he had the posters on his wall. Eddie bought into the rock myth, totally.

Forty years later, he's still a true believer. Forty years later, if I want to know what's going on in the British music scene, I still call him.

In return for helping out on his paper round, I got inducted into that teenage male world ahead of time, the world of girls and aftershave, racing bikes and clothes, penny round collars, Oxford bags, tight-fitting Fair Isle sweaters and platform shoes.

This was 1972.

I felt big when I was around Eddie and his friends. I got unconditional acceptance, like I got from Mum and Dad, but this was way cooler.

I remember the time he played me Bowie's *Hunky Dory* album, my first exposure to that cultural giant of the seventies.

'You just wait, kid,' Eddie said. 'Bowie's going to be huge. We've got tenth-row tickets for his town hall gig next week. Right, Stan?'

Ed's running mate Stan nodded obligingly. 'Yep, yes we do, Ed.'

'It's gonna be a good one, kid, have a listen.'

The record player's arm came down once more. The album played again. '*Still don't know what I was waiting for . . .*'

Unlike cousin Ed, who liked his singer-songwriters, I found myself connecting with bands. I loved the interplay between the musicians, the guitarist and the singer: Rod and Woody, Mick and Keith, David and Mick, great alliances that spoke to me much more than the lonely troubadour pose. Two guys or more, maybe four or five, that was a gang, it was a cult and it was sexy.

The band that really got my attention, because all of them were stars and they all had extraordinary looks and musical character, was Roxy Music. Their debut on *Top of the Pops* in August 1972 changed everything for me.

It's hard to say which was the more innovative, the sound or the look.

Let's start with the sound: sci-fi trash and vaudeville, a driving backbeat and a crooning, Sinatraesque vocal. The look: lip gloss, fur, calfskin gloves on a keyboard player who didn't actually play keyboards, preferring to studiously turn knobs instead.

I couldn't have gotten closer to the TV screen if I tried.

This was my moon landing.

I never fantasised about being a front man, but I began to see myself somewhere within the corps, maybe a little to the left of the main spotlight.

9 Side Men

The world of concerts and live music sounded thrilling, and I wanted in on that too, but it was going to be a tricky negotiation with the parentals. Eddie and his mates would often join the long lines formed on Saturday evening outside the Odeon in Birmingham city centre, waiting overnight to get tickets when the box office opened at eleven the following morning.

'I'll tell you what, kid,' Eddie proposed, after a concert by Rod Stewart had been announced for Christmas. 'We'll do the overnight shift with our sleeping bags, and you and your pal come in on the first morning bus and relieve us in the queue – you boys can get the four tickets when they open up.'

Sounded good. And I wouldn't even have to mention it to the folks yet.

All went according to plan until the line started moving at eleven. What a rowdy lot! Stewart had a really boozy audience in the early seventies, and they'd been drinking all night. Little me

To Nigel,
love, Bill N...
x

and my mate got tossed and shoved and pushed aside, and we lost our place more than once, but we hung in there. I just couldn't let down my cousin who had invested so much trust in me, and I had that hot, sticky tenner (best tickets were £2 each then). But with maybe ten or twenty in the line between me and the Odeon lobby, the sign went up: ALL TICKETS SOLD. Did I lose credibility with Eddie and his pals? Actually, he was very understanding. All he had to do was fork out a little more of his cash for a pair of tickets from the scalpers – he wasn't going to miss the show.

Next year, when Rod Stewart and the Faces announced two Christmas concerts in Birmingham, I sailed into town on the first morning bus with my new friend Nick Bates. Amazingly, we found ourselves at the front of the line after little effort and were able to buy a pair of front-row seats.

It was so easy, and I saw this as evidence of magic. Nick, 'the man who would be Rhodes', always was and always will be someone entirely settled at the centre of his own universe. He is an extraordinarily creative individual blessed with good fortune. I mean, his mother even owned a toy shop! How lucky can you get? I knew from the beginning of our relationship that if I stayed close to him, life would be exciting.

I first met Nick in the winter of 1973. I was thirteen, he was eleven. The eleven-plus exam I had taken successfully turned out to be the last year the exam would exist in our area. It was replaced by something supposedly more democratic and less selective, so Nick didn't get a crack at it. He got sent to the local secondary modern school on the housing estate up the hill, Woodrush School on Shawhurst Lane. Basically, the government had decided everyone should go to the school closest to where they lived. One negative effect of this decision was that my school, the County

High, was now flooded with local oiks, some of whom just wanted to make as much trouble for the grammar school boys – *those ponces!* – as they could. I quickly became a skilled negotiator, friendly to the morons but staying as true as possible to my own tribe, particularly the cultured young ladies in their tight blue skirts. My closest neighbourhood friend went by the rather unusual name of David Twist. He was my age (we had been born together, as it were, on neighbouring beds at the same hospital), and his mum was one of my mum's few friends. David had failed his exam, so he was at Woodrush too, which was where he got to know Nick. Even though Nick was two years younger, David divined that Nick and I would get along, so he made the introduction.

In 1973, David Bowie was king, and deservedly so. He had pulled off a remarkable string of successes. The release of his masterpiece, *The Rise and Fall of Ziggy Stardust and the Spiders from Mars*, was just the beginning. He also wrote 'All the Young Dudes' for Mott the Hoople, one of his favourite bands, who had split up but regrouped when they heard the song. He produced *Transformer* for Lou Reed and helped to give Lou his first-ever Top 30 hit, and then, most amazingly of all, he muscled his way into Iggy and the Stooges, adding additional production work and mixing their new-metal colossus, *Raw Power*. In June 1973, DB was on a massive tour of the UK, at the end of which he announced his retirement from the stage of London's Hammersmith Odeon. It was a ploy, of course, as we would all learn in time (it was Ziggy retiring, not David), but I remember hearing it on the 8.30 news, sitting on the back seat of the school bus. It was as if the queen was abdicating her throne, which in a way, I suppose is what it was.

But Nick and I shared some secret knowledge about all this. While the Dame was taking the bows and plaudits, the real power behind the throne was lurking stage left, in peroxide and platforms: Bowie's lead guitarist, Mick Ronson.

Every girl at school was a fan of Bowie's that year, so for us, being a Bowie fan was too obvious. We shared a fascination with the subtle and silent Ronson instead, and that served to bind our friendship. The jewels were of Bowie's making, no doubt, but it was Mick who crafted the settings and made sure those stones were shown in the best possible light. In the serious music journals of recent years, there have been many stories about what Mick brought to the Bowie canon, as if, after years of investigative research and laser scanning, the experts had discovered that it was actually Michelangelo's assistant, Luigi, who did all of the really good shit on the Sistine Chapel ceiling while the boss was out to lunch.

Nick had already been to a couple of concerts – yes, this boy was advanced for his age – Gary Glitter and Slade, if memory serves. But I was yet to pop that cherry. So, in the spring of '74, the two of us lined up outside Birmingham Town Hall on Saturday morning and got a pair of seats to see Ronson's first solo tour that coming April. We got our tickets, in Row J, for £1.35 each. It was the first time my parents allowed me into the city at night.

Their approval was conditional on Nick's mum, Sylvia, agreeing to drive us in and pick us up afterwards. No need for the night bus.

No one arriving at the town hall that night had to pay for a programme. We were all given beautiful folders with photos, badges, a biography, a full-colour poster and a flexi disc. Nick and I would play and laugh over that flexi disc for hours, as dear Mick, in his deep Yorkshire brogue, would marvel about love: '*Luv . . . luv . . . when you're in luv . . . it's . . . it's the best thing in the WE-ERLD.*'

What do I remember most about the concert? Not so much what was happening onstage but off, a foreshadowing, maybe, of the experience I would have in the Brighton Dome just a few years later. The violence of it all; seats getting smashed, all this pushing and shoving, girls screaming, standing on top of each other. I had expected it to be like going to the movies – that we'd be able to sit back in our velvet seats in Row J and soak up the experience – but this was no passive activity. It was visceral.

Onstage, however, it was clear that Mick really wasn't up for this. The kids, caught up in Bowie-mania, were going crazy. Mick just wanted them to quiet down and listen to the songs, but that was not going to happen, not that night.

Mick may have been the greatest living sideman, perhaps second only to Keith Richards, but he was never really comfortable centre stage.

Nick and I both wore chiffon without needing much encouragement, and we both loved the clothes, the hairstyles and the make-up that helped make Britain's glam-rock era so great. Neither of us was old enough, really, or had the dough, to fully express ourselves in the way we would have liked, and besides, the glam movement had peaked on that Bowie tour the previous summer, but we found our level.

Bryan Ferry's sartorial direction was having its effect, and all the boys were going through their dad's wardrobes to find his old demob suit; the forties stylings, the baggy double-breasted suits like Bogie wore in *Casablanca*.

Dad's fit me perfectly. But then there was the transsexual glam aspect, and we found ourselves mixing it up with ladies' blouses. At British Home Stores, in the city centre, there was a huge floor filled with two-piece ladies' suits from the forties and fifties to be had for a song. Vintage heaven. Some of those jackets were divine, and fitted both Nick and me. Throw in a little chiffon, maybe an animal-print scarf from Chelsea Girl, and you were away.

'You're not going out dressed like that?' our parents would cry.

'Don't you worry about it, Father,' Nick would tell his dad defiantly, as I applied a little lip gloss in their bathroom.

'Oh, leave them alone, Roger,' Sylvia would say. 'They're just having fun.'

We often drew insults from construction workers.

Nick was a little more outré than I, having the protection of a girlfriend, Jane, which gave him some cover.

One evening, on the train back to Hollywood, we were sitting in the front seat of the carriage behind a glass panel. A gang of denim-clad bozos started banging on the glass.

'We are gonna get you! You fairies are fucking dead!'

Nick and I were shitting ourselves, but we edged ourselves as coolly as we could to the far end of our carriage. Where was the guard?

I needn't have worried. Being with Nick, somehow we magicked ourselves out of danger. By the time the train pulled up at Whitlocks End, the bozos had disappeared.

We had other things in common as well as our dangerous tastes in clothing and music: he was also an only child, our birthdays fell in the same month, June (we are both Geminis) and our favourite board game was Chartbuster.

'Throw a six – your first single advances ten places!'

This pop music business looks pretty easy.

The next concert Nick and I went to together was Roxy Music in September at the Odeon. It was a Saturday, so in the afternoon, during our usual trip into the city, we found ourselves in the theatre lobby, where we made the acquaintance of two guys, Marcus and Jeff, older than us and both serious Roxy fans. They told us that the band were in the building and if we hurried down the alleyway that led down the side of the Odeon, we could hear them playing. This is where I learned about the secret world of the sound check. The logistics of an artist's show almost always require a visit to the venue in the afternoon, when the wires and mics and amps and drums are tested to make sure the triumphant arrival onstage later that night is not hampered by any technical oversights. There were a dozen or so kids standing there in Roxy regalia – T-shirts, scarves, haircuts – beside a purple articulated truck that had been backed up to the stage door to unload the gear. We couldn't see Roxy, but we could hear them, vaguely, playing songs from their new album, *Country Life*. Then the music stopped, and as if on cue, a black Mercedes limousine rolled down the alleyway.

In a sudden frenzy of activity, the band rushed out of the stage door and, without stopping, piled into the comfort of the car, which then took off at speed up the ramp towards New Street.

A girl yelled, 'They're going to the Holiday Inn! I know a shortcut!' and off we went, Birmingham's twelve biggest Roxy Music fans sprinting across the city at full pelt.

This was a club I wanted to belong to!

She knew her stuff, this girl; we were waiting under the hotel awning when the car drew up.

I don't remember Ferry, but I do remember guitarist Phil Manzanera, who was the tallest man I had ever seen in my life. Maybe it was the platform boots. Keyboard player Eddie Jobson took time to say hello and sign autographs. I asked one of the drivers to give me the champagne cork I spotted on the back shelf of the limo. I was proud of that. Was this strange behaviour for a fourteen-year-old suburban boy? I didn't think so.

Nick's and my gig-going gathered momentum. I still have the

ticket stubs from those years. The Faces show came in December, Queen, Genesis – big gigs by big bands, usually at the town hall or the Odeon. And if it was an artist we were *real* fans of, such as Iggy Pop, touring with David Bowie, or Mott the Hoople, we might find ourselves standing under those hotel awnings again or waiting by the stage door listening to the sound check.

10 The Birmingham Flâneur

I took my skiving up a notch when I began spending the entire school day in the city of Birmingham. I didn't ride the bus into Redditch any more; I just crossed the street from the school bus stop and got on the city bus instead.

I loved the Midland Red double-decker buses. Even though they were older, they ran better than the slower, sloppier West Midlands buses and they were more pleasing to the eye, with a tidier, more compact design. The sight of one coming over the hill and down the dip towards the stop on the Alcester Road never failed to cheer me.

I always sat upstairs if possible, grabbing one of the two front seats. I liked to watch the journey from the best vantage point the vehicle could offer. Past the Maypole and Bates's Toy Corner, through Kings Heath with its massive Sainsbury's supermarket where I now worked a weekend job, past Neville Chamberlain's old residence in Moseley and the Edgbaston Cricket Club, up onto the Bristol Road and past the ABC cinema (now a McDonald's), peeling off at the Albany Hotel, taking a right at the Crown pub and past the Jacey cinema, where Mum and I used to watch cartoons and shorts, but by then showed twenty-four-hour porn. Then, in a moment, out of the daylight and into the depths of the bus depot.

Where the adventures began.

Is there anything more exciting than the sounds and smells of the city? Never mind the architecture; the noise inside that torpid black bus terminus was something else. The fighting of gears, the firing up of fifty-year-old diesels, the honking in D-flat minor signalling departure. And the smell: of engineering, of fire and oil being kept a-simmer, just below boiling. Ah, the Midland Red fleet, that industry of freedom, bringing the country to the city and the city to the country!

From the terminus, I walk through the double swing doors into the Bullring market, more noise and stink. The fish market, florists, hardware, butchers in white cotton aprons and hats shouting attention to their wares, and one small record stall where I first heard Bob Marley. I head to the lifts conveying me to the newer Bullring shopping centre and its relative calm and finesse.

The most astounding feature of the Bullring was its indoor shopping bridge, a seventies take on Florence's Ponte Vecchio. It was one of the seven wonders of Birmingham.

There was another record store actually on the bridge, then the entrance to the Mayfair Ballroom, locked tight now, and maybe I'll make a stop at Hawley's bakery by the entrance down to New Street train station for a cup of tea. Then into Threshold Records, owned by Birmingham progressive rock group The Moody Blues. Yes, The Moody Blues have their own record label – which has a chain of retail stores – inconceivable now.

I liked to look in at the imports and second-hand vinyl at Reddington's Rare Records behind the Co-Op. We all sold our souls to Danny Reddington over the years. He was the punk-pawnbroker. In '77, I had to take the pittance he offered me for my album collection in order to be able to buy my first electric guitar and amplifier.

I was Birmingham's teenage *flâneur*, walking idly along New Street. It wasn't Paris, but it worked for me.

At 10.00 a.m., I would head over to Moor Street station, to meet fellow Roxy fan Marcus, coming off his shift around 10.30. Marcus would be taking tickets from a line of commuters coming into the city off the train, see me and smile, 'I'll be finished in a minute, and I'm starving!'

He would park his cap on a hook on the office door and we would quickly walk off, hands stuffed in pockets, through the pedestrian tunnel that passed under Queensway, catching up on gossip and ideas, mostly about music. Marcus was a few years older than me and his tastes were advanced. He loved Eno's solo records, especially the latest, *Another Green World*, which I found a little heady. The prints that came with the album adorned the living room of the flat he shared in Moseley with his girlfriend, Annette.

Annette worked in the city and often met us on her lunch break. The three of us would get a sandwich or go to Oasis, the indoor clothes market or Bus Stop (one of the cooler boutiques) for Annette to look at clothes. This was 1975; lots of sparkle and glitter still, but also Northern Soul influences like star sweaters and skinny-rib tees. The baggies had gotten baggier. Six-button Crimplene pants with side pockets. Cheap as hell from the out-door market.

I had the city mapped out according to a three-tier system. You must have guessed it by now: record stores, food stops and clothing. I could spend the day going from tier to tier to tier.

And then there was Virgin.

Virgin Records was how the Virgin corporate empire began. Before the airline, the moneylending, the media empire, the cola, there were the record stores. They were the least corporate record stores imaginable.

Virgin was the most Bohemian place I had ever been in; a hippy enclave, the floors lined with aircraft seats and no limit on the time you could sit and listen to music on the improbably large headphones. It was radical. They had turntables behind the counter and you could ask them to put on whatever albums you liked. The manager would give me odd jobs and reward me with used display posters, which I would recycle onto my bedroom wall. Once he gave me tickets to see Gong, of Planet Gong and 'The Pot Head Pixies'.

When Virgin moved into its shiny, upscale megastore on New Street, I was the first customer to buy an album there – the Doctors of Madness debut – and was rewarded with a free copy of Mike Oldfield's *Ommadawn*, which I never opened. Mike Oldfield? Who cares?

Everywhere in Birmingham there are monuments to heroes of the steam age, heroes of manufacturing and engineering. The Victorian aspect of the city, built at the peak of its wealth, was its DNA, supposedly so solid and unshakeable, but Birmingham never stops changing.

In 1975, it was the perfect modern city, and I never envied kids like Sex Pistols guitarist Steve Jones, who grew up in London. How on earth you find your way through that pile of bricks at sixteen I just don't know. At sixteen, I had my city mapped out. Everything about it I loved. I never stopped wanting to spend time there. I could make my daylight guerrilla raids, filling my head with the culture, then step onto the red bus back to Hollywood. I never left town empty-handed and, on my upstairs perch, would inspect the booty, an album or magazine, the city receding as the bus heaved south, carrying me towards the safety and comfort of my bedroom, my sanctuary.

Towards the end of my schooldays I could time that trip to perfection. I would be walking up to the front door of 34 Simon Road just as the school bus was dropping off my classmates. The suckers!

11 Neurotic Boy Outsider

If the city was the classroom, the *New Musical Express* was the textbook. The *NME* in the seventies had the most amazing, hip writers; Nick Kent, Charles Shaar Murray, Ian MacDonald. They looked like rock stars and they lived like rock stars, hanging out and taking drugs with them most nights of the week. Or so we were led to believe.

The world of music that the *NME* opened up was a revelation. From one week to the next it might be Miles Davis on the cover, or a report from Bowie's New York concert, or a dispatch on Bob Marley from Jamaica.

For my little alienated self, not connecting at school, not connecting at church any more, the *NME* allowed me to feel part of something. Part of a clique, with its own language, which I was learning to speak.

In a book review in the late nineties, the *Guardian* newspaper would write, 'The *NME* in the '70s was responsible for creating a generation of neurotic boy outsiders.'

I was one of those boys.

I was being drawn inexorably towards pop music and the culture around it. I had completely stopped going to school, but it never felt to me as if I was going off the rails. Music was nourishing me, and as long as I was getting my nourishment, what did it matter where it came from?

The music of the 1970s touched a lot of us teens, sitting in our suburban rooms, living with the claustrophobia of Dad's wartime drama and Mum's religious fanaticism.

Everywhere I went now, I was tapping my foot, drumming on the car dashboard, or playing keyboard on the kitchen table. But Mum and Dad were slow to get it, and it took ages until one of them said, 'Maybe we need to put a musical instrument in front of him.'

The only instrument in my family ever, as far as I knew, was an out-of-tune piano at Nan's house, which I used to love stomping on. Then, in 1975, my parents finally bought me a guitar, an all-black classic acoustic model that was a copy of something I had seen Bryan Ferry play, but I had no idea how to tune it, and it never occurred to anyone that a lesson or two might be helpful. A couple of strings got broken, and it was shoved to the back of the cupboard within a month.

I didn't know I could be a 'musician'. Musicians went to music school, became virtuosos, or plied their trade for years up and down the motorways in Transit vans. That's how I imagined it, because the artists that were drawing my attention in the mid-seventies were 'big' bands like Genesis and the Who, with extraordinary soloists, progressive rockers like Van der Graaf

Generator or Queen. You didn't just jump up onstage and begin to play like that. It took years of dedication.

But something happened in 1976 to change all that. The Sex Pistols released their first record. Only 'Anarchy in the U.K.' wasn't just a record, it was a revolution. A song that changed everything, not only for me, but for my entire generation.

I remember coming home after I bought it. I was sixteen. It was November. I charged up the stairs to my bedroom – Dad's hi-fi had been relocated – carried the speakers to the window sill and faced them outwards, opening the windows wide, playing the record as loud as the system could handle, out over the neighbourhood, over and over and over again, on repeat as loud as the volume would go.

Fuck the neighbours. Fuck them all.

'I'm not who you think I am! *This* is me!'

After I had played the song a dozen times, I was seized by an urge.

'Where's that fucking guitar? Where *is* that guitar?'

I dug it out, and started banging away at it, two strings, out of tune, ting, ting, ting, ting, ting, ting, ting, ting, ting, ting, ting, ting, ting, ting, ting, to 'Anarchy in the U.K.'.

And it fucking rocked.

The acoustic guitar salvaged from the cupboard wasn't going to cut it. I needed an electric guitar and found a Fender Telecaster copy in a second-hand music store for £15.

It had a tired 'authentic' sunburst finish that did not suit my aesthetics. With Dad's help, I sprayed the guitar body Ermine white, a colour Dad had knocking around in his garage, the colour of his second Ford Cortina. I acknowledged that six strings was above my capabilities and decided, made a choice as it were, to use only five strings. In actual fact, I didn't need all of those. On the Buzzcocks' defining punk classic 'Boredom', Pete Shelley had played a guitar solo using only two notes. This was the mood of the times.

I was still best friends with David Twist, the kid who had introduced me to Nick. I loved spending time at the Twists' house, because his parents allowed us, even encouraged us, to bang away at our instruments in his bedroom, David having a small amplifier his dad had built for him.

Nick was spending more and more time with his girlfriend, Jane. Whenever I visited Nick's house, I felt like the third wheel. That was not the case at David's, who was another single, solo loser like me. As cool as making music felt, the level that we were operating at was downright nerdy – no girls allowed, yet.

David sang, I bashed my guitar, and we created mock concert events, complete with 'lights down', 'lights up' and 'intro music'. Songs were written, and John West and the Sardine Cans gave their inaugural performance to both sets of parents at Christmas. Classic stupid name. Meaningless.

Needing to expand the sound, I convinced one of my friends from school, Roy Highfield, who had a snare drum and a hi-hat, to buy a tom-tom, and then another friend emerged with a bass guitar. We were a band.

And that was it, man, that was it. It was like lighting the blue touch paper. *This* is what I wanted to do. I *knew* I didn't want to play football in the park.

We moved our gear into Gareth's, Gareth 'the bass'. His family lived in a big house with a drive and space around it, so it was a suitable place for us to practise. Plus he had two sisters, Heidi and Debbie, who liked to sit and watch us, which was encouraging. Even Gaz's mum was cute, so there were women in the house that you could play to, which was super-important.

I believe it's known as the muse.

12 Shock Treatment

David, Gareth, Roy, and I were on Punk-rock 101, and we renamed our band Shock Treatment, from the Ramones song 'Gimme Gimme Shock Treatment'.

We started writing songs. Simple, to the point and very much of the time. 'Freedom of Speech', 'I Can't Help It' and 'UK Today' could have been written by almost any British teenager that week, although titles such as 'Cover Girls' and 'Striking Poses' suggest interests other than the political. There was nothing profound though, it was almost all imitation, but they *were* songs, with verses and choruses and rudimentary guitar solos. A couple of cover songs were learned also; The Stooges' three-chord dirge 'I Wanna Be Your Dog' was a song anyone could get right, and The Who's 'Substitute', which the Pistols had done.

I wasn't the singer, the front man, but I knew what we had to do. I knew we needed a gig, so I got us one, sweet-talking the

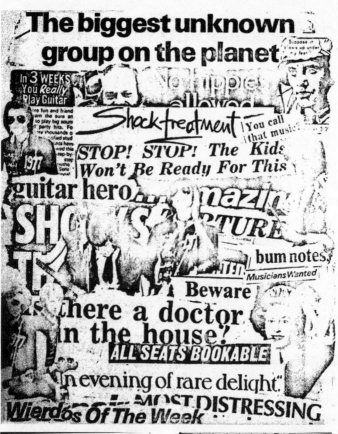

school committee into letting us play at the summer dance, a few weeks away in June 1977.

I had lost my taste for *Top of the Pops* and supergroups like Genesis. It was much more exciting and satisfying to see young bands perform in the clubs that would allow punk. Watch them grow over months.

The next step was to follow local groups around town. Watch them grow over *weeks*. There was an even greater sense of connection.

My friends and I would analyse the performances on the bus ride home – 'Did you notice they had a new guitar amp?' 'Did you like that new song they opened with?' – and we would also critique the posters and the flyers that had been handed out.

Hockley Heath Rugby Club was the venue that had been chosen by the Sixth Form Committee for the summer dance. A bar lined the back of the room, with a few tables and chairs laid out casually and a dance floor in front of them. There were floor-to-ceiling windows on both sides of the room so, being June, it was never properly dark in there. There was no stage, so we set up our meagre collection of instruments on the floor, our onstage sound augmented by the loan of a genuine Carlsbro 100-watt Stingray combo amplifier from our friends in the Prefects.

I had never experienced anything quite like the thrill I got from plugging my Telecaster copy into that machine.

Standing in front of my classmates, holding this weapon, all the rules changed. I was no longer nerdy Nigel who never got the team call-up, who had eschewed prizes and attention and competition. Before tonight I was nobody, but now I was in charge.

I was the bomb.

I had taken no lessons and I was no virtuoso, that much was clear, but I had written a few songs, and despite my limited technique, when my guitar was fed through the Carsbro and the Big Muff distortion box, it sounded big.

I wielded enough power and electricity with my £15 guitar and a borrowed amplifier to shake up everyone's perception of who they thought I was. I could see it on all their faces. They didn't quite understand it, but they all knew, boys and girls alike, that some substantial, chemical, hierarchical shift was taking place.

At the end of the night, there were two new facts that I knew for certain:

1. Shock Treatment were awful.
2. I couldn't wait to do it again.

Shock Treatment played a handful of gigs – we even got a review in local music fanzine *Brumbeat* – and then morphed into the Assassins. I have flyers for both bands at the Golden Eagle on Hill Street, both times supporting the Prefects. Then David and I met Mark Wilson, a DJ on the scene, who asked us to join the band in which he sang and played guitar – Dada. Dada was a much more inventive musical concoction than Shock Treatment. Boutique owner John Brocklesby played a pink Vox bass and sang his own songs. We brought in Roxy fan Marcus to play Stylophone, mounted on an ironing board (very Dada), and David switched from voice to drums. How crazy is that?

John's wife Heather made us some beautiful clothes – a white jacket with a leather collar, beautifully tailored, the kind of stuff they'd be selling in the shop – that gave us a certain classical flamboyance.

The Dada songbook opened with 'Toyroom', Mark Wilson's off-kilter paean to the joys of childhood, sung over a stuttering disco beat. The chords were DA/DA and it was seven minutes long. This was not intended to be mainstream music.

We went to the Crown on Hill Street and asked them if we could have the use of their upstairs room on Tuesdays. So in May of 1978 we began a residency there.

I am a big believer in residencies – getting to play in the same venue, the same night, week in, week out, you get to really develop a sense of what you are and where you are going. You have an objective – to improve – and each week you get feedback from anyone who chooses to come along. At first, the audience will almost always consist of friends and family, but after a while, if you have anything to offer, word will spread and people you have never met or don't know will show up at the door and pay money to hear what you play.

That summer, after telling a sceptical high-school careers officer that I wanted to be a 'pop star', I enrolled at Birmingham Polytechnic's College of Art and Design for a twelve-month foundation course. I had never stopped drawing at home and had filled up books with ideas for posters and band logos. This work, and my enthusiasm, was enough to get me a place, in spite of my underperforming at the grammar school.

A Foundation course offers a fantastic buffet of basic art training in graphics, fashion and textiles, fine art and photography all in one year, with the aim of helping you decide which area you wanted to specialise in for your degree.

For me, however, the decision to go to art school was inspired more by musical heroes – John Lennon, Keith Richards, Bryan Ferry – who had gone to art school. I hoped to hook up with other like-minded souls, just as they had.

Which I did.

The student that I was most drawn to was Stephen Duffy, the

future founder of the band the Lilac Time. In drawing class, when the rest of us were striving to reproduce each detail of the subject as accurately as possible, Stephen would grab a stick of charcoal and violently maul his paper with three or four rough strokes, handing it to the teacher as if to say, 'I don't care about *any of this.*' The teacher would invariably announce, 'You see everybody! Stephen *gets* it!'

What's more, Stephen was a songwriter and he played bass. Fretless bass. He was way ahead of me. He wore the signature chiffon and make-up to college and spoke knowingly of Kerouac and Zimmerman. One of his songs bore the enigmatic title 'Newhaven to Dieppe (And No Wonder)'.

Dada had hit a wall and would go no further. Now I wanted to be in a band with Steve, but I was going to need reinforcements.

I suggested Steve meet Nick Bates.

Like everyone else that year, Nick had wanted to play guitar, and I was supposed to be showing him how. Talk about the deaf leading the blind.

13 Barbarella's

*W*e walk through the double doors. The music is louder inside, the smell of beer and cigarettes. Pay the entrance fee to the girl at the table. One pound thirty. We fumble to count out our money, mine earned at a local supermarket, Nick's working weekends at his mother's toy shop. Get the look-over from the bouncers. Be cool and don't attract attention, like that scene in Saturday Night Fever. The age limit at nightclubs in England is eighteen. I'm seventeen and Nick is fifteen, but we've been here often enough to know we can get away with it. We walk down the carpeted hallway, the music ahead already at an impressive volume. At eye level, on the wall to our left, the place announces itself: 'The biggest night-club in Europe, Barbarella's'.

Everything is shades of dimly lit red. It feels red. It smells red. The carpet is orange-dark, and it's nice and warm inside after our twenty-minute walk through the city centre to get here. Walk another twenty feet or so past the entrance to a small bar into which I have never been – and don't remember ever being open – past the loos (avoid if possible: one is

always vulnerable standing there, open to attack, especially after the alcohol has had its way with the more violently minded punters). At the end of the red tunnel, Nick and I turn into the main club room.

The music is now so loud that everyone has to shout to have an outside chance of getting heard. Communication adjusts to a new level of minimalism. Instincts surge. The DJ, Wayne 'the Plastic Poser', is playing reggae – 'Cocaine in My Brain' by Dillinger, music that is dark and black and dangerous.

Music has never sounded better than it sounds in this room.

Beneath the DJ booth there is a dance floor the size of a double-width garage, filled with punks and New Wavers. Nick and I definitely qualify as the latter. We both still wear our hair quite long, and I'm still in glasses, a punk no-no. No more glam-rock duds. He has on a plain white shirt and skinny black tie, I have a black shirt on which I have stencilled '1977' across my heart, in homage to the Clash.

To the right of the dance floor are a few tables and chairs, and immediately in front of us are three dimly lit steps that lead up to a long, bright bar packed with kids aged between eighteen and twenty-five, all trying to get served. Looking across the dance floor from where we now stand is the stage, about three feet off the ground, where tonight's band will be appearing. Already there is a group of punks gathered at the stage, waiting. They are taking up valuable dance floor space 'cos they ain't dancing. They are here to see and hear live music. They check every action from the side and rear of the stage, looking down to inspect their watches.

It's after eleven, and this is a school night for Nick. I am in my first year at college and wonder how many nights I have had to lie to my parents, who think I'm doing work at Nick's house. On the stage, roadies check mics, keyboards, amps. We go up the steps to the bar, order two Cokes, and I light a cigarette. A Player's No. 6, 'The Schoolboy's Choice'. This is the best view of the stage and there's no danger of getting showered *in spittle, which has happened to me a few times watching the Clash and Generation X.*

Tonight the club is as full as I've ever seen it. It's Blondie's first head-line show in Birmingham, and they are about to explode. This is February 1978, and tomorrow they'll film their new single 'Denis' for a spot on Top of the Pops. Debbie Harry will become an overnight sensation.

Time ticks by slowly. We are making those Cokes last. More cigs get smoked. Both of us secretly hope the band won't be on too late, that we can maybe make the one o'clock night bus. The opening act has been and gone. The night now belongs to the headliners. The crowd has grown and no one is interested any more in what DJ Wayne is playing. Every new song just means another three minutes before the lights go down and the band hits the stage. The kids down front are chanting, 'Blondie, Blondie, Blondie . . .'

Nick and I smile to each other.

We've made it.

14 Ballroom Blitz with Synthesizers

I don't know whether it was the times we were living in or if that's just what it is like being seventeen, but it seemed to us there was so much music happening at that moment; punk rock had transitioned into New Wave, which was a catchall phrase that seemed to embrace just about anything made by anyone under the age of twenty-two. There were so many new forms of music that were inspiring us. Siouxsie and the Banshees were a favourite, and I felt I had a stake in them because I had watched them play to sixty people, then to a loud hundred, then to a thousand, then they got a record deal, which put them on *Top of the Pops*.

Another band I loved to follow was the Heartbreakers, formed by ex-New York Doll Johnny Thunders. Malcolm McLaren flew the Heartbreakers over to the UK to play with the Sex Pistols on their 'Anarchy in the U.K.' tour, and they never really went home. They connected with the British punks and found they could play

DURAN

DURAN

DURAN

DURAN ЯФК ЯФК

duran

duran

STEVIE
DUFAIT   FRETLESS BASS
              VOCALS
              RHYTHM GUITAR

NIGEL
TAYLOR   GUITARS
              BACKING VOCALS

NICK
BATES   SYNTHESIZERS
              TAPES
              RHYTHMS

SIMON
COLLEY   BASS
              SAXAPHONE
              CLARINET

HOW   ЯФК

FRETLESS BASS   DURAN DURAN ЯФК
VOCALS
                             ЯФК
VOCALS
FRETLESS BASS   STEVIE DUFAIT   ЯФК
RHYTHM GUITAR
                 NIGEL TAYLOR
GUITARS
BACKING VOCALS   ЯФК
                 NICK BATES
SYNTHESIZERS   NIGEL
TAPES   ЯФК   TAYLOR
RHYTHMS
                             DURAN
ELECTRIC BASS
BACKING VOCALS   ЯФК   DURAN

to much bigger audiences than in the States. There was something about Thunders onstage that was thrilling, dangerous and unpredictable. That New York attitude. Maybe it was his heroin habit. He came over as the real thing.

Steve Jones is open about the influence Thunders' playing style had on him. In the documentary *The Filth and the Fury*, there is a hilarious sequence where film of the two guitarists is intercut, showing quite clearly just how much of Thunders' attitude Steve knocked off.

Something similar could be done with me. I would learn to take Thunders' signature slurs and guitar runs and transpose them to bass, along with the accompanying sneers. The first time I saw the Thunders' magic was onstage at Birmingham University. The opening act was a band I had not heard of before, the Police. At that time I would sneak a cassette recorder into every gig I went to, and I set the machine to record when they began to play, even though I had no idea who they were. It was quite possible a band you had never heard of yesterday could become your favourite band tomorrow.

The singer with the Police also played bass, which struck me as quite clever and quite 'un-punk'. After the second number, he struck up a rapport with the audience of mostly students. A little too familiar, I remember thinking at the time, not knowing then that Sting had been a teacher and spoke 'student' way better than he would ever speak 'punk'.

STING: 'We've got the Heartbreakers coming on next.'
(*Cheer from me and one or two others*)
STING: 'They can't play, you know.'
ME: 'Fuck off!'

STING: 'Who said "Fuck off?"'

ME: 'I did.' (*all of this going down onto the cassette tape*)

STING: 'It's true. They're great guys but they can't play.'

ME: 'Fuck off, you wanker!

STING: 'You'll see. This next song is called "Fall Out"! 1 2 3 4 . . .'

He was wrong about the Heartbreakers. They were awesome that night. At the BBC in 1993, filming 'Ordinary World' for *Top of the Pops*, I was standing next to Sting watching a playback of our performance on a monitor. I thought to myself, I've got to tell him about that night, but before I opened my mouth he half-turned to me and said, 'I wish I'd written that song.'

Let's leave it at that then, I thought.

Seeing the Human League for the first time was another turning point. Nick and I saw them supporting Siouxsie and the Banshees and Penetration at the Mayfair Ballroom in the Bullring shopping centre and watched in stunned, amazed silence. They had no drummer. No guitars.

They had three synthesizers and a drum machine instead.

So what made for a much more exciting proposition than me attempting to teach Nick guitar was for us somehow to get hold of a synthesizer and make that his instrument.

Nick's mum, Sylvia, made a £200 purchase of the first Wasp synthesizer to arrive in Birmingham, at Woodroffe's music store. It was the best investment she ever made.

We also bought a Kay rhythm box for £15. It had presets such as 'mambo', 'foxtrot', 'slow rock' and 'waltz'. So with Nick controlling the keys, setting the tempos and pushing the buttons on the Kay, Steve Duffy singing and on bass, and myself on guitar, the three of us made our first recordings on a cassette tape recorder in the space above Nick's mum's toy shop. The resulting 'album' was called *Dusk and Dawn*. We named the band Duran Duran.

Where did the name come from? Every fan knows that. From the film *Barbarella*, which starred Jane Fonda as the most gorgeous astronaut detective the galaxy has ever seen, who is sent on a mission to 'Find Durand-Durand and . . . preserve the security of the stars.'

So why not Durand-Durand the band? Because you can't hear the final ds in the film, nor the hyphen, and there was no imdb.com back then.

Poor old Duran(d), played by Milo O'Shea, had stolen the Excessive Machine – a machine guaranteed to give women extreme pleasure and more – and who could blame him? Woody Allen would parody it with his invention of the orgasmatron. *Barbarella* is a masterpiece of Euro-kitsch and we have been forever proud of our association with it.

We brought in Steve's friend Simon Colley to play clarinet and occasional bass for Duran Duran's first live appearance, in our college lecture hall on 5 April 1979 at 6.00 p.m. – practically during class time. It was performance art in a sense. I listened to a recording of it recently. It's hard to imagine that band selling out Madison Square Garden, but as a shoe-gazer, noise-making concern, along the lines of My Bloody Valentine or the Jesus and Mary Chain, we could have had an entirely different career experience.

Our friends showed up – maybe twenty or thirty in all – to support us, and we took advantage of the projection screen to show abstract slides that were meant to enhance the meaning of the songs. The Human League had done that too.

Music was moving on and we were moving with it. We were

the zeitgeist. Since Shock Treatment, we had been unconsciously tapping into all the changes that were happening in the culture. We were evolving away from the three-chord angry noise. We aspired to something else, something fresh. Multimedia, fashion, dance, art. We wanted it all in the mix.

The cover of *Dusk and Dawn* featured a black-and-white photocopy of a New York streetscape shot on long exposure, car lights trailing up and down Park Avenue. In the top right-hand corner, we dropped in a photo of the three of us, with our facial features strangely absent. Maybe it was art – or maybe I just overdid the contrast on the college photocopier.

The song titles were: 'Soundtrack', 'Aztec Moon Rich', 'Take (The Lines and the Shadows)' – which could be one of Simon's titles – 'Hold Me/Pose Me', 'A Lucien Melody' and 'Hawks Don't Share'.

I was very proud of this first attempt at album-making and decided to offer it as my year-end project. Each student was allotted a certain amount of space in the main hall to display the fruits of their labour. I covered my wall space with a shiny black plastic dustbin liner and placed the solitary cassette tape on the table in front of it. It looked pretty good.

There was a certain amount of chutzpah required to keep a straight face as the college faculty and my fellow students circled my presentation. I had taken the Steve Duffy model of freedom of interpretation to another level.

Professor Grundy picks up the cassette, handles it gingerly.

GRUNDY: 'And what is this exactly?'
ME: 'It's what I've been doing for the last six months.'
GRUNDY: 'And what are you hoping to do with it?'
ME: 'Get a record deal.'

GRUNDY: 'It doesn't really relate to your course work though, does it?'

ME: 'Why should it? Haven't you been encouraging us to think more freely, about what is and isn't art? This is art because I say it is.'

(I couldn't have cared whether he passed me or not.)

GRUNDY: 'Well, I am glad you've learned something in your time here, Nigel.'

That was my last day in academia. A few weeks later I got a letter telling me I hadn't been accepted for a place on any of the BA courses I had applied for.

Secretly, I was happy. All I wanted to do was make music, refine these ideas we were having as a band and play as often as possible.

But I had to explain this to Mum and Dad, as I wanted to carry on living at home.

I approached them with far greater humility than I had my college professors. What I was proposing – to not get a job – went against the grain of everything they knew. They saw my music-making as a hobby at best, something to smile about but not to make a career of.

My cause wasn't helped by the fact that Dad had been made redundant – he liked to call it taking early retirement – at fifty-seven, and if I could get this through, for a while we would be signing on for state benefits together.

'I just need some time, Mum, Dad. This is what I really want to do.'

'I don't know. Jack, what do you think?'

Their disappointment was palpable. They both had dreams of their son at university. This was a big lump for them to swallow.

I had to further my argument. 'I'm not saying I don't want to do anything. I'm not going to be sitting around the house. I'll be working at the music. But I need to do it full time.'

Dad was pretty out of it. The debacle at work that had led to his 'early retirement' had left him stunned and out of ideas. The rebel in him wanted to support me.

'I suppose we could give it a try. One year only.'

That was all I needed. I could feel it. I could barely contain myself. In a display of emotion that was rare at number 34, I hugged them and cried because I knew the significance of what was happening.

Mum and Dad giving me the benefit of the doubt and allowing me to pursue my goal for twelve months was the best gift they ever gave me.

There was not a moment to lose.

15 Everybody Dance

Duran Duran played next at the Cannon Hill Arts Centre on 8 May (tickets fifty pence) and then at Barbarella's on 1 June.

Walking back to Hollywood from the Maypole bus terminus, Nick and I were convinced Duran Duran were going somewhere. We had really connected with the Barbarella's crowd. There was enough positivity in their reaction to what we were doing to encourage us. We were on the right track.

And then, disaster.

Days and days passed after the Barbarella's gig where neither Nick nor I could get hold of Steve or Simon. What the fuck was going on?

And then the word came down the wire; they were both making music at a Cheapside squat with several members of TV Eye, another local band, my oldest friend, David Twist, among them.

I raced around to Nick's home on Mill Close.

'Can you fucking believe it?' I said.

'Wankers!' retorted Nick.

This was not a time to play Chartbuster. The stakes had gotten too high for that.

We were distraught. But not destroyed. We were angry.

Anger is good.

Anger is galvanising. Have you ever noticed how often a football team performs better after one of the players has been sent off the pitch? Surely Malcolm Gladwell must have a theory about that. Our backs were against the wall. Steve and Simon had dared to count us out, thought they could do better without us.

We retreated to the room above the toy shop and plotted our revenge.

We had to turn this crisis around.

What did Nick and I do? We called Andy Wickett, the singer of TV Eye, who we knew was now out of a job, and asked him to join Duran Duran. He jumped at it. It was an incestuous game of musical chairs with a Birmingham accent.

Andy organised a meeting with Roger Taylor, the drummer with one of Birmingham's better bands, the Scent Organs. The four of us met at a house party the following Friday.

Roger Taylor is one of the nicest guys anyone could ever meet. He was working on the production line at the Rover car plant in Solihull, as was his dad, but he wanted to make music full-time.

For a guy who liked nothing better than beating the hell out of his drum kit, Roger had a very laid-back, easy-going manner. There was something casually fifties about him, with his James Dean hair and preppy style. And his reputation preceded him. When the Damned had played Barbarella's the year before, their drummer, Rat Scabies, had gotten up from behind his drum kit and dared anyone in the audience to take his place. Roger did.

I never imagined Roger wanting to play with us. I thought of him as being on another level. But he could feel the way the wind was blowing and did not want to just thrash away any more. He wanted to make music that had the energy and attitude of punk but was also new and different. He agreed to come and jam with Andy, Nick and me.

Duran Duran version 2.0 moved out of the toy shop and set up its gear on the second floor of the TV Eye Cheapside squat, where Andy Wickett still lived, enforcing a future-friendly new music zone, while the Subterranean Hawks, Steve and Simon's new band – the bastards! – were on the third floor, working on their Rolling Stones/Bob Dylan legacy.

The scene was set for a serious battle of the bands.

Inevitably, the parties would meet; there were encounters at undesignated times in neutral demilitarised zones such as the dilapidated ground-floor kitchen where the washing up never got done, and sneers and cigarette papers would be traded.

A sniffy elitism crept down from the third floor at times, especially as we began to upgrade our sound to incorporate dance-friendly grooves. When Roger first joined the band, I was still playing guitar, and I began to hone a more rhythmic style that would lock in with his drumming.

We were venturing outside the punk bubble musically and had a social life to match. We liked going to wine bars such as Hawkins, next door to Virgin Records on Corporation Street. The girls were more appealing there, and we were made welcome and treated better than we were in Birmingham's grimy pubs.

The wine bars also gave us exposure to a broader musical diet. The first time I heard Chic's song 'Everybody Dance' was in a wine bar. The impact of that song on me was huge, because the bass guitar came across as the lead instrument. I had never heard bass played that way. This record was as revolutionary to me as 'Anarchy in the U.K.' had been. I picked up a bass guitar that Andy Wickett had in his bedroom and started playing around on it. I found that I could quite easily imitate the style of the Chic bassist, whose name I had no idea of, along with the bass lines of other popular disco hits such as Sylvester's 'You Make Me Feel (Mighty Real)'. What I lacked in technique, I made up for in attitude.

Roger and I got excited at the idea of playing in the style of these disco bands and began to forge a sound together. We even began to talk about a rhythm section, a term that I don't believe had ever been used by a punk rock band. The bass was taking over, locking in the low-end notes with Roger's bass drum. I liked the interplay and exchange of energy that took place between us.

This is what my instincts were telling me: focus on bass. The guitar-player question would be answered soon enough. I made the decision to invest some of my meagre cash resources in a bass guitar of my own – an inexpensive Hondo copy that looked meaner than it was.

I often think, given the number of hours that I have spent looking at Roger's face over the years, how lucky I am to have such a pleasant, non-judgemental, friendly face to look upon. He is also the least moody guy I know. A nice yin to my yang.

16 Plans for Nigel

The next step was to enter a real recording studio. Bob Lamb was about to become a legend among Birmingham bands. He had been the drummer in the Steve Gibbons Band, staples of pre-punk-era Birmingham rock. Their success had not been huge, but they had made it to *Top of the Pops* with a cover of Chuck Berry's 'Tulane' and toured US arenas opening for the Who, who were fans. Bob had invested his royalties in a small but perfect four-track recording studio built into the sitting room of his Kings Heath flat.

He was a sympathetic and encouraging producer, the midwife who would be responsible for the birth of UB40, producing their first hit single, 'King', and their debut album, *Signing Off*. This would be inspirational for Birmingham bands, because UB40 were unique; they danced to their own drum – recording their album on a miniscule budget, releasing it on their own label – and ended up with a global hit.

Andy Wickett, Roger, Nick and I booked a day at Bob's studio.

This was our first exposure to multitrack recording. The first thing Bob did was to lovingly mic up Roger's drum kit. I had never seen that done before. He took time to get the sound on each drum correct. I was intrigued by the cables and plugs and knobs and buttons. I could not understand what was taking so long until I heard the first playback. We recorded four songs, among them a first draft of 'Girls on Film'. I laid down the bass guitar lines with Roger playing drums and then overdubbed the guitars separately, as we had not yet found a full-time guitarist. Listening back to the first rough mixes, we could not believe what Bob had done to our sound. He totally got the disco influence and had Roger record the hi-hat separately, a trick he had learned from American disco producers. We were tight and funky, and with Bob's help we had moved on from our brittle art-school atmospheres to create a danceable, viable, pop group sound.

On the demo cassette liner, I appear credited under my birth name, Nigel. It wasn't long after this that I decided that a pop star named John Taylor sounded better than Nigel Taylor.

I'd been sick of Nigel for years. It had been the nerd-name of choice for so much satire. In Monty Python's 'Upperclass Twit of the Year' TV sketch, the biggest twit of them all was called Nigel. The day at school following that broadcast had been a nightmare. And XTC had just released 'Making Plans for Nigel', about the neighbourhood Goody Two-shoes.

Nigel had to go.

But John — Johnny — was a rocker. Johnny Rotten, Johnny Thunders, Johnny Ramone.

It was more than just taking a stage name. I needed to reinvent myself. Not be Mum and Dad's son. I didn't want to be called Nigel by anybody: the band, my friends, my family. It would take Mum years to get with the John plan.

Do people treat a John differently than they treat a Nigel? It's like blondes and brunettes.

If I had had a greater vision for myself, I would have kept Nigel and been the only Nigel in a music business crowded with Johns and Johnnies. But I wasn't *that* confident.

For all that, changing my name was a commitment, a statement of intent, like a new haircut. A permanent one.

Nick and I were as one on this line of thinking. But he liked his first name. It was his surname – Bates – that didn't fit the picture. We would discuss our respective alternatives at length.

John, Johnny, Jon Ravel? Maybe.

Nicholas, Nick, Nik Dior?

In the end we settled on the more prosaic John Taylor and Nick Rhodes.

'Rhodes' seemed to have the right blend of high and low culture, drawing as it did from the Clash's manager, Bernie, and fashion's high priestess, Zandra.

17 Legs for Days

To accompany our new names and to take the new sound Bob Lamb had helped us create in the studio onto the stage, we needed a full-time guitarist. It was becoming clear I had a better feel for bass, and the drum/bass dynamic Roger and I were developing was working. Plus, in 1979 there were hundreds of kids who wanted to play guitar and very few who wanted to play bass. We met Alan Curtis, a Londoner who lived in Cradley Heath with his girlfriend, and asked him to join. We brought in our friend Fozzi from Vision Collision as an occasional extra to add soulful harmonies. The band's onstage confidence grew.

In the squat, our new musical direction aroused scorn and suspicion. Moving our gear back up the stairs to Andy's room after a gig, we were confronted by the words 'DISCO SUCKS!' daubed in red paint across the front door.

We were far too energised by the progress we were making to be bothered by such childishness. In their puritanism, the Hawks –

for it had been they with the paintbrush – were out-of-date. We were doing something new, drawing inspiration from what was happening now, not twenty years ago. We were attempting to innovate. They were being left behind.

But all was not rosy. Our relationship with Andy began to fray, and after a couple more gigs with him, we decided to cut him loose. It wasn't personal, but Nick, Roger and I just couldn't imagine taking the long ride with him, and the long ride was what we were in for.

We replaced Andy with Jeff Thomas, the singer from Roger's old band, the Scent Organs. In an act that created further indignity for the departing singer, Andy's girlfriend Jane stuck with us, now dating Nick and helping to manage the band. At the same time, I started dating the Hawks' guitarist's ex-girlfriend.

She was the first girl I slept with. We went to church together the following morning, good Catholic girl that she was. That settled the battle of the bands.

I wanted a girlfriend, to be sure. A little eye candy never hurt any musician. But I wasn't going to get hung up on it. I had absolutely no interest in marriage and was far too dedicated to the boys in the band to really make a good boyfriend. In fact, I would not be anyone's idea of a good boyfriend for another twenty years or so.

Jane, Nick and I went on our first expedition to meet record companies in London that winter. We took our latest demo tapes to Island, Phonogram and EMI.

We actually got into the A&R offices at Island and played the songs to someone there.

'Where you boys from?'

'Birmingham.'

'North of the border, eh? What's the band's name?'

We told him. He tapped the tape against the palm of his hand, considering.

'All right, let's put it on.'

We listened. He nodded along appreciatively. I needed to pee.

After the last song, he popped the tape out of the deck and offered it back to us.

'You can keep it. It's got our number on it.'

He looked more closely, as if to make sure we weren't lying.

'Oh yeah, right. Good to know. Thanks for coming in.'

And we were back out on the street in St Peter's Square.

By Christmas, Jane had drifted away. Shame. She had legs for days. They just weren't enough to get us a record deal.

18 Enter the Eighties

As we glided towards the end of the seventies, no one I knew was giving much thought to what the eighties were going to look or sound like. Maybe it was being discussed in the pages of big media like *Time* or *Newsweek* or the *Guardian*, but I wasn't thinking about it. I was too busy living.

No one knew then just how important the music that Kraftwerk had been making at their home studios in Düsseldorf, with their handmade keyboards and effects pedals, would turn out to be. They were inventing techno, and not just the sound.

The cover of 1978's *The Man-Machine* took its look from Fritz Lang's twenties monochrome masterpiece *Metropolis*, adding Russian Constructivism's signature colours and shapes, red, black and grey, all hard angles and triangles. The influence of that cover alone would take a year to fully enter the cultural stream. By late 1979, there wasn't anyone doing anything that mattered who wasn't in some way influenced by that album. Everything that was

worth saying visually could be said in black and white, with the ubiquitous grey and accents of red.

Manchester's Warsaw renamed themselves as Joy Division and wore smart grey shirts, dark ties and military surplus raincoats.

Visage would sing 'Fade to Grey'. Ultravox recorded in Cologne with Conny Plank, Can's producer, and filmed a black-and-white video in Vienna as an homage to Orson Welles's *The Third Man*.

No one who had a clue was dressing 'punk' any more. The punk look had moved on. In Birmingham, designers and boutique owners Patti Bell and Jane Kahn would honour the spirit of punk regalia, but soften it, romanticise it. They would provide some perfect looks for Duran over the next year or two.

Vivienne Westwood continued to innovate. She never got hung up on her iconic punk creations, she kept moving forward. The clothes she would unveil on Bow Wow Wow in 1980 were extraordinarily beautiful, and we would be adding some pieces from that collection to our wardrobes once the money came in.

The shapes right now were sharp and structured. Gary Numan got that right. He would have a number 1 song in the UK with 'Cars'.

The military look was back. Ground Control to Major Tom. Bowie in Berlin. *2001*. Keyboards were in, guitars were out.

No more 'No Future'; the future had been reinstated. The Sex Pistols' message was already passé.

The original punks drifted back to Bowie and Ferry, disillusioned with Sham 69 and the 'Oi' crowd. Back to dressing in sleek suits, slicking their hair back. People wanted to dress up again.

Glamour came back – Decadent Empire Dressing. The machismo of punk disappeared overnight. Disco was winning the war on rock. Halston, Gucci and Fiorucci all made it to the Midlands. Fonts were modern and democratic. Kidnapper typography and ink splatters were out. Avant Garde became the font *du jour* and **Helvetica** continued its ride to the top. Girls and boys began to cross-over-dress again, as they had done during the glam-rock years. The nihilism that had been so crucial to fuelling punk rock's beginnings had been replaced by something equally, if not more, motivational: the will to win, to succeed, to triumph. The UK elected a woman prime minister. Ambition was cool.

I didn't know any of this then, could not have articulated it if I tried. It takes perspective to recognise the shifting of trends. But 1979–80 was undoubtedly a cultural crossroads.

I learned lessons watching the paths taken by my idols. Turned out the Clash wanted to be the biggest rock and roll band in the world, the new Rolling Stones. I didn't get that when I was following them around the country, screaming along with their anthems, 'Complete Control' and '1977'.

Sadly, the Sex Pistols had not been able to ride out the insanity their notoriety had brought them. They had the most acrimonious breakup, and now Johnny Rotten, who had reverted to his given name of John Lydon in a very postmodern move, was doing something new. He would have a place in eighties culture with Public Image Ltd almost as significant as he had with the Pistols in the seventies.

Buzzcocks were proving to be tremendously resilient, turning up every other week on *Top of the Pops*, performing a string of perfectly composed pop masterpieces, one after another, as did Blondie. Both bands set a blistering pace.

1980 would see the death – almost – of the music weekly. Only the *NME* would survive long-term. There was a new, glossy, full-colour pop press gaining in popularity, exemplified by *Smash Hits*, who liked putting full-colour photos of Adam Ant on their covers because they sold well.

A taste of the zeitgeist as it stood in December 1979. The Culture Wave. Wherever it was going, I would be going with it.

19 Music Never Sounded Better

In February, Nick and I were going around venues in Birmingham looking for unconventional places to play, like art galleries and cafés. Although our residency at the Crown had served Dada well, we now agreed that we would do anything to avoid the pub circuit. The dank, beer-sodden, Victorian carpets and gloomy stained glass would have been a death knell to us.

We used to make fun of the bands that seemed to be constantly in residence at the same old, tired pubs that made up the less inspiring end of the local Birmingham rock scene. On BRMB Radio, late-night DJ Robin Valk would always be saying, 'And Wednesday, Bright Eyes will be sparkling at the Barrel Organ.' We would collapse in hysterics. They'd been sparkling at the Barrel Organ for so many years now, it was hard to believe there could be any sparkle left.

One band that had got it right was Fashion. The Police had introduced the term 'white reggae' into the music lexicon, and

Fashion had a lot of that. They also had an interesting electronic synthpop aspect that we found appealing and the most entertaining drummer on the scene in Dick Davis. Plus, thanks to Mulligan, the keyboard- and bass-playing dreadlocked blond art student, the best flyers the city had ever made.

We watched Fashion closely, in much the same way as we were following UB40, except with Fashion it was more about concept; the strength and substance were in the ideas.

One Friday afternoon, Nick and I, as part of our continuing search for special venues, visited the Ikon Gallery in the city centre and discussed with them the possibility of staging 'a happening'. From there, walking up Hill Street, we noticed posters for a 'Bowie night' at a nightclub called the Rum Runner. 'New Sounds, New Styles', the poster promised.

Looks interesting.

We walked up to Broad Street and knocked on the door of the Rum Runner.

The only thing I knew about the Rum Runner was that it was very old-school. I had never been there. Neither had Nick. It was not on our radar. I had always assumed it drew an older clientele, much like the Opposite Lock jazz club around the corner. It had been used as a location in the drama series *Gangsters*, a BBC Birmingham production.

We were directed up an external fire escape to the club's office, where we met Paul Berrow, a tall, rather debonair guy, suavely dressed in very un-Birmingham clothes; silk scarves, cravats, seersucker suits and handmade shirts were Paul's thing.

We had recorded another set of songs at Bob Lamb's, this time with Jeff Thomas at the vocal mic, and we handed Paul this tape, hoping he would have a listen to it at some future time.

But Paul wanted to hear it there and then. He responded

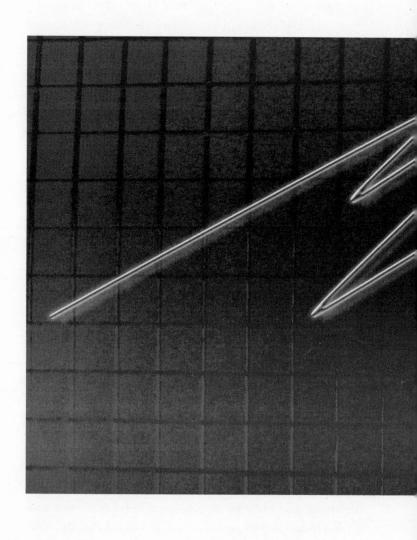

eagerly, 'Follow me, chaps. Let's have a listen to this downstairs.'

Undoubtedly, part of the reason Paul wanted to put our tape on right away was because he was very proud of the Rum Runner's sound system and was happy to have someone to show it off to. He and his brother Michael had been to Studio 54 in New York and had their minds blown, and were in the process of creating something similar at home. Their father owned a string of the city's top venues – clubs and casinos – and had gifted his sons the Rum Runner.

Michael, the more circumspect brother, was not there that day. If he had been, I don't know if any of the rest of this story would have happened.

Paul fired up the power amps, and four six-foot-high speakers – one on each corner of the dance floor – hummed into life.

He slotted the tape into the machine and pressed play.

Music never sounded better than it did in that room.

Paul loved what he heard on the tape, and he seemed to like Nick and me. He was by nature an optimist and an idealist.

'This is very bloody interesting,' he said. 'My brother and I have been thinking about getting into management. Why don't you come down to the club tonight, and bring the rest of the boys with you?'

So later that night, Nick and I showed up to introduce the band to Paul – our five-piece with Roger on drums, Alan Curtis on guitar and Jeff Thomas on vocals. We all seemed to get along, so Paul agreed to put on a gig at the club in March with Fashion headlining and Duran opening.

A few days later, we moved our gear into the Rum Runner. One of the bars wasn't being used, and that was where we set up our stuff. Paul said we could practise in there during the day.

Having a connection with the Rum Runner was crucial for Duran Duran. Paul and Michael became our patrons, and we effectively had this establishment representing us.

The deal was clear: our job was to write the songs and develop the sound, and it was the Berrows' responsibility to find us places to play, buy us whatever gear we needed and, ultimately, find us a record deal.

On 12 March we played for the first time in the club, on a low, makeshift stage set up next to the DJ booth. At the time it felt like our best performance to date, and I was happy with where we were at and where we were headed. But at 8.00 a.m. the following morning I got a call from Alan Curtis; he was at a motorway service area on the M1. Anxiously putting coins into the callbox, he tried to explain to me, 'I don't like that scene. It makes me nervous. I'm going back to London.'

I just didn't get it.

He must have been watching *Gangsters*.

Then Jeff and Paul started arguing. Musical differences, *between singer and manager*? One of them had to go. It wasn't going to be Paul. Another singer we could find, but a manager like Paul comes along once in a lifetime.

We held on to Paul, Jeff was out the door. Now we are looking for a singer *and* a guitarist.

And yet it didn't feel that daunting. Our commitment to Paul, Michael and the Rum Runner bought us a degree of comfortability that we had not previously experienced.

Paul and Michael invested in some gear for us. I needed to step up from the cheap Hondo bass I was using and the cumbersome amplifier combo I was schlepping around with me. I replaced that with a slick Peavey amp head and matching speaker cabinet. For my next bass, I was looking for something I could call my own. Something with style.

Another example of how the rules were changing at the beginning of the eighties was in musical instrument manufacture. Fender and Gibson had the monopoly on seventies music; everyone played one or the other, and most bassists used Fender Precisions. I didn't want to be part of any tradition. Was that the times or was that the teens? As I have gotten older, tradition, and being part of a continuum of bassists, writers and performers, has become more important to me.

But in 1980, I wanted to stand apart from what had come before as much as I could. There was a wave of manufacturers coming out of Japan, producing instruments that were strong and stylish, and the common knowledge was that they made the grade. The same thing would happen with cars ten years later.

I liked the Ibanez basses that Sting used, but they were expensive. At Jones and Crossland on Queensway, I saw and tried out a bass I liked the look of by a Japanese manufacturer I had not heard of before, Aria. It had a similar look to the Ibanez, and there were two models on offer: the 1200, which had two pickups and active electronics – which required six-volt batteries to power it – and the 600, with a single pickup, no active electronics, but sleek and very pretty, with a two-tone wood grain. It was also half the price; maybe the Berrows were footing the bill, but I had no intention of taking advantage of them.

It was a good choice; the Aria would become my signature instrument and get me around the world.

I've never had the kind of relationship with my basses one often hears guitar players talk about having with their six-string lovers. I don't cook breakfast with my bass strapped on, and I've been known to take it to bed with me only once or twice in really desperate times. I never became a real tech-head, and I am still using Peavey amplifiers.

Every night at the Rum Runner, we were exposed to the best of contemporary music – European dance music, funk, disco and jazz funk – all accompanied by a steady stream of vintage wine, champagne, a little smoke now and again and even a little toot.

The next few months found us auditioning for singers and guitarists. They would come to us from all over the Midlands, some from farther afield, having answered ads that we had taken out in the music press. We would tell the guitar players that the singer was sick, and we would tell the same story to the singers about the guitar player. And all the time, Roger, Nick, and I were refining the backbone style of what would become the sound of Duran Duran.

Andy Taylor was born on the northeast coast of England in Cullercoats, Northumberland, a hardy boy from a hardy land. He had decided he wanted to be a guitar player early on in life. He was a year younger than me and had not gone to college, so he had already been a professional working musician for several years. He had a band that regularly toured the airforce bases in Germany. Andy sang, played guitar, drove the Ford van and could fix it if it needed fixing. His was an entirely different experience from ours.

The night before Andy came down to Birmingham to meet and play with us, I had been watching guitarist Gary Moore on television. I was taken by his ability to switch from bluesy rock to choppy funk styles. I felt our band needed a similar level of skill and versatility. Gary Moore happened to be Andy's favourite guitar player. Andy didn't look like one of us. He showed up wearing a T-shirt with a logo in the style of a Kit Kat chocolate bar, saying

'Have a break/Have a kwik kwap'. Nick would always say the writing was on the wall right there and then.

And it's true, he didn't talk or think like one of us, but we connected over music, and that was what mattered.

Andy liked what happened the day of his audition and agreed to move to Birmingham. Paul's brother Michael installed him in the spare room of his flat, and pretty soon Andy was spending most of his nights there with the Page Three model Janine Andrews. Birmingham life suited him.

A third Taylor? Is that a joke? For weeks, Nick thought it was. Now we were back to four.

A part-time business associate of Paul and Michael's named Keith Baker began to obsessively insist that we install local beauty and Rum Runner hostess Elayne Griffiths as our singer.

For a few weeks, this idea had some currency. Cameras were brought into the club to film her singing two of our songs. I took my glasses off, as we were only miming and I didn't need to see the fretboard in detail. After the filming, the beautiful Elayne remarked, 'You should get contact lenses. You look cute without those glasses.'

I did?

The feeling among Andy, Roger, Nick and me was that Elayne was not the right singer for the band. It was not our vision. In effect, we'd become her backing band.

The auditions continued.

20 The Poetry Arrives

Until we found a singer, we were restricted to the rehearsal room. And I wanted to get back out in front of an audience. Despite the bonhomie and champagne, I was ready to resent Paul Berrow for not getting along with Jeff Thomas. But I couldn't get hung up on that for too long. Securing Andy was a major step forward, and we weren't wasting time. The band sound was finding its groove.

We offered the vocal job to Gordon Sharp from the Freeze, who had come down from Edinburgh and looked and sounded the part. I called him from my parents' phone in the hall and asked him when he planned to return to Birmingham.

'I've thought long and hard about it, John, but I am going to stick with my own band.'

Another blow.

The Berrows had more ideas about who could fill the vocal role, but on this subject they were clueless. The answer would

come by way of an angel, a student at the university who worked part-time at the Rum Runner on weekends.

She knew what we were up to and suggested to her roommate that he come down and meet us.

Simon Le Bon (his real name), grew up in Bushey, an outer suburb of London, the eldest of three brothers. We never did find out what his father did for a living. 'Dodgy things in Whitehall' was the most anyone could get out of him. But his mother and his mother's mother had both been dancers on the stage, and Simon had been encouraged to follow them into the limelight.

As a child, he had acted on TV and been given small roles in commercials. He had gotten caught up in the punk euphoria, as we had, and had sung in several bands. The one of which he was most proud was called Dog Days.

He had chosen to go to university to study the dramatic arts, so he had put his music-making on hold. Thankfully for us, he was offered a place at Birmingham University.

He was two years older than me, and our relationship, as it developed, would often feel to me like I was one of his younger siblings. But at that first meeting, what struck me most violently about Simon was his presence. He was tall and well spoken, and there was something noble about him. His Huguenot blood perhaps.

And then there was that name. Quite fantastic.

Hair cut short, bleached dirty blond; it gave him an edge. I can't forget what he was wearing for our first meeting, as it's become part of band legend: skin-tight leopard-print ski pants with loops under the boots. Undoubtedly a dubious look, but, you know, he was studying Shakespeare. In fact, he could have easily been Shakespeare's idea of a rock star. You knew he'd look good in a doublet. He was lean and he was punk and he was ready to move on up, like the rest of us.

We didn't play together the first day he came by but talked about music, working each other out. Simple Minds had just released their second album, *Reel to Real Cacophony*, which John Leckie had produced. It was an important album to us, and it was on Simon's radar too. I remember that as being significant.

He returned to the club a day or two later, bringing with him a battered blue book, his Dog Days lyric book, which was filled with lyrics and ideas for songs. That book contained the basis for many of our future compositions, perhaps most notably 'The Chauffeur'.

The four of us plugged in our instruments and played Simon a track that best represented the sound we had been working on. It started with a synthesizer sequencer and a 'four-on-the-floor' disco drumbeat. After eight bars Andy, Nick and I came crashing in together: the working-man's guitar, fat and no-nonsense, Nick's delicate, melodic keyboard riff and my tightly honed New York bassline. It was all too much, but it fitted together like sex and leather. Simon knew where he wanted to be. He sat and listened as we played the song through a few times, making notes in his book. Then he stood up, all six feet two of him, sauntered over to the mic, book open, and began to sing:

I've been in this grass here for the last ten hours.
My clothes are dirty but my mouth isn't dry.
How does it happen? Does it fly through the air?
Oh, I gave up asking days away.
And now I'm lying here waiting for the Sound of Thunder.

I wrote in my diary that night, 'Finally the front man! The star is here!'

The poetry had arrived.

21 The Final Debut

We set a date to play downstairs in the club under the neon lights and MirroFlex-covered walls; Wednesday 16 July 1980.

Everyone worked with the same determination and enthusiasm. Simon had one acting commitment left, an appearance at the Edinburgh Festival. Upon his return, he dropped out of his university course altogether to focus on the band full time.

Typically, musicians are not the most verbose of creatures. They are at their most articulate when they are playing music well with others. We hadn't – yet – become a band of huggers (I had to move to LA to get that habit), and back in the summer of 1980, acknowledgment and praise of each other, as we all contributed to this great forward-moving musical project, was made by way of the slightest nods, winks and half-smiles.

There was no leader. Despite the fact that Nick and I had been through so much and, together with Roger, had carried the

JULY 16

Duran Duran banner around Birmingham for several years, we never told any of the others what to play, what to sing or what to wear. The notes, the beats, the rhymes came out of everyone's individual soul.

That is how it should be, everyone holding down their own corner. No bosses. No one needing to be told what their gig is by another. I had to work on my basslines; every note I played had to be stronger and better than the last. No one needed to tell me what to play, and we all approached the work the same way. Work and play.

Our sense of equality was apparent in just how rarely we commented on each other's contributions. Bands rarely have that GOAL! moment where one person scores and everyone jumps on top of him. You play a song together well, and everyone knows it. You don't, and the only acknowledgement of that comes by way of no one looking back at you. I hadn't ever been a team player, but right then and there, everything we were doing felt good to me.

And there were no more auditions. Thanks be to God.

The five of us would now meet every day around two, play through the afternoon, then retire to the Rum Runner office to plot and strategise. We never once doubted that we were going to make it. Whatever confidence Nick, Roger and I had, it was now reinforced substantially by the confidence of Paul and Michael, Andy and now Simon. We were getting to know each other personally and musically, and building trust and intimacy.

The club would wake up around seven. The Berrows had given us all part-time jobs to help justify the cash outlays they were making. As I was still living at home, a job also helped quiet my parents' concerns. I got a twelve-month extension to my home-stay plan.

Simon and I worked the door some nights, and sometimes we

were behind the bar with Roger. Andy donned an apron and worked in the kitchen, cooking up the locally famous club chilli. Nick got the best gig; he got to DJ.

What was he playing? Let's have a look:

Yellow Magic Orchestra: 'Computer Games'
Mick Ronson: 'Only After Dark'
The Psychedelic Furs: 'Sister Europe'
Roxy Music: 'Over You'
Iggy Pop: 'Nightclubbing'
John Foxx: 'Underpass'
Wire: 'I Am the Fly'
Siouxsie and the Banshees: 'Hong Kong Garden'
Grace Jones: 'Pull Up to the Bumper'
Kraftwerk: 'The Model'
Donna Summer: 'I Feel Love'
The Cure: 'A Forest'
Lou Reed: 'Walk on the Wild Side'
Japan: 'Gentlemen Take Polaroids'
Magazine: 'Shot by Both Sides'
Bowie: 'Always Crashing in the Same Car'
Orchestral Manoeuvres in the Dark: 'Electricity'
Bryan Ferry: 'The "In" Crowd'
Public Image Ltd: 'Public Image'
The Human League: 'Being Boiled'
Marianne Faithfull: 'Broken English'
Joy Division: 'Love Will Tear Us Apart'

Years later, Nick and I would make a mix tape CD of all these songs, which we named 'Only After Dark'.

*

All these influences were coming at us thick and fast. On top of which, each band member brought something particular, something unique, from their own experience. Andy was not a member of the Glam & Punk Rockers Club. His influences came by way of heavy blues-rock, like AC/DC and Van Halen, as a result of which our sound leaped forward, and that would be the reason why, when every other English band of our peers was getting held up at customs, we cracked it in the Unites States.

But that was to come.

Right now, we had to finish the songs we had started before Simon had come along, and write some new ones too.

The template for our songwriting modus operandi had been set, to some degree, that first day.

Jamming, coming up with grooves, chord progressions, melodies. The songs started to develop quickly.

I'm fast. As a band, we all are. When we start writing a song together, we almost always hit on something interesting quickly. At this point, it's all just pure energy. And it's exciting, because every idea has the potential to become something fabulous.

'Sound of Thunder' had written itself that first day Simon had sung with us. Other songs, such as 'Night Boat', were suggested by technology, built around Nick's drifting keyboard sample and Andy's enthusiastic use of his new Roland guitar synthesizer. We introduced Simon to the 'Girls on Film' hook, which we had never let go of, and he immediately set to work rewriting the verses.

As mid-July rolled around, we were right on target. We had a short but perfect set of songs with which to introduce the latest and hopefully final incarnation of Duran Duran to the people of Birmingham.

Standing on the edge of the quay
No lights flashing on the water for me
Fog in my mind darkens in my eyes
Silently screaming for a distant sound
Ripple river yellows, rising for a breath of breathing and drowns
Stillness overcomes me in the night, listen to the rising water
   moan
I'm waiting, waiting for the Night Boat.

'Night Boat' was the first song we played live with the defini-
tive Duran Duran line-up, and we played it exactly as it would
appear on our debut album.

It was a remarkable development from our previous public
appearance. Andy and Simon had both brought with them a
supreme level of cool, ability and musical creativity. And they were
both so different. They expanded the band sideways, as it were.
Simon's post-punk intellectualism and Andy's raw but well-
wrought playing style multiplied the band's appeal by any number
of degrees.

They made us a million times more interesting, and we knew
it.

The audience at the Rum Runner were a pretty cool lot, that
was the vibe, so we didn't expect roars of applause; a cool appraisal
with a positive look was the most that could be hoped for. And
that was what we got. But, looking out at them, I could tell that
we had something now that we had not had last time. Call it the
'X' factor.

We followed 'Night Boat' with 'The Sound of Thunder',
rolling out the stomping four-on-the-floor rhythm section that
would define our sound. Roger had never played live this way,
like a New York session drummer out of Parliament-Funkadelic

or something. His friends in the audience were aghast.

We were nervous, and there was even less acknowledgement of one another onstage than there had been in the rehearsal room. But cool detachment was so 1980.

My nerves were not helped by the fact that it was my first time onstage without glasses. I had just about gotten used to the contact lenses, but I still felt like a toddler swimming without his water wings.

Simon addressed the crowd.

'We're Duran Duran, and we want to be the band to dance to when the bomb drops. This is "Late Bar". We wrote it for you to dance to.'

Roger counted it off: '1-2-3-4.'

And in we went.

I liked Simon's Home Counties accent, the Cockney accentuated. We weren't just a Birmingham band any more. Between Simon's origins and Andy's North Country background, we had unconsciously morphed into the perfect pop group of Old England, but it was so camouflaged by the nouveau hair colours and the make-up and the clothes that no one saw it. It would be our most potent secret weapon. When London was everything in the pop-music culture of the UK, with only occasional nods to Manchester and Liverpool, we would become the Everyman band that the whole country could get behind.

Looking at photos from that first gig, at those of us onstage and in the audience, I am struck by how eclectic and outrageous the scene was.

Pretty standard for a Tuesday night in 1980.

Everyone had dyed, styled or shaved their hair. Most were wearing make-up. It was a fashion interzone between punk, Goth and asymmetric forties makeovers that would between them define the next few years of pop-culture style.

Nick and I were still neighbours, the Hollywood twins, so at the end of the gig we travelled home together in a taxi. Naturally, we spent the ride home talking about where the last few weeks' work had gotten us. Although we would always remain the master planners, we had never been dictators. Despite some mockery from our peers, we had kept the faith.

Now, as the dark streets of Birmingham flashed past the cab, we plotted an audacious goal for this band of ours that had so far written only ten songs: to headline shows at Hammersmith Odeon by '82, Wembley by '83 and New York's Madison Square Garden by '84.

It was a plan that seemed perfectly achievable.

22 Taylor, Taylor, Taylor, Rhodes, Le Bon

Shortly after that gig, we made a decision to split all our earnings equally. Every penny of every ticket sold and the proceeds of every album that we would make, every song we would write, we would split five ways.

Just as importantly, every song was going to be credited 'Taylor, Taylor, Taylor, Rhodes, Le Bon', a most fashion-conscious business partnership if ever there was one.

It gave us all an equal stake in the band, and we each had to respect the others. It's the reason we are still together today.

There are very, very few bands that work that way. But Duran was always different. We had been formed by the sidemen – Nick and myself – working inward from the outside, rather than being built around a singer-songwriter, which is the more usual way bands come into being. So having that equality came naturally. Duran was a teenage democracy.

When you are grinding out those hours in the studio, making those all-night drives from Philadelphia to wherever, everybody *is* equal. This is one of my basic beliefs. Anyone can come up with the germ of an idea, but it's worth nothing unless you have a team that is prepared to push and develop that idea until it becomes something tangible. And then it had to be sold.

This philosophy of equality was something we wore with pride. We were excited by the idea. It felt modern. I could imagine meeting record company people and saying, 'Yeah, we write all the songs together and we split everything five ways. What are you gonna do about it?'

The sound was evolving, as was the picture. Time for a logo. Something different. We met John Warwicker, who was also at university in Birmingham (he would later start the design company Tomato) and asked him to design some posters for us. He came up with something pretty spectacular, totally different and totally now. The posters were triangular, in neon blue and pink. The Rum Runner's MirroFlex formed the backdrop. We went out at night with glue pots and covered the city in our new identity. Mike Berrow didn't run fast enough and got arrested, further proof the Berrows were as committed as the five of us were.

The arrangements we came to with Paul and Michael, including the percentages they would receive from our recordings, live appearances and merchandise, would be the subject of many heated debates in years to come. Some of us are still angry. Some of us are philosophical. Whatever decisions we made back then, however naïve it may seem with the perspective of thirty years' experience, I tend to feel that what we did was cool, because it got the show on the road and motivated everyone. There were five stars onstage, and our managers were stars too. They were no schmucks put in place to simply follow our dictates. They were creative and they had vision, and that allowed us to concentrate on what was most important.

They bought us time at AIR studios, my first experience of a 24-track studio. One of my favourite bands, Japan, was working down the hall. We recorded our new version of 'Girls on Film', which was still not quite right, and a version of 'Tel Aviv' that would also change considerably by the time it found its way onto the debut album.

We were getting a look together so that when we walked out onstage, we (a) looked like a band and (b) didn't look like any other band, so they bought us clothes, then organised, and paid for, photo sessions with big-name photographers.

We got an agent in London, Rob Hallett at the Derek Block agency. He became our first champion in the capital, someone in the business talking up the band, and Rob had a big mouth.

Rob had connections in Birmingham, as he represented both UB40 and Dexys Midnight Runners. He heard from Dexys' manager that we were going to be the next success out of the city.

An agent's primary function is to book gigs. Rob got us a coveted spot at London's Marquee club.

Another Berrow investment was required to get us up and down the motorway to London in style. No Ford Transit vans for us. We acquired a late-seventies six-seater Citroën CS in French blue. Man, we nailed that accelerator to the floor once we hit the motorway.

At the wheel would be Simon Cook, a friend of ours from the Rum Runner crowd who was now being employed by us as a driver and minder. He was a great spirit to have on board, and ex-army, so we would never again have to worry about encounters with aggressive football fans. The Citroën would cover a lot of miles, most of them up and down the M1 motorway. Our equipment would follow in a rented Ford van driven by another member of the growing team.

It was Simon Cook who indirectly gave Simon Le Bon the nickname 'Charlie'. One evening, Andy got frustrated at having two Simons around and said, 'I can't fucking handle this. You, Le Bon, what's your middle name?'

'Charles,' SLB replied, reluctantly.

'Right,' says AT. 'You're Charlie. And you' – pointing his talon at Simon Cook – 'are Simon.'

We were beginning to learn not to argue with Andy when his blood was up.

Rob Hallett soon followed up the Marquee booking with a prestige slot at the Lyceum Theatre, opening for Pauline Murray and the Invisible Girls. John Cooper Clark was also on the bill. Pauline had been the singer in Penetration, the band for whom the Human League had opened when they had made such an impression on Nick and me with their multiple synthesizers and drum machines.

Anyone who has visited the Lyceum in London knows what a beautiful theatre it is. In terms of architecture and décor, there is nothing like it in Birmingham. It was the biggest stage I had ever walked out onto, and it was intimidating, not just because of the architecture but also due to the London punters, who tended to look down on Brummies from a very great height, and also because of the possibility of a writer from *Melody Maker* or the *NME* turning up, or record company A&R men. We had to be at our best, and we were up for it.

There was something reassuring about the feel of the springy boards under our feet. For over a hundred years, the greatest entertainers in the country had been walking on that stage, and a heritage like that cannot help but rub off on you.

When I stepped out onto that stage, under the most lights I had ever faced and playing through the biggest sound system I had ever plugged into, I was stepping into a tradition and couldn't help but get caught up in it. Simon would have felt it too, with his stage upbringing, his mother reminding him, 'Eyes and teeth, Simon, eyes and teeth!' It was possible his grandmother had appeared on that very stage.

Our opening-act set lasted just thirty minutes, but it stirred up the right amount of interest in the audience and in the industry players who were there to see us or one of the other acts on the bill. We were certainly as much discussed as the headline act.

One of the reasons I had the confidence to grow into these bigger venues was because of what I was beginning to understand about Roger: that he was entirely reliable, that there was never any drama, anger or bullshit. As a drummer and as a man, he is always on time. For a bass player trying to become a better bass player, trying to become a performer, that was of critical importance.

Roger and I are always the first to congratulate each other on a job well done after a show, albeit in an extremely low-key way.

ROGER: 'I thought that was pretty good.'
JT: 'Best one yet.'
ROGER: 'It took me a while to get into it. My fucking headphones fell off in the second song.'
JT: 'Really? I thought you were good.'
ROGER: 'One or two good-looking chicks out there.'
JT: 'Definitely.'
ROGER: 'I think I'll go and have a drink at the bar, watch Pauline Murray.'
JT: 'Okay. See you out there.'

Of course, 'chicks out there' would not have been any use to us that night, as we would all be crammed back in the Citroën by midnight, heading back to Birmingham, arriving home just in time for a nightcap at the Rum Runner.

HAZEL O'CONNOR
HAZEL O'CONNOR
HAZEL O'CONNOR

AND
MEGAHYPE
MEGAHYPE
MEGAHYPE
+
DURAN DURAN

7.30PM SAT. NOV.22
LANCASTER UNIVERSITY

23 Bidding Wars

In November, the Berrows bought us onto a tour supporting Hazel O'Connor. Buying artists onto a tour was common practice back then. The idea was to give the up-and-comers showcase opportunities where they could strut their stuff on decent-sized stages, with sophisticated sound and lights, in front of decent-sized crowds.

It cost about twenty grand, and Michael sold his flat to pay for it.

Hazel O'Connor had been a wild child – a singer, actor and exotic dancer who had lived all over the world. She landed in the studio with Tony Visconti in 1979 and recorded an album of songs that formed the basis for the film musical *Breaking Glass*. Hazel starred as Kate, an angry singer-songwriter who is managed by a firecracker played by Phil Daniels. The film was directed by Brian Gibson who, many years later, would sell my wife Gela and me his Los Angeles house. The executive producer of *Breaking Glass* was a young Dodi Fayed.

After the film was a hit, she put a band together, Hazel O'Connor's Megahype, and went on the road playing big venues – the Odeon in Birmingham, Colston Hall in Bristol – and sold out most nights. The idea of playing on that particular tour was appealing to us, as she didn't attract the kind of fanaticism some artists had, which an opening act could not get past. We wouldn't be banging our collective heads against a wall of apathy. We could take her on.

It was a three-week tour, from 18 November until 6 December. We joined the 'Megahype' tour on a Sunday night at the Top Rank in downtown Cardiff. They may not have been fanatics, but the crowd we were exposed to there was not like any audience we had played to before. Beer-drinking rugby hooligans would go close to describing them. Nick and I had gotten used to insults being hurled at us for our choice of wardrobe years ago. They would shout 'Poofters!' 'Fairies!' and 'Wankers!'. 'Wankers!' was pretty much the catch-all phrase back then. We were not above using it ourselves, either. That was probably the insult we most frequently shouted back at the mob. We were happy to end our Cardiff set.

On this tour, I was wearing a silk Dior blouse that had belonged to my girlfriend and black PVC pants. I was starting to dye my hair dark red, and make-up was back. It was hardly Ziggy Stardust, but out here in 1980 it was still provocative, as was the music, which was anything but good-time rock and roll. It was going to take longer to connect in cities like Cardiff. A hit would help. Something on the radio. Someone like John Peel saying, 'These cats are cool.'

*

The world of the Rum Runner was a protective shell. It was our own world, and one could easily forget that most people didn't dress the way we did, that we were part of a cult.

When we took our act out of clubland, away from the cult, we often would hit walls of resistance, indifference or even hatred. It didn't stop us or make us want to tone down our appearance; on the contrary, we just got more outré.

From Cardiff, we went on to the Manchester Apollo with its velvet seats and high balcony, for our first theatre experience. We continued to feel more and more at home on these bigger stages; our act breathed into them. Then we hit the universities of Sheffield and Lancaster.

The highlight of Hazel's set every night was the ballad 'Will You?' from *Breaking Glass*. We would all line up at the monitor desk, stage right, and watch the band perform this gorgeous song, in which saxophonist Wesley Magoogan would deliver the solo that was the emotional peak of the show. There was never a dry eye in the house.

As we were going from town to town in our rented Winnebago camper, Paul and Michael were making connections with the London music business, bringing representatives from different labels to see us. We must have made for an appealing package. Paul and Michael were grown-ups. They were hard-working and they had vision. That is what the record companies were buying, as much as anything. A band with looks and songs with hooks but also, importantly, a sense of 'this is where we are going'.

We would meet the label guys backstage after the gigs and they'd ask us what we wanted to achieve. We would trot out what was becoming our mantra: 'We want to play Madison Square Garden by 1984.'

It was we, we, we.

'We want to be the biggest band in the world.'

RECORD GUY: 'Right, yeah, we can help you do that. That is a very appealing idea.' (*Record Guy turns to management*) 'How much is it going to cost to get on board with you guys?'

Paul would reply, 'Perhaps here is not the place to have that discussion, chaps,' and usher them away to somewhere more private.

For the labels, it's a punt, a bet. In the car back to London, they would be discussing us among themselves, maybe saying, 'I think they could do it. They seem so determined.'

THE OTHER: 'Have you ever met a more ambitious bunch of kids in your life? Who do they think they are?'

On Friday 4 December, after playing in Norwich the previous night, we drove to London in the RV. We had been invited to the offices of EMI and Phonogram, the two favourites in what had now become, to our delight, a race to sign us, a bidding war.

We visited EMI's global HQ first, a seven-storey office building built in the early sixties from glass and concrete, next door to the Wallace Collection on Manchester Square in W1. The building is featured on the front of the Beatles' first album, *Please Please Me* – the Fab Four peering over the edge of the balcony.

EMI made sure we got the full treatment. The general of the charm offensive was Terry Slater, who ran the A&R department. Terry was a Cockney, a bearded bear of a guy who'd been a musician himself, having played bass with the Everly Brothers.

Standing to the left of Terry was Dave Ambrose, whom Rob had introduced us to a week earlier in Leeds. As we followed Terry and Dave to Terry's ground-floor corner office, every secretary gave us the eye, a warm welcome and a smile, and they got as good as they gave.

There was a piano in the corner of the room. I sat down on the stool in front of it. Terry's eyes misted over. 'When Freddie sits at that piano, there's nothing like it! That's where he first sang "Mama, just killed a man".'

Freddie Mercury had been one of Terry's earlier signings.

Terry drove a Rolls, unashamedly, and he would later manage A-ha. Dave Ambrose was the alkali to Terry's acid, a lovely, damaged, sweetheart of a guy who had an instinctive feeling for music. He walked slowly and carefully around the room while we talked.

Within an hour, we had been swept off our feet by 'The Greatest Music Company in the World'.

They were a hard act to follow, and consequently, when we walked over to Phonogram's offices, on the third floor of an office building they shared above Chappell's music store on New Bond Street, we were bound to be less impressed. Not that Roger Ames, who ran the show there, wasn't impressive, he was, and he had an equally interesting vision for the band. In fact, Paul and Mike connected better with Roger than they had with Terry, and when the seven of us filed out onto New Bond Street, they made their case.

'They're the guys,' said Mike.

'Absolutely. A very smart man. I like him,' said Paul.

'We like EMI,' said we, in unison. 'We're signing with them.'

It was a coup. We had taken Mike and Paul's advice on business from Day One, and they had not steered us wrong, but we had been entranced by the EMI charm. The possibility of signing to the Beatles' label, Queen's label – even the Stones were then under contract to EMI – was too big to ignore. And after the Sex Pistols debacle, EMI were keen to make restitution to the modern world. It was no coincidence that one of the first guys we met in the Manchester Square offices was Malcolm McLaren. He knew EMI was the best London-based international music label; that's why he had signed the Sex Pistols to them in the first place. EMI had dropped the Pistols after the scandal surrounding their appearance on daytime TV hit the headlines, but it had been a mistake. They should have held on to them.

Malcolm was now managing Bow Wow Wow, and he had promptly taken them straight round to EMI. Dave and Terry, not wanting to lose out a second time, signed them eagerly.

They wanted us too, and we wanted them. It was that simple.

The following night, the 'Megahype' tour came to an end at London's Dominion Theatre. Simon and Andy jumped onstage for an encore of Bowie's 'Suffragette City'.

After all the excitement of our first national tour, we went home with an international record deal. Mission accomplished.

The apogee of working class family life

A young prince of the neighbourhood

Nigel - a most unconventional choice!

A pretty cosy life, that of an only child

Jon Ravel and Nik Dior? Maybe

And that's it —
we were a band:
Shock Treatment

duran:duran
duran:duran

SCENE»2

The Final Debut - July 16, 1980

OCTOBER 22nd HOLY CITY ZOO -

duran duran

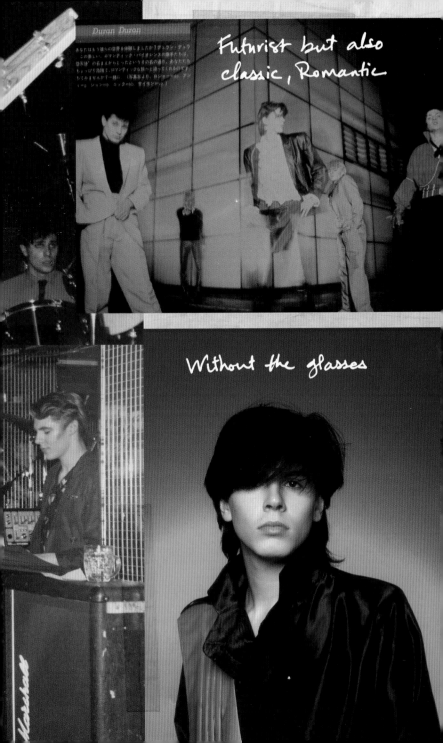

Futurist but also classic, Romantic

Without the glasses

Sri Lanka - totally at odds
with who we were as a band

Quite comfortable with the surreality
of it all

A long way from Birmingham

*My Golf GTi —
An Eighties Icon!*

with Theodore & Theodore
at Madison Square Garden

the last
photograph for
eighteen years

24 Divine Diplomacy

There was now a team around us. Dave Ambrose brought a producer named Colin Thurston along to meet us. Colin had engineered the famous Bowie/Iggy Berlin sessions that had yielded the milestone albums *The Idiot* and *Lust for Life*. Now, as a producer, he was doing great work with contemporary artists that were all interesting to us: Bow Wow Wow, the Human League, Magazine.

We didn't need any persuasion. Dave had made a great A&R call.

Colin had been born in Singapore and was a natural outsider, and it would become clear to me that he was most at home in the studio with strange and hungry young musicians.

Between management, ourselves, EMI and now Colin, the decision was made that 'Planet Earth' was the right first single, and 'Late Bar' was chosen as the B-side.

EMI were on point with our strategy. We had already printed

up several thousand labels for what would have been an independent pressing of a 'Planet Earth' 7-inch single to be funded by Mike and Paul (with 'Anyone Out There' as the B-side), but the keenness of the record labels to make a deal with us so quickly pre-empted our need to go it alone.

EMI scheduled the single release for February. A plan was made to record the single, get that delivered to the pressing plants and then put the rest of the album down on tape.

We were on the fast track.

Colin's favourite recording studio in London was Red Bus, across the city on Edgware Road. We drove the Citroën down the M1 and checked into the Lindsay Hotel on the Fulham Road.

Colin was absolutely the right producer for us. He knew how to take what was best about us and magnify it, and boy, did he take our sound to another level.

Colin specialised in giving individual attention to all of us. There was no preferential treatment. He lavished as much detail as was necessary on the recording of the bass, the tom-tom overdubs and the keyboard sequences, just as he did on the lead vocal parts. Or at least it seemed that way. Being the focus of that kind of scrutiny for the first time in the studio made me a little nervous. I could no longer stay in between and out of sight. I was uncomfortable subjecting my playing to such detailed analysis, but Colin was a divine diplomat.

COLIN: 'That's great, John, great.'
JT (*taking off my bass, perspiring slightly*): 'Cool. Thanks, Colin.'
COLIN: 'Hold on, hold on. We're not done yet.'
JT (*plugging my bass back in somewhat reluctantly*): 'Oh, okay.'
COLIN: 'Most of what we have is great, John. But it can

be better. I think you could approach the B-section
slightly differently. I've an idea.'

JT: 'Okaaaay . . .'

The tough love would continue until the track was completed
to Colin's standards. Listening back years later, I am grateful to
Colin for raising the bar on what I thought was the limit of my
abilities. It has been said that 'Planet Earth' was the first truly
'eighties' pop song, and that is as much a testament to Colin's production skills as our efforts.

'Planet Earth' was influenced by German techno as much as it
was by punk and New York disco. Andy's heavy-metal lead line,
strangled through the Roland guitar synth, gave it power, but
under a dark light. Lyrically, it was new. 'Planet Earth' was a cel-
ebration of youth, of the possibility of youth, about feeling good
to be alive.

After three years of songs about hate and war, it was fresh.

After I had cut my bass tracks, I got sick and couldn't function. I
was a right mess.

I was beginning to discover that I did not relish sleeping away
from home. The Hazel tour had taken us away from Birmingham
for a couple of weeks, and the recording in London did the same.
Mostly, I still spent nights in my own bed. As much as I was desperate for freedom from Mum, Dad and the paper-thin walls of
Simon Road, being away from home meant taking responsibility for
looking after myself, feeding myself, keeping my clothes clean.
Getting to bed at a reasonable hour.

Andy and Simon were already well trained, both essentially
having left home years before we had met. They were both in
their own flats in Birmingham, so it was no odds to them whether

they were there or at hotels on the road. Nick, Roger and I were all still living with our parents. Andy knew the gig was of primary importance; it was the gig for which you got paid. Simon's years in his student digs had obviously taught him something, but me, I was a pampered poodle, and without Mum and Dad spoon-feeding me, I was not eating properly, drinking too much and staying up until dawn, not wanting to go to bed in lonely and anonymous hotel rooms that I would sometimes be sharing with other band members.

I wanted to make music, and in this sense my dreams were being realised. The time spent onstage was becoming more fun the better at it we were getting. But what to do with the time in between, the time when I didn't have my bass strapped on in front of an audience?

Those were turning out to be the challenging times.

25 Divine Decadence

After the work in Red Bus was complete, we returned to Birmingham. On Christmas Eve we played the Cedar Club, one of the city's bigger live-music club venues. It was the first of what would be many triumphant returns to our hometown.

Although it was yet to be released, it was good to be able to say, 'This is our new single.' We played 'Planet Earth' twice, the second time as an encore, and streamers rained down as we invited many of the Rum Runner stars, like Koryn Foxx and Gay John, to join us, in their glamour and finery, on the stage.

Divine decadence was in the air.

After the warmth and conviviality of a Simon Road Christmas – relatives, friends, Father Christmas Cassidy, checking in with Nick around the corner in Mill Close – a sense of change and expectation hovered in the atmosphere. It became clear to me that my entire family would be taking this journey with me, that I was to be the torchbearer of the family name. It was going to be Nigel – 'sorry, John' – who was going to put the family on the map.

For New Year's Eve, it just had to be the Rum Runner. Bearing in mind that the Rum Runner knew how to party pretty much any day of the week, this was going to be a spectacular night.

One of the benefits of our newfound glory was a cab account, and either Nick or I would call and order a pick-up. As we sat in the backseat of the Maypole minicab service, you would have been troubled to find two more delighted, excited and happy-to-be-who-they-were-just-at-that-precise-moment-in-time individuals on the planet.

It had been less than a year since we first walked into the club, but the changes we'd experienced since that moment had been staggering. One of the things that had changed was that we didn't have to wait in line any more: a nod from doorman Al and hostess Elayne, and the velvet rope was raised to let us pass. There was no need for us to count out our change, as we had at Barbarella's a few years previously; Margaret, looking up from the cash register, smiled a welcome and gestured us to go on through. This was privilege.

The lines were longer tonight than they had been a year ago, because the Rum Runner's star was rising along with ours. It seemed that more and more of Birmingham's night people wanted to play among the MirroFlex and oak-barrelled booths.

Paul had appointed a new club manager to allow himself more time to work with the band. Smoking a cigar, he smiled and beckoned us forward. We checked our coats and walked past the steps to the empty bar – which lay dormant now that our gear was properly flight-cased and stored, ready for the new year's studio sessions – and into the sound, the pounding rhythms of Yellow

Magic Orchestra, Grace Jones and Bowie. The MirroFlex and pink neon lights told us we were home. Like all great nightclubs, just being in it made you feel special. One of the chosen ones. I guess that's the beauty of the velvet rope. As long as the velvet rope chooses you.

I had a new girlfriend. Roberta Earl-Price. A lovely brunette, whom only a few months ago I would have considered out of my league. She had been dating one of the city's flashier fashion-conscious gents, a man whose cool was known and acknowledged by all, and yet she left him for me.

I still couldn't quite get my head around that. But who cares? Here she is.

'Hey! Hi! Johnny!'

We kiss. She smells good. Of perfume, hairspray and alcohol. I inhale her. We walk arm in arm to the bar. It's the last day of 1980, so it must be a glass of chilled white wine.

The club is packed and it is barely ten o'clock. There is no one here who has not put a lot of time and effort into the way they look. How would they have put it in *Cabaret*? 'Even the straights are beautiful.'

It is the hyper-fashion-conscious stars like Patti Bell and Jane Kahn leading the way, who raised the sartorial temperature, taking dress to a new level of outrageousness and modernity. Adam Ant is an influence on some – he's definitely in the house – and Gary Numan: black tie, black shoes, blond hair. Then there are the lacy, frilly, stretchy, corkscrew-haired girls, adherents to the church of Vivienne Westwood. There are punks attempting to change it up – not too late, a little rockabilly with quiffs and grease – and it all fucking works so well together.

At three minutes before midnight, the kick drums and synth basses take a break. It's time for Sinatra. 'New York, New York', a club anthem. Everybody on the dance floor, singing, toasting, happy, joyous and free.

Roberta and I were right there in the centre of it, and the music never sounded better.

PLANET EARTH
LATE BAR

DURAN DURAN

PLANET EARTH
(NIGHT VERSION)

26 Manic Panic

At the beginning of January, with barely time to get over the Rum Runner's New Year's Eve party, Duran Duran hit the ground running, and we were back in the studio with Colin, recording the rest of the songs that would make up our debut album. At Red Bus, we cut the bass and drum tracks for 'Careless Memories', 'Night Boat', 'Anyone Out There', 'To the Shore', 'Faster than Light' (which we would use as the B-side to 'Girls on Film'), 'Tel Aviv' and what would become 'Khanada'.

Colin's plan was to complete the basic tracks of sequencers, bass, drums and rhythm guitar, along with 'guide' vocals (quick vocal sketches that help everyone keep the song's arrangement in mind), then move into Chipping Norton Recording Studios, a live-in studio environment in Oxfordshire, to work on keyboard parts, guitar overdubs and final vocal tracks. The rhythm-section recording sessions for *Duran Duran* took about ten days in all, including the time before Christmas we had spent recording 'Planet Earth' and 'Girls on Film'.

We also recorded an extended version of 'Planet Earth' for the clubs. We rearranged the single, creating a lengthy four-on-the-floor bass drum-driven intro, and further extended the middle breakdown of the song to make it longer and more dynamic. We added over two minutes to the length of the song, taking it to six minutes ten seconds. Unlike dance mixes of later years, there was no cutting and pasting; we played every note live, and proudly so, in imitation of the great extended club mixes that had come out of New York, and particularly Chic. Colin brought in a horn section, 'the 'Gosport Horns' – Andy Hamilton on sax and Spike Edney on trombone – to add bluster and funk. It was our first encounter with session musicians, an experiment with augmentation. Roger piled on layers of percussion. I added some slap bass. As the new version was intended for nightclubs only, we named it the 'night version' and scratched 'Duranies rock on' into the run-out groove, a little message from us to the world.

We all got to appreciate another aspect of EMI's munificence when marketing man Rob Warr introduced us to Perry Haines, the man-about-town go-getter who had just launched *i-D* magazine with Terry Jones. Haines's *i-D* was to our scene what *Sniffin' Glue* was to the punks. Rob Warr instructed Perry to take us into London, buy us some clothes and get us haircuts at Antenna, just off Kensington Church Street.

I thought our haircuts were working just fine, but whatever. We had all been getting our hair cut and coloured by a Rum Runner mate named Mitch Wilson, who ran a salon in Wolverhampton with his sister Tracey. This was a fantastic moment for hair colour, as the 'Crazy Colour' and 'Manic Panic' hair-dye brands had been launched the previous year and had definitely helped us define our look. Simon was no longer a blond, he was now a brunette, which gave an opening for Nick to go all the way blond. Andy trailblazed the black-and-blond two-tone skunk look that Kajagoogoo's Limahl would popularise, and Roger was adding blue to his black. I set up camp in the bordeaux/burgundy corner. I've always felt the best haircuts come courtesy of a devoted girlfriend, and Andy would marry Tracey eventually.

Seriously, there was nothing London could teach us about hair, but Perry was a fantastic personal shopper. First stop was PX in Covent Garden, Spandau Ballet's dressers, so we had to be careful in there. I picked out a musketeer shirt in deep red, another in white, and a scarlet-and-grey waistband out of Adam Ant's wardrobe. From there, Perry took us to Antony Price's store Plaza on the King's Road in Chelsea, immortalised by the Roxy Music song 'Trash'. In contrast to PX's historically skewed nostalgia, Plaza's wares were ice-cold cool. In the window stood a single mannequin in a sharp grey sharkskin suit, slick hair, shiny shoes. Inside Plaza, the clothes were arrayed on chrome racks that lined each side of the store – one side for girls, the other for boys.

I got away with the most fabulous butt-length, torso-hugging leather jacket, unlike any leather jacket I had ever seen. Roger and Nick got baggy suits in the forties Bogart style, in powder blue and lavender. The clothes we bought that day would form the basis of our wardrobe for the next few months.

For our first EMI-sponsored photo session, photographer Andy Earl took us to the modern Milton Keynes building complex. This would be an important step in the initial branding of DD. The photos suggested something that was futuristic but also classic, romantic. New Romantic. We all look cool, calm and confident. Arrogant even. Sexy.

27 Perfect Pop

BBC Radio 1 responded well to 'Planet Earth' when it was released to the record stores on 2 February. John Peel played it, Andy Peebles and Peter Powell played it. On *Roundtable*, Radio 1's Friday-evening review programme, Jonathan King remarked that it sounded like 'someone had tried to make a Blondie record', which was not too far off the mark. Local radio picked up on it too, across the country: BRMB in Birmingham, which we had expected, but also Piccadilly in Manchester and Capital in London.

The press release makes interesting reading.

Nick says, 'We wanted to pick out all the good elements of various musics, but focusing on disco where it's just the total beat that counts.'

'When we first formed,' says John, 'what we were playing was very much avant-garde English music.'

Andy says, 'My guitar isn't a lead instrument, it's not predominant at all. It just adds flavour and energy.'

The press release goes on: 'Unlike Spandau Ballet, Duran Duran love playing live. "We don't see any point in not trying to get across to as many people as possible," says Nick. "What's the point in being a group otherwise?"'

The British love music and love novelty. That is why the UK Top 30 has always reflected the cutting edge of contemporary popular music better than any other nation's chart around the world. When fifties rockers Little Richard and Jerry Lee Lewis first came to Britain, they received a greater welcome than they were getting in their home country. The same for the Motown stars. Jimi Hendrix came to Britain because his manager knew he could make it happen there. Britain created the Beatles, Bowie, Pink Floyd, Led Zeppelin. The list is endless.

What succeeds in the UK carries around the world. Every other country that cares about modern music looks to what is happening there. Canada, Australia, the United States – anywhere, in fact, where there is a decent core of Anglophilia. It has less effect on mainland Europe: Germany, France, Italy – countries that have their own pop sung in their own language. But pop is an English–American phenomenon, sung in English, and progressive pop almost always happens in England.

It is certainly far easier to have a hit in the UK than it is in the United States, which, because of its size alone, requires a campaign of military proportions to get a song into the Top 20. In the UK, a couple of half-decent reviews in the music weeklies and one or two plays on Radio 1, a TV appearance or two, and then, unless your song is 'complete and utter gobshite' (as Bob Geldof might say), it will make it into the lower reaches of the pop chart.

Which is when the work begins.

On 10 February 'Planet Earth' entered the UK pop chart at

number 97, and the following day we filmed our first British TV appearance, on a now-defunct popular-culture show called *Look! Hear!* at the BBC's Pebble Mill studios in Birmingham. The BBC sent a huge limousine to pick me up, which caused quite a furore on Simon Road.

The day after that, we drove down the motorway and assembled at a studio in north London to make something called a 'video'.

Thanks in part to support from Molly Meldrum, 'the Aussie John Peel', 'Planet Earth' was racing up the pop charts in Australia faster than in the UK. There was no way we could all fly down there to give it any help; that just wasn't practical.

One particularly interesting woman – who liked to sit provocatively on her office desk, showing off her rather nice legs – introduced Paul Berrow to the concept of the 'promotional video'.

'Artists are having a lot of success with them,' she said, encouraging him to look at the videos for Ultravox's 'Vienna' and the Boomtown Rats' 'I Don't Like Mondays'.

Consider Queen's 'Bohemian Rhapsody' clip, she advised, pointing out what a fantastic job that video did of selling both artist and song.

Videos, she continued, were quite inexpensive to make – certainly cheaper than five return flights to Australia – and, in the hands of the right director, could sell the band's image much better than a conventional TV playback. There was quite a cottage industry building up around video production in London – the best director working there, the man who would do the best job for Duran, was Russell Mulcahy.

Russell had come from Australia and had directed the video for 'Vienna'. There was no denying how impressive that was and how well it worked, so Paul engaged him to direct 'Planet Earth'.

We met him at a TV studio in St John's Wood, not entirely sure what we were supposed to be doing there.

Russell was a live-wire, compact sort of fellow, with great energy and an easy sense of humour. We found him very comfortable to be around, and he seemed to take to us equally well. I rented a red vintage Rickenbacker for the shoot, not even bothering to bring along my Aria Pro. I have had to explain many times to younger players since then that I did not use the Rickenbacker on the recording of 'Planet Earth'.

More wear for the new clobber, Simon choosing the white PX shirt that I had worn in the Milton Keynes photo shoot, me all in leather again. We brought Gay John and Patrick down from the Rum Runner to do the 'New Romantic' dance – swinging arms, bobbing heads, side-to-side finger clicking – for the cameras.

What was most impressive, we would discover, watching the results back a few days later, was the painted glass work – the revolving earth at the beginning and the crevasse that Simon appears to jump off at the end; cool special effects that none of us expected.

I've never liked lip-synching. It's all the work of a gig with none of the juice. But it was clear that at £10,000, the video was a good investment. It was shipped off to Australia immediately, where it helped 'Planet Earth' reach number 1.

Our first British headlining tour had been booked to help the single get attention. We returned to Aston University campus for the opening night, then on to Liverpool, Manchester and London.

That Monday, we got the longed-for call to appear on *Top of the Pops*, still the most important music television programme in the country.

An appearance on *Top of the Pops* wasn't quite as simple as it looked. The Musicians' Union had an agreement with the BBC specifying that all artists booked to play on the show had to re-record the song in front of union representatives and BBC officials, to make sure the musicians seen presenting the song on TV were the same musicians who had made the recording.

The intentions may have been noble, but the reality was a serious drag for any recording artist who might take any longer than six hours – the BBC's allocated re-recording time – to lay down their track. In particular, 10cc had gotten into a serious mess attempting to recreate 'I'm Not in Love', their multitracked Spectoresque masterpiece, one rainy Manchester Monday and had made their complaints public, exposing the lie, as it were. Reproducing days or weeks of work in one day was idiotic and frankly impossible.

So a nefarious compromise had evolved between the artists, the label representatives, the BBC and the MU. It went something like this: on a Tuesday morning, the producers and engineers would enter a London recording studio with their equipment and set up. The artists would take their places around midday, and at 12.50 p.m. the union rep would arrive in the company of the label rep. He would walk in on a scene that could not have been scripted more imaginatively by Kafka. Introductions were made. The band would wave through the glass and appear to be animatedly digging into their work.

At 1.00 our label man would turn to the MU rep and say, 'Fancy a spot of lunch?'

'Good idea.'

And they would disappear for a liquid lunch on the firm, to return, slightly pissed, around 4 o'clock, just in time for the producer – Colin, in our case – to play back the final mix of the 'new recording' that had allegedly just been made, despite the fact that half the time we weren't even miked up. Papers were signed and everyone went home happy.

What a load of bollocks! This charade would go on for another ten years until the rules were finally relaxed.

Wednesday was the big day. We had an eleven o'clock call at BBC Television Centre in Shepherd's Bush for the first of three rehearsals.

The recording of the 'live' show – (where the 'prerecorded' track would be played as we mimed over the top) – would be broadcast the following night – Thursday.

We all knew it was an amazing break, but it couldn't have been more badly timed, given that we had our first headlining London show that night. Somehow, we found the time to get over to the Sundown on the Charing Cross Road for a quick sound check in between rehearsals.

Despite all the bullshit, actually being inside those studios was a real trip, after all the years of watching the show with Mum, or at Nick's or Dave Twist's.

The Who were on – real big guns, old-timers now – and Soft Cell, New Wavers from Leeds with an extremely cool presentation of 'Tainted Love' inside a padded cell. I watched both their playbacks in rehearsal. There wasn't a chat as we all gathered around the monitors, but there was some acknowledgement. The Who gave off a friendlier vibe than Soft Cell, but that was hardly surprising. The Who could afford to be magnanimous. We were hardly in competition with giants like them.

It was all so pragmatic in reality; there was nothing in there that didn't have a function. It was interesting how they got the show's look, which had been fine-tuned considerably since *Top of the Pops* first aired in 1964, with an increasing role being played by the audience, who contributed as much to the colour and currency of the show as the artists. The audience were herded between the three principal stages that made up the set and were given rigid guidelines on when they should applaud, when they should dance and how much noise they should make.

The show's director sat in his control room, high above the studio, and his directives came down through the PA system as if from a higher power. The cameras roved around us, picking out our poses, accentuating the positive, mostly. Simon crimped his hair for the occasion. Roger was almost drowned in dry ice.

It was hard to take seriously. Watching the playback on the monitor after we had been processed by the *Top of the Pops* machine was seriously amusing. But we were in the club now. A bona fide chartbusting pop band.

The tour picked up the next evening at Rock City in Nottingham, where I experienced my first onstage contact-lens calamity. In reaction to a sudden head move halfway through 'Anyone Out There', my left lens fell out. The room dropped out of focus. Instincts surged. I saw it, glinting cheekily up at me, standing out against Rock City's carpeted floor. I swooped down on it and, in one sleek move, picked it up and put it in my pocket without missing a beat. At the end of the song I had a mirror brought to me so I could reapply it into my eye. It was a nerve-racking moment, and the thought it might happen again became a nightly worry. Thank God and the Russians for Lasik eye surgery, which arrived in time for the 2002 reunion.

When our first national tour was over, we were ready to complete the album. Nick, Simon and Andy decamped with Colin to the residential facility in Chipping Norton for a few weeks of overdubs. Roger and I, our work done, had time to kick around. We were scheduled press interviews to do, which I found easy and didn't require the kind of discipline that playing did. Throughout the course of a press day, I could get slowly hammered, and it wouldn't matter one bit because there was no show to play that night.

I found myself struggling to fill the time when I wasn't working, particularly if I was away from girlfriend Roberta in the capital. A great deal of my identity was now caught up in the late-night club world, and my nights out were becoming longer, more often than not stretching into the next day. I was developing the habit of mixing my drinks, and discovering the even higher-octane thrills that came from mixing my drinks with drugs.

Cocaine was a big part of the seventies rock mythology I grew up with. It went with the territory of fame, success and record sales. It wasn't even a secret. I'd read about it in the pages of the *NME*.

I had already gotten a taste for coke at the Rum Runner, where it was popular with some of the more louche clientele, who were always happy to share with the golden boys. In London, in the music business, cocaine use was as normal as drinking a pint of bitter in the pubs of Birmingham. Everybody was doing it and no one felt bad about it. The business took account of the hours that were lost due to hangovers and scrambled thoughts. Hundreds of grams were being charged to record company accounts across the city every week.

It was all a bit of a laugh really. No one took it seriously. No one had been to rehab. Yet.

PART 2
HYSTERIA

28 The Whole Package

We asked Fin Costello, a photographer whose work we liked, to shoot the album cover. I wanted an old car in the picture, to give it a Gatsbyesque, neoclassical vibe. But I paid the price for the suggestion, getting stuck at the back, my eyes barely visible. I'm not crazy about the photo that was chosen for the cover of the album. None of us were, as there were many better pictures of the band taken that year, but the design that wraps around the image is superb.

At Nick's suggestion, EMI brought in Malcolm Garrett, who had designed all the Buzzcocks artwork. Malcolm created designs that were thoughtful and clean. His Duran cover is a classic. It could have been designed by the great minimalist architect John Pawson. The band logo – my favourite of all our logos – was expensive to produce, with silver foil strips added for emphasis.

It was classy.

It said, 'We are the new breed.'

'Planet Earth' peaked at number 7 in the UK pop charts. We all wanted 'Girls on Film' as the follow-up and were keen to get it out quickly, but EMI claimed to know better, saying 'Careless Memories' was the right follow-up to 'Planet Earth'. It had more integrity as a song, apparently, and would show the audience our deeper, more serious side. Maybe it did all that, but it didn't sell, and in some corners of the industry we were swiftly written off as one-hit wonders.

At this point, in an attempt to stanch the flow of blood, EMI's press and public relations department kicked in. Press and PR was run by Janice Hague, a strawberry blonde who coordinated publicity for a most diverse roster of artists: Kate Bush, Angelic Upstarts, Queen and Bow Wow Wow.

She dealt with the national tabloid newspapers, the weekly music press, and the now-burgeoning glossy colour pop press. *Smash Hits* was the market leader, and they took to Duran right away, giving us our first cover.

When the magazine came out, we were all surprised that they had chosen a picture of Nick and Roger for the cover. They didn't use a band shot or a picture of Simon, which would have been a more conventional choice.

People around the band saw that as a signal. There was clearly depth to Duran Duran and a wider appeal.

Our policy of equality was justified.

We took photos at Chipping Norton for *The Face* magazine, which had also just started and was already being thought of as important. That was a great session – off-duty, having a laugh in and out of the farm buildings, playing pool.

As if in retaliation for the embrace of *Smash Hits* and *The Face*, my beloved *NME* declared us the enemy. They gave our Rock City show the meanest review I had ever read. 'Duran Duran are going to be huge,' ran the last line, 'and the sad thing is, they don't deserve any of it.'

I couldn't get my head around that. Should we have put in more time in the Transit van on the motorway? Should I have gone to Juilliard? The *NME* never altered their position on us once they had formed it.

The other area of press that Janice handled was the teen-oriented girlie press, magazine weeklies like *Jackie* and *Diana* and *My Guy*. I knew *Jackie* and *Diana* well. All the girls at school read them and would often tear out the Bolan or Bowie centre-spread for me if I asked. I didn't see anything wrong in Duran appearing in those mags, and one afternoon, when I was sitting in Janice's office, I raised the subject.

'What about the teen press? What about *Jackie*? Is that still popular? It was a couple of years ago, when I was at school.'

'Oh yeah, it's huge!' says Janice.

'So why don't we send them some pictures?'

'I could put a package together,' says Janice, a bit doubtfully.

A week later, back in Janice's office again, she said, 'I heard back from *Jackie* and they really like you. There's a girl there, you should call her. In fact, do it now.'

She slid me the number across the desk. I picked up the phone and called her. The editor's name was – by pure coincidence – Jackie.

And so began a love affair with the British teen press, a courtship that would last years and trigger a level and type of fame that none of us had intended or could ever have expected.

Like all the best seductions, it only worked because we weren't really conscious of what we were doing. We weren't trying to seduce the teen press. Never had we envisaged ourselves as having that kind of appeal. We were just trying to get the music out.

Once we made ourselves available to *Jackie*, all the other teen mags wanted in, and once they had a taste, they couldn't get enough. What's more, we were as equal in their eyes as we were in our own. Each of us, independently of the others, turned out to be pin-up material. Together, we now had real power.

Back at the Rum Runner, we started receiving fan mail.

It was a lot of fun. We would gather in the club restaurant some time in the afternoon and pass out the mail, letters and packages, like something out of a Beatles movie: six for you, six for him, one for you.

We sat there, all of us diligently doing more homework than we had ever done at school, signing photos and writing replies to the letters. Building bridges, forging relationships with girls – for these letters were written almost exclusively by teenage girls – around the country. We would respond to the letters and often receive responses to our responses. I got to recognise the handwriting of some enthusiastic early adopters and would know whom a letter was from before I opened it.

What began to happen was that girls aligned themselves with their favourite Duran star. Some gangs of friends formed sub-groups of five, mirroring us, where each friend could have a favourite Duran without stepping on the toes or desires of the other four friends, because if you were an Andy fan, clearly you could not be friends with another Andy fan. That would not work. You could be friends with a Nick fan, however, because there was no conflict of interest. Both friends could live together in harmony with Nick and Andy on that designated fantasy desert island for ever and ever, without a hint of envy.

The fans would do some pretty crazy things over the years but my favourite has to be the girl in Atlanta who was present at a press conference we gave on the reunion tour. I had a cold, and was sniffling into a series of tissues, absent-mindedly throwing them into a waste-paper bin under the table.

Next time we were in the city the girl called out to me at another public appearance, 'I was the girl who got your cold.'

I wondered what on earth she was talking about. 'After you left the press conference last year I stole your used tissues. I wanted to get your cold.'

In June, we toured again, kicking off with that fateful night at the Brighton Dome when Durandemonium officially began.

The fans were as much of a surprise to each other at Brighton that night as they were to us. They had thought that as they were the first in their school to get into DD, maybe they were the first in Brighton. But that night they realised they were members of a rapidly exploding club.

Duranies rock on.

Every night on that tour, Simon would try to take control.

The stern teacher pose seemed to work. It could at least create enough of a pause in which to say, 'Good evening, Newcastle,' or 'This is our new single, "Girls on Film".'

But what did that matter, really? They already knew that. What they really wanted to know was this: Can we be theirs? Individually or collectively? Do we want them as much as they want us?

The tour concluded with a triumphant night at the Birmingham Odeon. This time it was *our* sound check, *our* limo getting chased across town. We were now strapped in for a ride, and there would be no getting off. The mania that we had witnessed inside the concert halls enveloped us 24/7.

Being a teen idol means you become the focus of a very unique kind of energy, midwives to adolescence. Everywhere we went, there were young girls trying to get our attention, catch our eye. More often than not, the eyes were teary and bloodshot. They were sad and happy at the same time.

The most negative aspect of our fan-driven fame was the degree to which we found ourselves in competition with each other. The fans really were comparing Nick with Andy, Andy with John, John with Simon, and so on. Who was the most hand-some, the smartest, the most artistic, the most popular? At first we didn't take it too seriously, we had all studied at the school of *A Hard Day's Night*.

It had never occurred to us that any one of us might be more important than the others.

But, one afternoon, as the driver attempted to back our tour bus out of the Glasgow Apollo car park after a matinee perform-ance, the kids swarming around the bus were banging on the steel sides, chanting, 'We want John! We want John!'

I wanted to crawl into a hole. I still didn't like the attention that came with coming first. I would much rather they had stuck to chanting, 'We want Duran Duran!'

Confusing. And not at all the kind of confusion that I had expected to have to deal with as a member of a modern art-school band, and one that prided itself on its democracy.

29 All Aboard for the Promised Land

In September, we left Heathrow for our first trip to the States. It was a long flight by Air India. Air India economy.

When we finally emerged at JFK, it was dark. Manhattan had been glimpsed out of the aircraft window, and Nick, Simon, Roger, Andy and I were all incredibly excited as we made our way into the arrivals hall, to be greeted by long lines waiting to clear immigration.

Finally, it was my turn to face the terrifying-looking customs officer; paunchy, mirrored shades, you know the look.

I must have neglected to fill out my immigration form properly, because the officer in charge wanted to know where I would be spending the night.

I had no idea. So I called back down the line to our tour manager: 'Where are we staying tonight, Richard? What's the name of the hotel?'

Richard cupped his hands either side of his mouth and shouted back, 'The Holiday Inn.'

That answer didn't satisfy my officer. He took off his shades, the better to glare at me. 'The Holiday Inn *where*?'

'The Holiday Inn *where*, Richard?'

'Long Island.'

'The Holiday Inn, *Long Island*,' says my man, ironically.

'I'm sorry, I'm ... in a band.'

That seemed to work. He put his shades back on and sighed. Stamped the papers. Handed back my passport and said, 'Well, if we need to find you, we'll just put out an APB for a funny-looking guy with purple hair.'

'It's burgundy, not purple, you wanker,' I muttered under my breath, walking over to the baggage carousel.

We collected two self-drive rental cars from Avis. I sat in the passenger seat of one, alongside Richard, and eagerly unfolded the map. I always fancied myself the navigator. Roger and Nick were in the back seat, and Andy and Simon were in the other car. We had to get onto the Van Wyck Expressway, but all I could find referenced on the map were expwys.

'I can't find the fucking expressway, Richard, and what's a fucking expwy?'

'I think they are one and the same,' said Richard, who had been to the United States before.

We had all assumed that our first New York gig would be in Manhattan. Kojak's Manhattan, the place with the high homicide rates, the streetwalkers and the Empire State Building. But, as the signs directing us to Long Island made clear, we were heading the wrong way. A low moan gathered force as we realised that the best view we'd be getting of Manhattan that night was in the rear-view mirror.

Duran Duran's first US gig was actually in New York State, on Long Island, and the Holiday Inn was in a town called Hicksville. By the time we checked in, it felt like we were paying a good-times tax before we could enter the promised land.

When I woke up the next morning, I was amazed by two things: the size of the breakfast and the number of TV channels.

I ate: bacon, sausage, scrambled eggs, hash browns, bagels, pancakes, maple syrup.

I watched: *The Munsters*, *The Addams Family*, *Mister Ed*, *I Dream of Jeannie*, *Lost in Space*.

I liked this place.

The gig the following night, at the Spit Club in Levittown, was even more amazing, jam-packed with kids who seemed to know all the songs from the album: 'Planet Earth', 'Girls on Film', 'Careless Memories'. They were friendly and enthusiastic, just like the kids back in Birmingham, and we felt at home. The fashions were different; not so extreme, but you could tell that they wanted it, that they were ready to break from the chains of denim and T-shirts.

In the States, we were always thought of as the epitome of a New Wave band – the terms *New Romantic* and *Futurist*, which were being attached to us by the British press, all got rolled into this one catch-all term. We were fortunate to have had massive support from a radio station on Long Island, WLIR, which was known as the East Coast 'knowledge' for new British music. The station embraced Duran from Day One and was responsible in large part for turning young Americans on to our music.

As well as through the independent and college radio stations, our music was also becoming popular thanks to the RockAmerica network of video clubs. These were extraordinary venues – mostly large ballrooms – that had taken to projecting videos onto giant screens above the dance floor. The artists that were most successful with this audience were those who were combining cutting-edge visual material with groovy dance beats: Adam and the Ants, Ultravox, Depeche Mode and us. The energy and creativity that was coming out of the British video boom was finding its place in America.

There is a fantastic clip on YouTube of a video club mocked up in a TV studio. *MV3* was a short-running music video show that could only be seen in a few West Coast cities. If you check out Romeo Void's performance of 'Never Say Never', when the cameras pull back from the band's video to reveal a dance floor crowded with teenage kids dancing the 'Planet Earth' dance, that's the closest I've seen to what those American audiences looked like that year.

The last thing we had done before leaving London was film our latest contribution to this new art form, the video for 'Girls on Film'. Two versions: one for the single and one to accompany the longer dance mix of the song, the 'night version', which was specifically intended for these video clubs.

This night version video became the biggest hit across the RockAmerica network that summer – in no small part because it was very, very raunchy. It was filmed in a warehouse in St John's Wood, London, with the band playing on a makeshift stage at one end of the set. At the other end was a boxing ring, in which there took place a succession of increasingly lurid scenes – the sumo bout, the shaving cream on the pole, the mud wrestling and, of course, the ice cube on the nipple. So many guys have said to me over the years, in hushed tones, 'Oh my God, that video, I watched it over and over.'

*

Is there a wow quite as wow as the crossing of the East River into New York City? We could barely contain ourselves as Manhattan unfolded in front of our eyes. This was the city of the Ramones, the New York Dolls, Frank Sinatra – and now Duran Duran.

We checked into the elegant St Moritz Hotel on Central Park South. Outside, a line of horse-drawn carriages waited to take tourists on romantic tours of Central Park. Inside, red velvet splendour enveloped us. I had a room the size of my suitcase, but I didn't care because it was a room with a view. Twelfth floor, corner. I was not planning on spending much time in here, but standing at the window, looking north across the park, it was breathtaking.

I had to call Mum and Dad to share my excitement.

'4742163.'

'Mum, it's me.'

'Hello, luvvie.'

'Mum, I'm in New York. What time is it there?'

'Oooh, are you? It's almost six o'clock.'

'I'm in the hotel, standing at a window overlooking Central Park. It's amazing.'

'There have been a lot of fans here today. Your dad's been talking to them.'

'We're playing tonight, at the Ritz.'

'That sounds fancy. Do you want to speak to your father?'

'Sure . . .'

After I'd hung up, Richard called to tell me to be in the bar downstairs at 8.00 p.m. and reminded me, not for the first time, to change my watch.

The ground-floor lobby bar of the St Moritz still lives in my memory as the most beautiful, sexy, suggestive drinking establishment I have ever ventured into. The smell of perfume and cigars, dollars, furs and jewels, glittering glasses brimming with the romance of *highballs* and *cocktails*. The pianist played Cole Porter. I sat on a bar stool and ordered a rum and Coke, helping myself to the snack nuts.

One by one, the band gathered. Everybody was buzzed. There was a great sense of occasion. If you want to know what we looked like that night, what we were wearing, look at the 'Girls on Film' video. Simon had taken to wearing military-style suits by Antony Price – he had one in blue and one in beige – and a scarf tied around his head as a headband. Actually, everyone was wearing headbands. The blue-and-white-striped matelot shirts that Roger had started to wear had caught on; now three of us were wearing them. The suede pixie boots were still working, with trousers tucked in. Sleeves rolled up. (Antony Price hated that we did that, although Michael Mann would notice it when he was styling *Miami Vice*.)

Everybody was high on the energy of the scene. Outside, two white Cadillac limousines waited for us, paid for by our American label, Capitol. This gesture would endear them to us for the next five years. Was there a more fabulous moment in the band's history than stepping into those cars that warm, fall Friday evening in New York? I don't think so.

The five of us got into one car, label and management into the other.

It was a decent drive downtown to the venue on Eleventh Street. One straight line, I noticed, then one left. It seemed as if somehow the ambience of the bar had been transferred into the limousine. Have you ever sat in an American stretch limousine? The crystal decanters – whisky, vodka, gin, with plenty of mixers on ice – and a TV set tuned to the local news, always with awful reception. There were neon pinstripes pulsing along the interior roofline. It was less a car, more a nightclub on wheels. We loved the buttons that pushed up the dividing wall between us and the driver's cabin. Spinal Tap got that right.

The Ritz had played host to U2's American debut the previous year and would do the same for Depeche Mode in '82. There was a balcony around the main dance floor and the club boasted a thirty-foot video screen, which made it our perfect venue.

It was like we were home from home. Like at the Spit, the kids in the crowd knew all the words. The difference here in New York City was the higher level of fashion consciousness.

These kids looked like us.

I wrote a postcard home to my parents. I was clearly having the time of my life:

'Well, what can one say? I'd stay here forever. Yesterday Simon and Garfunkel did a reunion gig in Central Park in front of 500,000 people. Ridiculous!'

30 Memory Games

The cities and venues we played on that first US tour will entertain us for hours years later, when we're on boring drives during the reunion tour. By then, many conversations will have been reduced to memory tests.

'What was the name of that place we played in Washington?'

'The Bayou?'

'That's right!'

'And the place with the pole down the centre of the stage?'

'The East Side Club.'

'In Philadelphia?'

'Remember Boston?'

'The strongest pot ever . . .'

'Oh God!'

'And where was the girl with the red Corvette?'

'It wasn't red, it was pink.'

'Little pink Corvette doesn't have quite the same ring about it though, does it?'

'Artistic licence.'

'Pink or red, it was Montreal.'

'The worst hotel, ever?'

'Detroit.'

'Great gig though.'

'At the Clutch Cargo.'

'Well done! Good point ... the Clutch Cargo.'

'And Chicago, of course.'

'Where Johnny and I got to go to the Playboy Club, didn't we ... and scored our first bunnies!'

'Who came with me to see James Brown?'

'I did.'

'So did I.'

'And we stayed at the Ambassador East.'

'As seen in *North by Northwest*.'

'Fantastic.'

'San Francisco?'

'The I-Beam on Haight Street, hard helmet night!'

'Then home.'

Home. The one word that has the power to reduce us all to silence. The game is over, for now.

31 Legal Age

One thing I discovered on tour in 1981 was that girls – in all languages – liked taking drugs with me. Even though I had a girlfriend back home, my horror of lonely hotel rooms meant I would go to any lengths to avoid sleeping in them alone. Coke, I was beginning to realise, was an effective insurance policy against that eventuality.

I had been a nerd at school. I wasn't a jock or an intellectual and had never had a regular girlfriend as a teenager. Now, I only had to wink in a girl's direction in a hotel lobby, backstage or at a record company party, and I have company until the morning.

So what's the problem, you might ask? Well, the trouble is – and I didn't figure this out until I was almost forty – that there is something about an intimate encounter of that nature with someone you barely know that jars against the spirit. You want it, but it doesn't feel quite right. And when you start doing it night after night, week in, week out, your ideas about love and sex begin to get somewhat distorted.

And jumping into bed like porn star Johnny is not as easy as you might imagine, especially with someone whose first name you're not even sure of. You feel awkward. Or at least I did. Maybe it was some residue of Catholic guilt? Plain old common decency? Hadn't Mother taught me something about this? The drugs and the alcohol served to take away all those doubts, plus any inhibitions or insecurities I – or she – might have.

I didn't want to be lonely, and the drugs ensured I never was. I'm a pin-up on thousands of bedroom walls, but the fear of lone-liness is turning me into a cokehead.

Of absolute necessity for any touring musician is the itinerary. It usually comes as a gift from the tour manager on the last day of rehearsal. Depending on the length of the tour about to be under-taken, it could cover any length of time between one week and two months.

Page one lists the principals, the inner circle and the crew who are going to get the show around the world. All the num-bers to call if in trouble are listed there: the management, the agencies, the travel agents, the local promoters. Then follows a page-by-page account of the destinations: 'October 3, Chicago. Band Hotel: Ambassador East. Crew Hotel: Crown Hyatt. Venue: Park West.' And so on and so on.

I had not noticed right away that in the left-hand corner of each page of the US itinerary there was a number, usually 18, 21 or 20.

It was months before I was let in on the secret. The numbers referred to the legal age for sexual intercourse in that particu-lar state.

The other necessity for the touring musician is the day sheet, usually slipped under the hotel-room door while the occupant is still asleep. Regardless of the degree of befuddlement, the day sheet information was always quite clear:

TODAY IS OCTOBER 3
IT IS FRIDAY
YOU ARE IN CHICAGO
TODAY IS A SHOW DAY
SOUND CHECK IS AT 4PM

You almost expected it to say YOUR NAME IS: JOHN.

32 Dancing on Platinum

For 12 November, my diary entry reads simply 'Collect Discs'. Our first commemorative disc awards. At last, a prize-giving ceremony I was comfortable with, being able to share it with my mates and, finally, something for Mum and Dad to hang on the wall.

The team assembled at Manchester Square in the office of the managing director, Cliff Busby. In the photo, we look like a veritable boys' club, albeit one with a predilection for leather and frills; Terry Slater's in there grinning like a proud father, Rob Hallett's there, so too are Dave Ambrose, Mike and Paul and Colin Thurston.

We are all happy and proud. Dancing on glass. Gold, silver and platinum.

At the end of November, we embarked on yet another British tour, our third of the year, kicking off in Southampton. We rode a luxury bus down through Hampshire and parked it outside the

Gaumont. It was a madhouse. In between sound check and concert, I sat on the bus and tried to collect myself. But with the chanting and the banging, it was impossible. By the time I hit the stage, I was a nervous wreck. And in all truth, trying to 'collect myself' was an absolute impossibility at this point.

A year earlier, we had been onstage at the Cedar Club in Birmingham, celebrating the recording of our first single, 'Planet Earth', by playing it twice. Maybe four hundred people present. Twelve months later, we were selling six thousand tickets over three nights at the Birmingham Odeon.

Yes, we may have been cute, but no band ever worked harder than we did in 1981.

My desk diary has over a hundred and fifty phone numbers. Ex-girlfriends are all present, as are all ex-band members: Steve Duffy, Andy Wickett, Dave Twist. I wasn't ready to let go of any of them yet. But next to them is a new cast of characters: agents, musicians, photographers, studio technicians, other celebrities, make-up artists and hair stylists and more than a few phone numbers for girls with foreign prefixes. The handwriting is studied and deliberate, every entry carefully catalogued, like trophies.

If an adult can be defined as someone with a reasonably full Rolodex, then I was on my way to becoming one. An adult, with a life and a career.

And I wasn't *that* messed up yet either, because fifteen minutes after midnight on 1 January 1982, I am back in my childhood bedroom at 34 Simon Road, soberly looking back over a year of achievement with extraordinary sincerity, almost like a prayer, writing my thoughts in my desk diary.

'How can 1982 be better? Retaining one's position commercially? Perhaps even *improving*?? Certainly socially, one would hope! How much must one change? So many questions one could not have dreamed of considering twelve months ago. Questions one hopes will be answered twelve months from now. At least before I could only go <u>UP</u> now for once I'm aware I could go <u>DOWN</u>. *Most unlikely*. Confidence (but never complacency) breeds results.

'Writing this my heart races with excitement. My four best friends are still DD. Set sights higher still in all ways, enjoy rock & roll three C's but not <u>too much</u>.

'Thanks. I do realise how lucky I am.'

33 Bird of Paradise

As 1982 broke, after an intense year of roadwork and recording, we were ready to record a masterpiece.

Does that sound arrogant? Hey, I'm only one-fifth of the story, one-*seventh* if you include the managers, one-*eighth* if you include Colin Thurston, still on board as producer for Album 2.

But *Rio* was a masterpiece.

In August of the previous year, we had been booked into EMI's demo studio on the ground floor of the Manchester Square office block. We recorded four new songs: 'Last Chance on the Stairway', 'My Own Way', 'New Religion' and 'Like an Angel'. These songs formed the backbone of the *Rio* album.

That recording of 'Last Chance' was identical to the version that would make the album cut.

'New Religion' started out minus Nick's gothic intro, which he would add during the album recording sessions. It was a little slower, more doomy, but confident. I felt the writers in us stretching out on this one, giving each other room to speak, which was just as well, because we all had something to say.

'Like An Angel' was the lightest of the four tracks and would end up on the B-side of the next single.

The version of 'My Own Way' was as close to pure disco as we would get, sounding like something from the early Bob Lamb sessions with Andy Wickett.

We were aspiring to the musicianship we were hearing on American R & B records, but our level of playing was not quite there. 'My Own Way' would get a makeover, twice. The second, 'single' version has more than a whiff of Michael Jackson as it would sound if played by a group of young punks. It would be our fourth single.

During the percussion breakdown on the 12-inch dance version, Simon would ad lib, 'I think I am going to Rio.'

All of the songs on *Rio*, with the striking exception of 'The Chauffeur', were fully arranged before we returned to AIR Studios on Oxford Street in February to begin recording. We had already demoed 'Hungry like the Wolf' at the Manchester Square Studios and 'Save a Prayer' back at Bob Lamb's in Kings Heath.

Having been worked out in sound checks on stages around the world, the song 'Rio' was ready to record.

The title was something I had thrown into the mix. Brazil still had the power to cast a spell, conjuring dreams of exotic calendar pictures from my bedroom wall as a child. Rio, to me, was shorthand for the truly foreign, the exotic, a cornucopia of earthly delights, a party that would never stop.

Simon chose not to make 'Rio' about the place but about a girl. His genius was infusing this girl named Rio with all the hedonism and romance of the Brazil of my fantasies.

Moving on the floor now, babe
You're a bird of paradise
Cherry ice-cream smile
I suppose it's very nice
With a step to your left
And a flick to the right
You catch the mirror way out west
You know you're something special
And you look like you're the best.

The writing on the *Rio* album is fantastic, all out. Essential Duran Duran. It is what can happen when a group of passionate, music-loving, fame-hungry guys are given some support, nurtured and put out to work harder than any of them thought possible. Take note, twenty-first-century recording companies.

Every one of us is performing on the *Rio* album at the absolute peak of our talents. That is what makes it so exciting. That doesn't mean that everyone is playing as many notes as they possibly can. There is no showboating. Every part is thoughtful, considered, part of a greater whole.

I had developed a relationship with Aria in Japan, and they were using pictures of me to advertise their products. They gave me a 1200 – the more expensive one, with two pick-ups and active electronics – which was a step-up sonically and technically. It was also heavier. This now became my go-to bass for all the recordings on *Rio*, and the 600 got left behind.

On the song 'Lonely in Your Nightmare', I experimented with fretless bass. I had held off playing that instrument as long as I could, as it is a far more challenging proposition than a fretted bass, almost like a classical instrument – a violin or a cello. But I had admired the fretless playing of Mick Karn, the bassist of Japan, for years and wanted to try something in his style.

For the main verse part of 'Lonely', I used the fretted 1200, overdubbing a second part on a fretless bass, creating melodic lines that wove around the lead vocal. The chorus bass part was played entirely on the fretless bass. Played well, the sound of the fretless bass is smoother, and the instrument actually has greater melodic possibilities, since there are so many notes in between the notes, as it were. I was very pleased with the results I got from the fretless bass, but it would always be a difficult instrument to play live.

The track we laid down for 'Hold Back the Rain' is almost ten minutes long – now *that* is confidence – and it's never boring. The song was edited to fit on the album, which compressed the energy even further.

And what about 'The Chauffeur'? That was a curveball, created out of nothing by Nick on a studio all-nighter with Colin, Simon responding with lyrics out of the 'Dog Days' book. 'The Chauffeur' has become a gothic classic in itself and is one of our most covered songs.

I first listened back to a mix of *Rio* sitting beside Paul McCartney, who was working in the next-door studio and, at my beckoning, came in to listen to what we were up to. His approval was denoted by a highly satisfying two thumbs up.

We'd become friends with Paul and Linda's daughter, Heather. Paul could see the through-line from his old band to ours. On one occasion, we went to see him play in New York. Backstage, he was happy to see us.

''Ello lads, what are you doing here? Long way from Birmingham!'

I explained we were in the city to hang out.

'Oh, John and I used to love taking trips like that. Sometimes you have just got to get away and have some fun, get some inspiration.'

Rio was recorded following the same blueprint as the first album. Colin had recorded Roger and me playing along with Nick's sequencer parts. Then came the guitars and Nick's other keyboards, with Simon singing whenever he had a lyric ready to try out.

The big ballad on the album, 'Save a Prayer', would be the biggest hit, reaching number 2 in the UK. A live version would make it to number 16 in the US charts in 1985. And that song began with Andy and Nick, who were probably the farthest apart from each other in terms of musical temperament, picking out chords together, building the most delicate and complex of our sequencer tracks to date. The rest of the song was hung upon that frame.

Then there is 'New Religion', which would become another fan favourite; a rapping, schizophrenic Le Bon in conversation with a funky rhythm section. Now that's a pleasure groove to play.

We were a finely tuned machine, bringing out the best in each other, raising each other's game, note by note, track by track. We had become the perfect band.

And by God, those managers were not hanging around, either. Paul came across Patrick Nagel's work in *Playboy* magazine. He commissioned Nagel, who was based in Santa Monica, to create an image for the album sleeve. Nagel provided us with the cover art, rendered on translucent plastic; there she was, the girl who was dancing on the sand.

The final painting Nagel delivered to us was a fully realised canvas. It was massive. Five foot by five foot. The acrylic paint is graphic and eye-catching. Of course, it doesn't say 'Rio' across the top. Malcolm Garrett, returning Nagel's powerful serve with a well-judged backhand, added that, as he did the burgundy surround.

That painting has a story to tell. Years later, with the band down to three original members and not on talking terms with Paul and Michael, Simon, Nick and I were at the BBC, recording for *Top of the Pops*. 'I Don't Want Your Love', maybe?

Suddenly we remember the painting, which we have heard is hanging on the wall at Paul and Michael's management company in Covent Garden. The three of us jump into our stretch Mercedes, taking security guy Jim Callaghan for support, pull up outside Tritec Music and march in while everyone's at lunch.

'It's our turn with this,' say we, carefully unhooking the sizeable canvas from the wall.

'If Paul and Michael want it back, have them call us.'

They never did.

Is *Rio* the greatest album cover of the eighties? Discuss.

The photo of the band on the inside cover was taken by Andy Earl on the roof of the BP tower, with St Paul's Cathedral and the City of London spread out beneath us. We are on top of the world.

And we are wearing new clothes, naturally, mostly by Antony Price. Malcolm Garrett smartly picked up on the colours of Nick's and Andy's suits – lavender and pistachio – and brought those hues into the design, effortlessly creating the New Wave colour palette that would echo around the pop-culture world for the next twenty-four months.

34 The Pleasure Habit

I had time on my hands in London, once again. Only now, I was a little more connected. I had good friends living in the capital, and I was spending a lot of time with our agent, Rob, often sleeping over in his Kilburn flat.

The place we most frequently went for after-hours amusement was the Embassy Club on New Bond Street, owned and run by an ex-guardsman, Stephen Hayter, with whom Rob and I got along well. The Embassy has a place in London's club folklore for a number of reasons, among them the fact that for several years, Motörhead's Lemmy was welded to the Space Invaders machine to the left of the main bar.

It was like an art installation; just add amphetamines.

It was understood that no one should attempt to interrupt him; he had far too many scary tattoos, and his interest in the Third Reich was well documented. I never saw him buy a drink or use the bathroom. He was an iron man on that machine.

Less of an iron man was Limahl, whom Nick discovered one night working at the Embassy at a fairy-and-princess party, or something equally daft. Seeing Nick, Limahl – fetchingly dressed in a white silk bodysuit and wings – ran up and slipped him a cassette tape. On it, Nick heard 'Too Shy' and recognised it for the hit song it was. He would in due course take Limahl and his band Kajagoogoo into the studio and produce their debut album with Colin Thurston. 'Too Shy' was Nick's first number 1 record, preceding Duran's first UK number 1, 'Is There Something I Should Know?'

One night, Rob and I were working the club restaurant when Stephen beckoned for us to join him in his inner sanctum.

'You're gonna like this. Follow me.'

In his office sat David Bowie with his friend Sabrina Guinness. I was almost struck dumb.

'Hello, boys,' said David. Turning to me: 'I've heard about you.'

'Oh, thank you, yes, we covered "Fame",' I tell him, 'and Colin Thurston is our producer,' trying to find some common ground with the Thin White Duke.

'Ah yes, dear old Colin, how is Colin?'

I hadn't met many legends at this point in my career. David was the perfect gentleman, and we spent the rest of the evening in his and Sabrina's company. When Rob and I finally declubbed, we were on cloud nine as we traipsed back home.

'I c-c-c-can't believe it,' Rob kept saying, in his stuttering south Londonese. 'Us and David Bowie.'

The Embassy really was it, the Rum-Runner-on-Thames – no problems at the door and free drinks as standard. And it was also a place I could score in.

*

I would sometimes get angry when work interrupted a binge. Along with the late nights came more hangovers, increasing in frequency and intensity. I got a call from Colin that I was needed in the studio one particularly sore morning, and my immediate reaction was, 'What a drag!'

A drag? Wasn't this my dream job, my fantasy? Duran Duran was succeeding on every level, and I wanted to spend my free nights watching Lemmy play Space Invaders at the Embassy?

I had broken up with Roberta at Christmas, not because I had a particular replacement in mind, but rather because I assumed that the girl-pulling powers I was enjoying on the road would continue when I was at home. This turned out not to be the case. There's something about being in a touring band performing onstage most nights of the week that acts as an aphrodisiac. Maybe it's all the strutting and preening, maybe it's being in a city for just twenty-four hours; the girls that want you have to act fast.

But back in London, Rob and I struck out most nights. We would start out the evening reeking of aftershave, hairspray and optimism, but our 'failures to launch' became something of a running gag. Years later, Stephen Hayter would tell Rob at least part of the reason we found it so hard to get the girls: 'We all thought you guys were gay.'

35 Music Television

In New York the previous year, Paul and Michael had met with a group of executives at Warner-Amex Satellite Entertainment who were trying to get a national music television channel together. They were calling it MTV. The problem was, they didn't have much sexy content. The rock acts that filled the daytime FM radio slots did not make videos. What they really wanted, they told Paul and Mike, was 'sexy, exotic travelogues, like James Bond movies'.

Paul knew just the place.

Sri Lanka.

We could stop off there on the way to Australia, where our 'Rio' tour was due to begin in April.

We staggered our departures from London. Simon left with the advance guard. Russell Mulcahy, Eric Fellner, Paul, Mike and I followed a few days later. Nick was the last to leave, not wanting to miss out on any of the final mix decisions Colin was making.

On the Air Lanka flight, on the last day of March, I wrote Mum and Dad a postcard.

'Hi Ma, Hi Pa, the first of many, flight seems good. Food and stuff great. Anyway it'll be 8am when we arrive so I am going to try and spend the day doing nothing. Love John XXX.'

On arrival, I checked into a rather rustic hotel in Galle, on the southern tip of the island.

Sri Lanka seemed totally at odds with who we, as a band, thought we were. Simon, however, was entirely comfortable with it. He also had the most to do, being in the majority of the scenes that Russell Mulcahy was filming. Eric Fellner, who would later have Oscar successes with Working Title, produced the six-day shoot, in which we managed to film the videos for three songs.

We shot on videotape. The budget was tiny: £30,000.

'Hungry like the Wolf' had shades of *Apocalypse Now* as Simon chased model Sheila Ming through the rainforest. Was she real? Was she a hallucination? Russell planted his fedora on Simon's head for a touch of Indiana Jones. It would move onto my head for the filming of 'Save a Prayer', in which the entire band, barefoot, took its only spiritual journey of the year, to a Buddhist temple in the Sri Lankan highlands of Kandy. That hat stayed on my head for the rest of the year.

The band made fun of me for being the one to receive the full force of an elephant's hosing while sat atop the beast at a jungle water hole. But I didn't care. I loved it. It is one of my most treasured memories.

Andy had less happy memories. He developed a recurrent stomach bug after the trip to Sri Lanka, which he believed was a direct result of shooting that scene in the muddy water, and he blamed the Berrows for putting him there ever after.

'We're a fucking rock band. What the fuck were we doing out there poncing about on elephants?' he'd say.

We also shot some footage sitting on top of processional elephants riding through the ancient city of Colombo several nights later. It was a breathtaking experience, but the footage was never used.

Nick and I shot another scene on the beach with me in a pink pastel suit strumming a guitar and Nick playing some local panpipes. This was a long way from Birmingham. But we were all quite comfortable with the surreality of it all.

Judging by another postcard I sent back home from Kandy, I was confident that the work we were doing was going to have a powerful effect: 'Videos are going to blow the world apart. They are so FANTASTIC! John XX'

On our last night there, we filmed the band reunion scene for 'Hungry like the Wolf' in a downtown Kandy hotel lobby, happy to be back in our Antony Price glad rags. Normal service was about to be resumed. We had been in Sri Lanka just eight days, but we had filmed iconic footage that would define Duran Duran – the eighties? – for a generation.

36 Down Under and Up Above

The next day, we boarded a flight to Australia, our first visit to the country that had been so supportive since giving us our first number 1 hit. We touched down at 8.20 a.m. – to be met by hundreds of screaming Aussie fans.

Now back on the road, and with tours planned to the end of the year, I felt like I had made a sensible decision at Christmas to part ways with Roberta. I wanted to be footloose and fancy-free, and it seemed impossible to have a relationship going honestly with a girl back home.

Although being single wasn't quite the pathology that it would become later – when I truly believed I could not have a career and a relationship simultaneously – in Australia I came to appreciate the rather strange phenomenon of meeting a girl in the hotel lobby upon check-in and being in bed with her less than an hour later.

What services those girls performed! It certainly helped dispel

the homesickness. What I didn't realise was how much I was giving. I thought I was just taking. In fact, I tended to fall in love at the drop of a hat, and I fell in love a lot in 1982.

I didn't see these microromances – some lasting a few days, some just hours – as emotional crutches; rather, it was just part of the life we had created for ourselves. Sex addiction? What was that? I would have had to take a real stand, ethically and morally, not to get laid a lot that year.

None of us were monks, but not all the other guys were as comfortable sharing their beds as often and with as varied a cast of actresses as I was – Andy's marriage was coming up in three months. However, my behaviour didn't strike me, or any of the others, as compulsive.

I loved Sydney – the air, the people, the food, the ocean. Australians struck me as Brits without the inhibitions.

The postcard home from Melbourne reads, 'Absolutely unbelievable. Just like the Beatles. Screaming kids. Had to get a police escort from the radio station and we were on the news as the amazing new sensation. FABBO!! John XX'

I was sad to leave Australia. It had been a very funky sandbox to play in for two weeks. But then so was our next destination on the 'Rio' tour – Japan.

Bands had been going out to Japan since the seventies, and the hunger there for western music was insatiable. On our arrival at Narita airport, we were once again met by hordes of young fans. The journey from the airport to the city takes almost two hours, and the band cars were trailed by a column of taxicabs filled to bursting with excited, giggling, crying Tokyo teens.

In Japan, we became familiar with service lifts and the

mechanics of exiting through the kitchen. Everywhere we went, we were hustled, smuggled. It was exhilarating but exhausting.

Tokyo was a sensory overload, a sci-fi fantasy; *Godzilla*, *Blade Runner* and *Thunderbirds* all rolled into one hallucinatory day-dream – neon-lit frozen faces, the morning mists of Hokusai and our first Sony Walkmans.

The language barrier was the most formidable we had encountered to date, a whole other level of trying to get ourselves understood and understanding what was required from us. From the moment we stepped off the plane, we had a team of interpreters. Everything that we said had to be filtered through them.

I didn't like that. Still don't. I often found myself saying testily, 'That's not what I meant,' like a bad-tempered Henry Kissinger.

The Japanese processed us. The promoters needed to control the experience, as if we were a potentially dangerous substance that must not be allowed to contaminate the calm and order of Japan. They were happy we were there, but they would be even happier when we left.

Compared to the freedom of Australia, it was almost as if we were under house arrest. The moment we tried to step or speak out of the prescribed boundaries, a siren went off and we would be firmly escorted back into the appropriate cultural holding bay.

On our day off, Roger and I went out of the hotel to the shopping area around Harajuku with our driver, Simon Cook, as well as the two Japanese secret service guys who had been assigned to our case.

Tokyo is a madhouse at the best of times, and there are always crowds swarming around the tiny boutiques and markets in the lanes and streets of Harajuku. Roger and I thought we could get some gifts for our families – maybe some souvenirs – what's the big deal?

Well, the big deal was that we were big. As big in Japan as Gulliver was in Lilliput. There was no chance of not standing out, of having anything remotely resembling a normal experience. After an hour the whole thing got too unwieldy, and our guys with the walkie-talkies were getting nervous.

The car had to be backed down a narrow side street, and we were manhandled into the back seat, the scene beginning to reach the point of hysteria.

The following day, I wrote another postcard home. 'Ma and Pa, Hi, had an awful day yesterday. The screaming hit fever pitch and I started to feel like a prisoner in the hotel. Then went to go shopping with Rog, and followed by 600 people. Back home Wednesday.'

37 Incongruous on a Yacht

'Hungry like the Wolf' was in the UK Top 5. The significance of video for pop in general and Duran in particular was becoming increasingly evident, as now all anyone wanted to talk about with us was the videos.

There is no doubt that the work we did in Sri Lanka created a huge shift in the way we were perceived by the global music-buying public. We were no longer just an urban club band, famous for our sharp clothes and snazzy haircuts. We were, thanks to that video, transformed.

I can't believe we got away with it. We had somehow morphed from city nightclubbers to backpackers who had just walked out of the *Rough Guide*. And it hadn't been such a big effort for us to transition like that. Even though Sri Lanka hadn't seemed like a natural fit for the band, it worked. So well received were the Sri Lankan videos that label and management would decide to capitalise on them sooner rather than later.

Simon, Nick, Roger and I decided to take a quick holiday in Antigua, in the West Indies, before the US tour started in June. We spent a week there on the beach at English Harbour and had the place almost to ourselves. Every morning we would routinely trot out of our villas, one by one, like another Beatles scene or something out of Monty Python – 'Good morning, Mr Rhodes', 'Good morning, Mr Taylor' – and set up our towels for a day's suntanning.

Postcard to 'Dear Momsie and Popsie: You wouldn't recognise your healthy blonde beach hunk. Building up my muscles, trying to master the art of windsurfing.'

A well-deserved vacation at a glamorous resort. Living the high life, onstage and off. We were making money now and didn't have to consider, 'Can we afford a holiday this year?' We had gone way beyond the lifestyles our parents had made for us. Family holidays with Mum and Dad had always been on English soil (Devon or Cornwall), while Wales and Scotland were considered holidays abroad. Now it was a given that I would be living my life as a member of the jet set.

After a short week, as we were getting ready to leave, we got a call from Paul telling us not to pack, that he was on his way with Andy, Russell and the video film crew. His plan was to film another two videos: one for 'Rio' and another, if time allowed, for 'Night Boat', from the first album.

The inspiration for the 'Rio' video came from a book of photos that Russell owned, *Foxy Lady* by Belgian photographer Cheyco Leidmann.

The photographs were provocative; jarring, high-contrast neon colours, surrealist images of girls on beaches with milky oceans, girls with razors and shaving foam.

Once again, the Antony Price suits were in the frame –

incongruous on a yacht, but on film it worked, giving an impression of bright and decadent sophistication.

It was a surprisingly controversial, polarising video. It became our most iconic video, making MTV's all-time Top 10, but it was also perceived by many in Britain as an arrogant portrayal of the worst traits of Thatcherite self-interest. There would be no going back to the underground after that one.

But we had no political agenda. We just went with the energy. We were riding a wave, living a dream of our own making. We didn't see what could be wrong with that.

38 Theodore & Theodore

In June, we were back in New York, back at the St Moritz, getting ready for our second US tour.

We were playing bigger clubs and theatres across the country, but first there were some festival-type bills organised up and down the East Coast – Philadelphia, Washington, New York.

On 2 July, we played the Peppermint Lounge in Manhattan, and Robert Palmer came backstage to meet us. We clicked right away. I was a fan of Robert's music, and he was known for his great style. Nick and I had seen him in concert at the Odeon in Birmingham and loved his most recent album, *Clues*, which was proving to be a big success for him, particularly the single 'Johnny and Mary'.

Robert and I were opposites in many ways. We had very different ways of tackling similar problems, sartorially and sonically. In him I saw a mentor; in me, I think he saw a fountain of youth.

I also became friends with Blondie's bassist, Nigel Harrison, after meeting him at an after-hours club. Blondie were preparing for their first tour in several years, and I floated the idea to him of having us as their opening act.

After a show in Boston, the Duran tour made its way westwards across the continent, taking in Edmonton, Winnipeg, Vancouver and Calgary. By the time we reached the Greek Theatre in Los Angeles for the final performance, we had gotten the official offer to join Blondie in Kansas for nine dates, taking us back east.

This would give us an opportunity to play larger stages in front of bigger crowds in America, as their tour venues were averaging around the 10,000 capacity mark.

In Los Angeles, Nick and I both met new girlfriends. After the Greek Theatre show, I went to Club Lingerie on Sunset, where I met a girl named Bebe Buell. She was the inspiration for Richard Butler of the Psychedelic Furs to write 'Pretty in Pink', and she had a daughter, Liv. At the time, she had said Liv's dad was Todd Rundgren, but it was later revealed Liv's dad was actually Steven Tyler. She was a model, singer and muse.

Sunday, while I was sleeping in, Nick went on a boat trip, floating lazily along the Santa Monica coastline. On board, he met Julie Anne Friedman, also a model, from Des Moines, Iowa – and his future wife.

Love must have been in the air.

Two days later, at the Chateau Marmont in West Hollywood, Andy got married to Tracey Wilson, who had been his sweetheart since she gave him his first haircut. I was an extremely hungover best man. Andy had to rouse me, after not a lot of sleep, reminding me that the tuxedos had to be rented and the preparations made. He actually trusted me with the ring. For a few hours.

Andy's wedding was further evidence of Duran Duran's rapidly expanding movable feast, with many of our friends flying in from England for the occasion. There was not to be a honeymoon for the Taylors, however. Tracey went back to England and Andy flew on to Kansas with the rest of us to join the Blondie tour.

As we had on the Hazel O'Connor tour, we gathered around the mixing desk every night to watch Blondie begin their show, Debbie descending onto the stage in a glass lift before singing one of our favourites, 'Rapture'.

It was interesting to watch and learn, up close, the level of stagecraft and theatrics needed to play to the bigger open-plan American venues.

We bonded with Blondie's drummer, Clem Burke, Nigel and guitarist Eddie Martinez. Debbie Harry and her partner, Chris Stein, were elusive, and it was hard to make a connection with them.

On Saturday 14 August, the tour arrived at New Jersey's Meadowlands Arena, with former New York Dolls front man David Johansen added to the line-up, which had to make it one of the coolest bills we were ever on. The most significant thing that happened that night was meeting two guys who showed up backstage, friends of Debbie's who would become great friends and mentors of ours – Nile Rodgers and Tony Thompson of Chic. We bonded in the backstage bathrooms over white powder and mutual admiration; Brummie man-love meets Manhattan man-love.

'You guys are awesome!' says Nile.

'Man, we fucking love you!' say I.

'Hear, hear,' says Tony, offering me a bump.

I took it.

'You're the reason we're here,' I enthuse, the words getting a little strangled as the line bites.

'Why, thank you, my good man,' says Tony.

The debonair shtick that Chic had always put on was for real.

'You guys are the reason I started playing bass.'

Exaggeration was assumed as part of any coke rap, although what I was feeling for Tony and Nile was genuine.

Nile turned to Tony. 'Where are we going now, Theodore?'

'You keep calling me Theodore and I ain't going anywhere with you, man.'

Wherever these guys were going, I was going with them.

'Let's go the Studio,' says Nile.

Recording studio?

Studio 54.

Nile likes to tell the story of how 'Le Freak' was written after the night that he and Bernard Edwards (the bass player in Chic) got turned away from Studio 54. The song was originally entitled 'Fuck Off'. But by August '82, Nile was a king of the Manhattan night. The DJ played a Duran song when we came in the door with him. It was the crowning achievement for a band born out of the Rum Runner club scene.

MTV was beginning to appear in a few states, and they were playing us a lot. Our records were being feted in a big way on the channel, and we were selling well in MTV territories.

What we weren't getting was any mainstream radio play. 'Hungry Like the Wolf' had been serviced to the powerful FM stations a second time but still to no avail. However, EMI in London were determined that we get a hit in the United States, because London could see that if Capitol could not get the band going commercially, the company could lose us worldwide, as our contracts would soon be up for renegotiation. EMI insisted Capitol pull out all the stops.

Paul and Michael were desperate to have a hit in the US too. They got their hands on a market research document called the Abrahams Report. It was an analysis of all the sounds that were most appealing to FM radio programmers. It literally spoke of the 'John Bonham drum sound' and the 'stereo guitar sound typified by AC/DC and Van Halen'. If you were trying to sell refrigerators to Middle America, this report claimed, the people most likely to buy your products liked these sounds.

'We need to take notice of this, chaps. This is how we are going to get on radio here,' said Paul.

I was appalled at the idea that we should remix our perfect album to cater to these philistines, but Andy and Nick listened, and I am glad they did. They went into the studio with producer David Kershenbaum and remixed side one of the *Rio* album with the intention of making the songs more FM friendly. The guitar levels were raised, the overall sound made punchier, but the integrity of the tracks was not compromised.

Rather than replacing the album tracks with the new mixes, Capitol released them as a stand-alone extended-play 12-inch single entitled 'Carnival'. With it, they launched a third and what would prove to be entirely successful attack on the American rock radio establishment.

Our first US hit was the remixed 'Hungry Like the Wolf'.

Back in London, Nick went straight back into the studio to finish up the Kajagoogoo project. Which made me jealous. I wanted a side project too. I told Dave Ambrose I wanted to make a record with Bebe, a version of the T. Rex song 'Get It On'.

'Really, John, can she sing?' said quiet Dave.

'I think so.'

The recording with Bebe got put on ice after the English tabloid press pointed out quite how many other musicians she had dated before me. We broke up, and the idea of covering 'Get It On' was filed away.

39 Coffin Sex

What is it about Munich?

On 5 October 1982, our tour bus was rolling down the A9 autobahn from Berlin. This was our second trip to Germany but the first time Munich was on the date sheet. The tour had started in the North, in Hanover, then gone to Bochum and Hamburg before playing the Berlin Sektor on 4 October.

We had a bus, which was unusual for us, and were sleeping half on it, half in hotels. Three-star hotels. Duran never really took to the bus life. Not that anyone ever said, 'I don't like sleeping on a bus, let's not do it any more'; it was just another example of our collective consciousness. We tried it in Europe in '82 and never did it again.

In truth, I wasn't getting much sleep.

I was squeezed into one of the bus's eye-level bunks, mid-fuselage, with Paul and Mike Berrow's younger sister, Amanda.

Is there any form of fornication less pleasant, less comfortable, than at mid-afternoon on a rumbling old tour bus?

Coffin sex. Capsule sex. The smells of sweaty socks and diesel. No air. I should have been over this; this was high-school stuff. Trying to get her bra unhooked, fingers down the panties – you know the drill. Fumbling and ridiculous.

To be fair, we both knew that this wasn't love, and neither of us had a great deal of enthusiasm for what was taking place, but in the moment, she was a girl and I was a boy.

When we arrived in Munich, we checked into the Hilton. There was no Duran show that night, so the local promoter suggested we go see Kool and the Gang perform at the Circus Krone.

I must have scored some blow before the concert, because all I can remember of it is a blur with a beat. We stood at the back and left before the end. We went on to a nightclub, the Sugar Shack, and who should be there but Roxy Music.

This was the first time I had met my childhood heroes since waiting to get their autographs under the awning of the Holiday Inn in Birmingham, a long seven years ago, in 1975. Bryan knew we were fans and invited us to join them at their table in the VIP section for champagne.

It should have been a moment to savour – a schmooze with the band we had loved for so long, an opportunity to exchange numbers, maybe put down a tent peg for a future collaboration – but my drug craving was keeping me restless. I could not keep still. From the bar to the restroom, back to the lounge and the VIP table, then off again. A moving target, I couldn't relax. My constant thirst needed slaking.

Then the night turns black. I am back at the hotel in Roger's room, and he is sitting on the bed, covered in blood, and someone is telling me that he has been involved in a fight at the club. He's just back from the hospital.

What happened? How did I miss it? Is Amanda wearing white? And why, more importantly, is she nursing his wounds?

I am suddenly consumed with jealousy over the attention that Roger is getting from Amanda. So jealous that when I leave the room to go back to my own room, I punch my right fist through a glass light fixture mounted on the wall. There is blood everywhere. My right hand. *Fuck*. I may be drunk, but I am conscious enough to know I am in big trouble.

I go to Andy's room and wake him up.

I can't remember going to the hospital but I did go, and I had several stitches. I wouldn't be able to play again for some time. The rest of the German dates had to be cancelled and everyone flew home the next day.

Almost thirty years later, the scar on my right index finger – my very necessary, playing, pulsing lead finger – still pains me when the weather is damp and cold. It's like one of those old war wounds that veterans talk about.

How did I feel about this obvious meltdown, and causing such disruption to the band? Embarrassment. Shame.

I was getting as much attention as any twenty-two-year-old ever deserved to get, and certainly as much as any of the other band members. I didn't need to sabotage myself to get more.

So why did I?

Fear? Fear that it was all going to be gone in a matter of moments? That deep down I was not deserving of all the success and attention I was getting?

I am trying to live away from home, live on the road, live out of suitcases and tour buses and hotel rooms and not die of loneliness.

I missed home.

I missed Mum and Dad.

I didn't know that then. It's taken me years and many therapist-dollars to figure it out. In my self-centred fear and loneliness, I just cracked. I never gave one thought to the consequences.

The organisation did, however. The next scene played out a few days later in the Rum Runner office, with all band members and Paul and Michael present.

I was the naughty boy in the headmaster's office.

They expressed sympathy and concern – poor me, with my right hand bandaged and in a sling – and they were all in agreement that losing the remaining German dates was not the end of the world, that we could overcome this slight setback in our scheme of things. However, there were three sold-out shows in Portugal, where the band was top of the charts, that could not be cancelled so easily.

They told me that I would still be going along to do all the peripheral stuff – the press conferences, TV interviews, etc. – but another bass player would be coming in to play my parts for the shows.

I accepted the news with grace. What else could I do? And they were quite clear that this must not happen again. What would happen if it did went unspoken and was left hanging in the October air.

Five days later, we arrived in Lisbon. At the airport, we had the latest of our many encounters with the local press, in which we would imitate the Beatles and they would imitate the press that interviewed the Beatles.

And I was back in my role as swinger-in-chief, not going to let any of that get me down. My shit-eating grin was back, laughing off any problems I or we may have been having. Only at that evening's concert, standing alone on the side of the stage, watching *my* band perform without me, did I pause for any introspection. My stand-in was a thoroughbred pro and had no difficulties in learning my parts.

The conclusion was gut-wrenching. I was not an irreplaceable component to the machine any more, and that seed of self-doubt would fuck with me for years.

Was Munich to blame? I pretended so.

40 Jacobean

A December British tour brought us back to Birmingham after a year away, living in hotels.

We booked into the Holiday Inn for the nights of the shows. After the last concert, and the traditional party at the club, it was time to go home.

I had to think twice about that. Home? Mum and Dad's? Simon Road? I was still living at my parents'! How could that be?

I wasn't still there because I couldn't afford my own place; we were making real money now. I just hadn't had the time to think about where I would live and to physically make the move.

Or was it more than that? There was an undeniable comfort in being able to go home, however infrequently, after all the travelling and the madness, to Mum's cooking and the familiar sounds and smells of the house I had grown up in.

One of the innovations that I brought to Simon Road from my on-the-road experiences was a 'Do Not Disturb' sign handmade out of cardboard. It even had 'Please Clean Room' written on the other side. Mum got the message even if Dad didn't.

Dad was good though, when it came to handling my first exposure to a sexually transmitted disease. I contracted crabs in the US and thought I had gotten rid of it. But in the shower at Mum and Dad's I scratched away at some scabby thing on my chest and the little fucker went scuttling away down my leg. Dammit!

I knew this one was not for Mum.

Dad rose to the occasion admirably. There was no judgement, simply, 'You better not let your mother know about this.'

He took off all my bedsheets and secretly put them into the washing machine, practically boiling them down to paper, then got me the necessary meds from the local pharmacy.

It was a good, if unusual, father/son bonding experience.

Almost proudly, he admitted, in an unusual show of candour, that 'picking the lice off his pals' skin and hair' was something he had learned in the prison camp.

'We all stood in line, each of us going through the hairs of the man in front.'

It was the first time that he had relayed to me any sense of the deprivations of prison-camp life.

But it was too late. I was not now in the mood to hear about it. I just remember thinking, 'How useful.'

But the buddy-movie moment did not last and I knew I could take no more of living at home when Dad came stomping up the stairs the following day and banged on my bedroom door, saying, 'You're not on bloody tour now, you know. Turn that music down!'

I had to find my own place, and fast.

I chose a two-bedroomed first-floor flat on Jacoby Place, Edgbaston, ten minutes from the city centre, and, in a mad flurry of credit card and chequebook purchases, filled it with European furnishings from the better local stores: Roche Bobois and Ligne Roset. Dad painted the flat and laid the carpet for me. The colour scheme was pure 1982; grey sofa, black glass coffee table and a single burgundy wall, with a Patrick Nagel portrait of Joan Collins to the right of the bookshelves. Nastassja Kinski by Richard Avedon hung above the bed.

I spent no more than a dozen nights in that Jacoby place.

Madness? I was just getting started.

We flew back to New York for New Year's Eve to take part in MTV's coming-out ball at the Savoy.

We had been introduced to Andy Warhol on our first visit to New York and had got to know him a little. Over the years to come, Nick would become great friends with him. After our performance, I was drinking at the bar when Andy wandered over, sipping his drink through a straw. He leaned into my ear and whispered conspiratorially, 'You should be the singerrr.'

'No thanks, Andy,' I said.

41 The Year of the Geographic

1983 was the year of the geographic. A 'geographic' is a term used in addiction and recovery. When a person finds some fact of their life unacceptable, they try to escape dealing with it by changing location. Change the backdrop, change the geography; that way you don't have to change yourself.

January saw the assault on the American charts of the *Rio* album and the 'Hungry Like the Wolf' single. They would peak at number 5 and number 3 respectively in March, just two of the many numbers in this year that would stagger us, as Duranmania began to grip the world.

Capitol saw the chance to cash in and relaunched the first album. They updated the car photograph on the cover with something from a more recent shoot that represented the band's democratic philosophy and popularity – i.e. we were all the same size – and changed the graphics so the album aesthetically matched the style of 'Is There Something I Should Know?' – the latest single, which we had recorded in January but was bolted onto the older album for the US release. That album would be platinum by the summer. I guess we wouldn't be leaving EMI after all.

In London, at the *Daily Mirror* Rock and Pop Awards, the forerunner to the Brits, we won everything that was going: best album, best group, best male singer and '*Daily Mirror* Personality of the Year'. 'Is There Something I Should Know?' went straight into the UK charts at number 1 in March.

I heard the news at the same time as the rest of the country, Tuesday lunchtime, listening to Radio 1 in Janice Hague's office in Manchester Square. It was a fantastic result, although our level of cocksureness was so high, it didn't come as a complete surprise. Still, hearing those words spoken over the airwaves undoubtedly had a real magic: 'And we've got a new number 1 this week, and it's a new entry, its first week on the charts, and they've made it. Duran Duran are number 1. Congratulations, boys!'

You could hear the champagne corks popping on every floor of the building.

The video for 'Is There Something I Should Know?' was a conscious attempt to strip away the artifice; it was anti-location, anti-style. We all wore blue uniforms more befitting Winston Smith from *1984* than New Romantics.

In February we were on the TV and the radio every day.

EMI released our first video album, a fifty-five-minute review of the first two years of our existence, featuring eleven of our most popular songs. It was unprecedented.

The fan club, based in the Rum Runner, was now receiving hundreds of letters and cards from all around the world every day. A team of staff had been hired to cope with the deluge. There was no longer any possibility of us handling our fan mail ourselves;

replies to fans were now made photostatically. Some staff members became adroit at simulating our signatures for photographs.

My parents were both energised by the success of their son. Dad, having been in a malaise since his enforced retirement, was now on top of the world, having fun with it all, and becoming someone in the neighbourhood.

The third act in their lives had begun.

The first of the year's geographics was made on the orders of Paul and Mike, who decided we should write and record the third album outside the United Kingdom. They also ended our relationship with producer Colin Thurston. It was one of many decisions that were made on our behalf without too much consultation. They just felt they knew what was best, and the record company must have felt the same way. Our feelings didn't come into it. We were too busy to process it anyway.

We were tempted away from Colin in part by the suggestion that we could produce ourselves. 'Is There Something I Should Know?' was produced by the band, with the help of Ian Little, who worked with Roxy Music on their *Avalon* album. The song was a smash, but for the album we were about to begin, the band were not going to produce. We would keep Ian Little on board, but to augment Ian's skills, we also took on Alex Sadkin, who had worked on the Grace Jones albums and with Robert Palmer and Bob Marley. Alex's credentials were impeccable, and it was his task to freshen up the sound for Album 3.

Employing Alex Sadkin was a statement of intent. We were not about to stand still creatively. We all knew that meant death. The vultures were circling. None of the critics thought we could follow *Rio*.

The South of France was chosen as a suitable relocation.

Management found a château for rent in Valbonne, five kilometres north of Cannes on the Côte d'Azur. It was beautiful and sophisticated.

One of the appeals of the move to the South of France was getting to drive down there. It was an opportunity to live out one of my James Bond fantasies.

Bloody James Bond, making it all look so damned effortless; the way he travels, checks into hotels, orders champagne in foreign restaurants, drives on the left, drives on the right.

Weeks earlier, I had finally made the time to take my driving test.

As a kid, I always knew that there were not going to be any of the problems with my learning to drive that Mum had. Just riding fairground bumper cars gave me a hard-on. In regard to automobiles, I was Dad's prodigy. Cars were for guys; that was obvious. Women were meant for the passenger seat. There was always something a little inappropriate when a friend of mine had a mother who drove, like Nick's mum, Sylvia. Suspicious.

Dad had given me practice lessons on and off since I was sixteen, and I always rose to the occasion. *I* knew what the clutch was all about.

However, the fame thing had created a bit of a complication in the plan to get my licence. I had been sure I would be driving at nineteen, or twenty tops, but Duran had taken over and I had not had time to learn how to drive.

The test was on 22 February.

In that way that the British have of reminding one to not get above one's station, the grey-suited examiner took a moment before the test began to address me.

'Now, Mr Taylor, I want you to know that I know who you are. In fact, my daughter has pictures of you all over her bedroom wall. But this will not influence me in any way. I hope you understand that. Now, pull away smoothly in your own time and follow the road ahead.'

I passed.

I had already decided exactly which car I wanted, and later that day it was delivered. A Volkswagen Golf GTI. Seven-and-a-half grand. Brand-new, colour scheme carefully selected to match my Duran wardrobe: black bodywork with red pinstripes, two-tone grey interior.

I named her Suky, after her licence plate, SUK 437Y. To celebrate our engagement, photographer Denis O'Regan shot us on the top floor of the Moor Street station parking garage in Birmingham city centre for the Japanese fanzine *Viva Rock*.

One eighties icon for another.

Driving Suky aboard the Seaspeed hovercraft to cross the English Channel, with my licence less than two months old, wasn't quite the James Bond experience I had hoped for. And those winding roads that looked so joyful to navigate in *Goldfinger* were bloody hard work. The final destination took some finding. As I drove up the château driveway, I was exhausted.

I parked Suky behind a Ferrari that turned out to be Mike's new ride. That didn't seem quite fair. I had been perfectly happy with my VW until I saw the manager's Ferrari!

By choosing to drive instead of fly, I was the last to arrive, so I got allocated the only bedroom left, a poky corner room the size of the single bed that furnished it. Simon, meanwhile, had set himself up in regal splendour in a beautiful master bedroom suite that looked over the grounds. Paul's room was not dissimilar.

It was a fantasy, just not mine.

Once we started working, though, things levelled out. Making music straightens out the bullshit. That's always the way with musicians. Well, *almost* always the way. We had to move the sound forward – that's what Alex was there for – and develop our song-writing and musicianship further. For me, that meant choosing to play far fewer notes.

The bass playing on the first two albums had been characterised by a busy, syncopated style, as I put my New Wave spin on the funky disco sound that was coming out of America. In trying to create a sense of musical maturity, I wanted to find a way of saying more by playing less. Basslines were getting less busy, as synths were now being employed to double bass–guitar parts, so the lines were getting simpler but fatter, as exemplified by the low-end work on 'Thriller' and Bowie's 'Let's Dance'.

The drums and amps and keyboards that had been driven down from London were set up in a bright, sunlit, top-floor room that was unfurnished and unused. It was a pleasant enough room and it had a veranda, but there was no power in the wall sockets, so the engineer had to run cables down three flights of stairs to the generator and recording equipment, which were located in a truck parked on the driveway. We all had to get used to the inconvenience of running up and down the stairs – *up and down, up and down* – trying to make sure that the sounds we were making upstairs were getting to the tape machines downstairs.

It was a frustrating experience. We had a lot of ideas, but we weren't getting them down on tape. There were too many snags with the gear, the power, the *stairs*, the whole fucking old house, basically. And then we learned, to our dismay, that when a piece of equipment broke or needed replacing, the new parts had to be flown down from London.

Cue lots of pool time, French food and trips to La Croisette in Cannes.

We got a handful of tracks going – the basis for several songs that are on *Seven and the Ragged Tiger*: the groove that would become 'New Moon on Monday' was given a working title of 'Spidermouse', and we had 'Of Crime and Passion', '(I'm Looking for) Cracks in the Pavement', and 'I Take the Dice'.

A Philly Soul-type groove we worked up became 'Seven and the Ragged Tiger' after Simon dashed down some vocal sketches. Simon reimagined us as a twisted Enid Blyton creation; the five band members plus Mike and Paul were the seven, and the ragged tiger was that intangible phenomenon that was beginning to swallow us up – fame. The song did not survive, yet strangely, the title did.

Paula Yates and Jools Holland came down to shoot a special for the UK TV show *The Tube*. We contrived a big barbecue party for the folks back home to see us living it large *and* getting work done.

Except we weren't getting as much work done as we made out.

Without fear of contradiction, I can state for the record that this was Duran's *smoke* period. There was rarely a time when a joint was not being rolled or smoked. This engendered a lot of philosophical conversations and considerations, spoken in a hashish hush, as if the *Bhagavad Gita* were being discussed rather than the snare-drum sound or a guitar part.

After a few weeks of that, despite being on the French Riviera, we were all getting restless and talking about making a move.

It was time for a geographic.

The BBC had made a documentary of the Police recording *Synchronicity* at AIR Studios in Montserrat and it looked like they were having a lot of fun and making great music, which was the combination we were looking to achieve also.

I was given the task of announcing this plan to the world in the April issue of the Duran Duran fan club newsletter, along with other news that I delivered with very specific attention to detail: 'I am very happy to announce that on Pan Am Flight 98 on Tuesday 19 July at 7.35 a.m., Terminal 3, we shall be returning to England. Rah Hooray! Why is this, I hear you ask? Well, what some of you will know is that on 20 July we shall be playing at London's Dominion Theatre for Charlie and Di for the Prince's charity trust. What you don't know is that on Saturday 23 July we will be playing an outdoor concert for Greenpeace, at some venue yet to be confirmed, so for the thousands of you who won't be able to go to the Dominion, there's one for you.'

I had always enjoyed answering fan mail at the Rum Runner, loving the feeling of connectedness I got from the back-and-forth with our most enthusiastic followers. Now I didn't open any of the envelopes, read any of the letters or reply to any of our fans directly. Taking it in turns, we would formulate a monthly missive that would then be reproduced by the thousand in colour on glossy paper and disseminated by our fan club organisation. Something was definitely lost in the expansion programme, but what else could we do?

I never again felt as connected to our network of fans until I surrendered to the social networking media of Twitter and Facebook in 2010. Now, once again, I see identifying traits before I read the comments, but this time they are icons and usernames, not handwriting, and I know instantly who they are, where they live, and where they sit in the Duran stratosphere.

A member of our road crew offered to drive Suky back from France. I flew back with the boys. Months later, I would get a summons for an unpaid parking ticket in Torquay. *Torquay?* It near drove me crazy trying to figure that one out. Had I driven there in a blackout? Then the penny dropped. After getting back to London, the roadie had used my car to take a family holiday on the south coast.

42 A Caribbean Air

Packing for the West Indies, I realised I was going to need a new wardrobe for the climate there. The five members of the band always had a strong collective consciousness when it came to putting a look together for a photo shoot, a video, a tour or a working holiday like this.

I expressed this idea in an interview with Steve Sutherland in *Melody Maker*: 'I don't think there was anybody in the band who wasn't sceptical about going to Sri Lanka. Our manager had been there for a holiday, and came back talking about this amazing, Utopian island. Durans go back to nature? How's my lip gloss gonna go in this? But when we got there, it just happened so naturally, the hair was let down without anyone consciously doing it.'

Duran arrived in Montserrat with an entirely integrated new look, wearing pale earth tones, pastels, pale blue and pink, cream and white. No black, no leather, no military! The staff of

the studio were delighted to welcome us and made commemorative T-shirts. I rented a red Suzuki jeep and had fun getting to know the island, racing along the beaches in and out of the surf. Another Bondian fantasy brought to life. Somehow I acquired a postcard of the Vue Pointe Hotel signed by Stewart Copeland, Andy Summers and Sting.

One concern before departure had been the lack of entertainment on Montserrat, particularly after work hours. So we had personal flight cases built, like those old steamer trunks you sometimes see in Louis Vuitton ads, except ours were built to road standard by the company that made the flight cases for our stage gear. You could drive an articulated truck over them and they wouldn't break, according to the brochure. The cases housed our clothing and personal effects and – most importantly – new Sony Trinitron television sets and brand-new multi-region video cassette players. We all stocked up on VHS movies and planned to swap and trade titles throughout our stay.

These monoliths weighed a ton. It took the entire road crew to get mine into place in the rented villa I was sharing with Andy.

At last, we got a couple of groovier tracks going. 'The Reflex' came into life on my birthday, 20 June, after some celebratory champagne, and a day or two later we hit on 'Union of the Snake', I loved cutting tracks in the studio, then taking off my guitar to do a running dive into the perfect blue of the studio swimming pool.

But there were problems in Montserrat, just as there had been in the South of France. Andy was not at all happy with the studio speakers, and the tape machines didn't seem to be running properly. There were breakages too, and now it took even longer to get the replacements flown in from London.

We did fly in two of Chic's superstar singers, Michelle Cobbs and B. J. Nelson, from New York. It was great having their energy around. They contributed the 'na na na nas' to 'The Reflex'.

But the moaning and whining gathered momentum, leading to a major ruckus with the technical staff. They were like, 'It's you guys. You guys are not working. Our studio is perfectly fine.'

They thought we were delusional.

Maybe we were.

Things eventually got heavy with AIR, and payment of bills was questioned on both sides. We received a stern letter from AIR London telling us we were no longer welcome at their UK facilities.

But looking at photographs of us taken on the island, either together or individually, we all look happy and relaxed. Maybe we were bored, as in my case, or frustrated, as in Andy's, but we still knew how to put on a show. No cracks could be seen in the images we chose to put out of ourselves.

We escaped Montserrat to fly back home to play the UK dates I had announced in the newsletter from France.

The Prince's Trust gig was held at the Dominion Theatre. Duran Duran, who were apparently Princess Diana's favourite band, were billed alongside Dire Straits, who were Charles's. We played for about an hour. There's a bootleg of the show called *Di's Big Date* which I would not recommend. I don't know if it was the jet lag or the perfume, but I had tuning problems throughout and played horribly.

The performance was of little importance, however. It was all about the photo op. The picture of Simon and me with Diana, our hands entwined, went around the world. It was Mum and Dad's favourite of all the photos taken of me. I only took it off the living room wall after Dad passed away twenty-five years later.

The outdoor concert was held at Villa Park football ground in

Birmingham. In a stroke of marketing genius, all of our merchandising for the event was in claret and blue – Aston Villa's colours. We gave a press conference at the Dorchester on Park Lane with four of the five Durans wearing Villa scarves and Nick – reluctantly – holding up a Villa rosette, aware of betraying the loyalties of his dad, Roger, a serious Birmingham City fan.

Robert Palmer and his band flew in from touring the United States to open up. We partied at the Rum Runner like old times. After that, I made the cover of the Aston Villa match-day programme, photographed with my bass in the Villa colours for their game against Sunderland in August. I am the only non-player or coach to have had that honour.

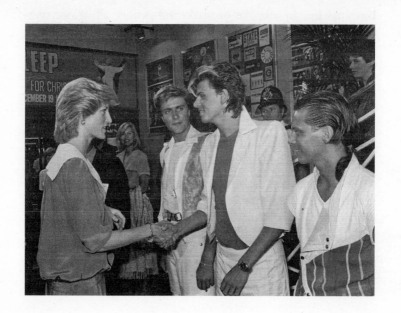

43 Resentments Under Construction

Where would we go now? We had intended to go to Compass Point in Nassau, Alex Sadkin's home base, but we were now completely turned off the idea of 'getting away from it all'. We wanted to get *to* it.

Like pop's General Patton, I carried a large-scale wall-map of the world with me wherever I travelled. I could monitor where we were selling well and where we could tour. If we really had to move again, to another country and another damn studio, if this exile was to continue, then let's go somewhere *fun*, for God's sake. I peered at the map and considered the question.

Where did we have the best time on tour last year?

Australia.

Or, more specifically, *Sydney.*

Ever since 'Planet Earth' reached number 1 on the Australian pop charts in the New Romantic spring of '81, Duran Duran and the Aussies had a special relationship. The concerts on that tour, at Sydney's Hordern Pavilion in particular, were the biggest-selling concerts we had played to date. Just as importantly, we had friends down there.

Alex and I rented a gorgeous twin-bedroom flat in the upscale George Street Apartments. Rumour had it George Harrison was also in residence there, but we never saw him. High above the city, with north-facing views of the ferry terminals, the Opera House and the Harbour Bridge, it was, in Bryan Ferry's words, 'penthouse perfection'. I rented a silver 7-Series BMW to get around in, intending to take full advantage of this town.

EMI owned studios in Sydney, which was convenient. They were named Studios 301 after the address on Castlereagh Street. It wasn't as sophisticated a set-up as AIR, but it was better than the mobile set-up we had endured in France. Any technical problems or breakages could be resolved in house, quickly.

We had an album's worth of basic tracks cut, so it was now a question of getting lyrics written and recorded. I chose to give Simon plenty of space. You can't have five or six guys sitting around staring at Simon, expecting him to deliver lyrics to order.

I would get out and about and take care of public relations.

I was a tiger loosed from the cage. A little ragged, appropriately, but a tiger nonetheless.

And I discovered a new drug.

MDA. Methylenedioxyamphetamine.

MDA would find more traction in the marketplace in a slightly different form and under a different name. Ecstasy.

44 Unlimited Latitude

It's Saturday, midnight, the peak of the weekend. I'm at a nightclub. Music plays. Grace Jones. Something familiar, something comforting. An hour ago, I took a small white pill that had been passed to me under the table at the restaurant I had been eating at. The effects of the pill are coming on. I'm warming up.

In fact, I have never felt so warmly comforted. I am opening up, open to everyone and anything, awake, receptive. My touch sense is exploding, gently. Touch me! Touch me again! The silk, the leather.

I'm aswim in textures that are both holy and new. A girl dances next to me in a dress that is so soft I can put my fingers right through it. And the lights are dancing too, and so deeply, deeply seductive. Nondestructive, creative. Pulsing profoundly like molten gold. Everyone in this room is in love with me and I am in love with them.

I have lost myself at a Sydney nightclub thousands of miles from home and it feels so good. Almost all my inhibitions have drained away. I have unlimited latitude. Lying on my back on the floor, a

beatific smile on my face, I am surrounded by a hundred starry dancers.

The music over, I scrape myself off the dance floor, head for the exit and climb behind the wheel of the BMW, accompanied by my new best friends, my soul mates. Set the controls for York Street. My last coherent thought before falling asleep hours later is, 'This MDA is incredible. I have to tell everyone about it.'

Fact is, I had never been one for hallucinogens. I liked speedy, chatty party drugs that kept me up all night and randy. There aren't that many of them. I had never gone in for the slower, introspective buzz that could be had from hash, which always made me want to retch, or pot, and certainly not LSD or any opiates.

The MDA had broken down my walls. It was the closest a drug had come to giving me a feeling of complete relaxation and oneness with the universe. It had brought me closer to God.

The following day, I was like the Mad Hatter on a mission. Beginning with Alex, who of all people I figured should be sympathetic to the transcendent spiritual qualities of my discovery, I worked my way around the band like a missionary as we came into contact throughout the day, some of us taking a late Sunday lunch out at Doyles fish restaurant, and back at the apartment afterwards.

'It's amazing, you have to try it,' I insisted. 'The music, the lights. It makes our lives up until now feel like a black-and-white movie. Last night I went into Technicolor, in turbo power.'

Andy, you at least could dig that, surely?

What was wrong with my own reality that I was so desperate to change it? None of the others seemed bothered; life was working well enough for them. And I can't have done too good a job as a salesman, because when I headed back out into the Sydney night that evening, determined not only to replicate the experience of the evening before but to build on it, maybe write a book about it, I had none of my bandmates on the ride with me.

Perhaps there was work to do.

'Expectations are resentments under construction.' One of my favourite lines from the addiction recovery programme I now follow. I loved it the first time I heard it and use it the whole time. It has entered the family vernacular, and the band all use it too.

When I went out into that Sydney night for a second run at the MDA mountain, I was loaded with expectations of what was going to happen and how it was going to make me feel when that small but powerful pill took effect.

I dropped it, with no alcohol. I had understood from the night before that the effect I wanted, what MDA was about, didn't need alcohol. That aspect would appeal to the ravers in a few years' time, when the drug hit big-time. You would see them in their thousands, in fields in the middle of nowhere, out of their minds on acid and Ecstasy, with bottles of Evian. This was a better buzz than booze could offer.

Waiting, waiting for something to happen. When is that shit going to kick in? This club is boring. It was so much more fun last night.

I need some space. Go to the bathroom and check my face. Tired. Bedraggled. Not a Jackie magazine face. Eyeliner up double-quick.

Return to the table. Who the fuck are these people? They aren't my friends; they're stragglers, hangers-on, waiting for something from me. I am their prey.

Somewhere to the left of me, a reptilian tongue flickers, catches a fly that flew too close. Closer still, that record executive has a tail – I hadn't noticed that before – a piece of scaly dinosaur meat that is thumping the leather banquette steadily, patiently, like a windscreen wiper stuck on slow. It does not surprise me.

One fast move and I'm out. Angry now; where is that fucking buzz?

This city is nowhere, man, it's too far from anywhere, no fun at all. Am I now just a bad actor who has forgotten his lines, onstage in a poorly written play that no one is watching anyway? The universe comes down hard on us sometimes. If this is the way you want it, John, raw and uncooked, here it is. Truth is as black as it is white. Last night was a gift but you want to make it a habit. That is going to be expensive.

I surrender, Lord. Send the servants home. Let's have an early night, just the two of us, like the old days, a front-row pew at St Jude's. Let's watch some bad TV and go to bed. I'll toe the line, Daddy, I promise, just let me rest.

But the trip will not stop, and alone in my high-rise Sydney fuck pad I am teetering on crazy. Slide the glass back on the balcony and take some air. Whoa! It's vertiginous! If I could find the phone I would use it, but who would I call? I don't even know.

I can't get out of my head and my head is three feet thick. Where is last night's poetry, because this is a fucking nightmare?

I am crying, 'Stop it, God, make it go away.' But there is no relief to be had, and the clock runs onward to another wasted dawn.

In the studio we were burning out everyone around us. We'd been on this album a long time. So when Alex announced one morning that some changes had been made to one of the arrangements ('Seven and the Ragged Tiger' was becoming 'The Seventh Stranger') and I was required to go down to the studio and make some alterations to my bass part, I freaked out.

I was in the bathroom shaving. In yet another moment of overreaction, I picked up a heavy glass and threw it at the shower door, smashing it into a million pieces.

'Fuck, Alex, this is bullshit! That song was finished! I'm finished! I'm done!'

'It's not such a big deal, John,' said Alex gently. 'It will be easy. Sometimes these things take time.'

Andy and I did our last overdubs on the *Seven and the Ragged Tiger* album that afternoon. He was fed up too.

'That's it,' he said. 'I'm having no more of this. I'm off.'

The thought of Andy leaving Duran was horrifying, and it snapped me out of my complacency. The balance that made the band great would be lost, along with our edge.

Maybe a side project could enable us to let out the pressure?

'Don't worry,' I said. 'We will do something different next, something tougher.'

It was the beginning of a rift that would deepen over the next two years; Andy and I on one side, Simon, Nick and the Berrows on the other. Roger did a balancing act between us.

Even worse than Andy not being part of Duran was the thought that Andy might not be part of my life. He was the only one I could comfortably get wasted around.

Alcohol and drugs were beginning to take control not just of decisions and choices I made, but also of who I hung out with.

One of the worst effects of this was that I didn't want to be around Nick any more, my oldest friend, simply because he never supported my using. Nick was just not a drug user, so it was uncomfortable for me to be around him when I was high. Andy was an easier playmate.

More and more though, I was keeping away from anyone connected with the group when I was using, seeking out lower companions. Instincts on rampage baulk at investigation.

I didn't want to be challenged on my behaviour, and outside the group and management, there was no one who would challenge me. Quite the opposite. Everyone wanted to party with me. But behind the party face, I was caught up in a vortex of fear, arrogance, loneliness and extraordinary popularity.

45 Anticlimax to Reflex

On 17 October, 'Union of the Snake' the first single from *Seven and the Ragged Tiger*, was released in the UK. We had a barbecue at Paul and Michael's villa in the swanky Sydney suburb of Vaucluse, where we awaited the phone call from London. The champagne was on ice. We were all expecting another 'Straight in at number 1, it's Duran Duran' moment, but it didn't happen.

'Union of the Snake' went in at number 3 – and that was immensely disappointing, which gives some indication of the pressure we were under and the expectations we had for ourselves.

The burgers on the grill cooled as the ice in the coolers warmed.

But at least after all the time, energy and air miles, *Seven and the Ragged Tiger* was finished. Nine songs.

'The Reflex' opens the set, followed by 'New Moon on Monday', which would be picked out as the second single. Side B of the album begins with 'Union' and continues with 'Shadows

on Your Side', a song about the darker side of the fame we were all living through. Then comes the instrumental, 'Tiger Tiger', and the album closes with 'The Seventh Stranger'.

We flew in Rebecca Blake, the New York-based fashion photographer who had shot us for *Rolling Stone* the previous year. In the film *Eyes of Laura Mars,* Faye Dunaway's character is based on Rebecca, and her work appears throughout the film. She shot through the night, preferring the drama that only artificial light can provide.

The shoot was certainly dramatic. A full-size, hot-blooded tiger was brought onto the set at the State Library of New South Wales. The clothes choices are decidedly uptown – back to black – Nick has the most gorgeous black lizard suit, with tight black boots and black tie, Roger and I are both in evening dress, and Simon and Andy are more casual-looking in expensive suede and leather. We all looked like successful, wealthy young men; still available.

Once again, Malcolm Garrett had the job of giving the photograph a graphic framework, this time placing it into an Art Deco board game frame filled with symbols and ancient runes. The Aston Villa colours remained on the logo.

The video for 'Union of the Snake' didn't work too well; it was too high-concept, overstaged and overdressed, and it lacked direction. After the immediacy of *Rio, Seven and the Ragged Tiger* would take some getting used to. In fact, I'm still just getting used to it now. It made number 1 on the UK album charts, but it was still somehow anticlimactic.

We made plans for what was to be our biggest world tour yet, and it made sense for the tour to begin in Australia.

Right before we left Sydney for opening night in Canberra, I met up with Janine Andrews, Andy's old flame from Birmingham, who had a part in the latest James Bond film, *Octopussy*, and had come to Sydney to help promote the movie. It was good to see her and spend time with her. We both felt a connection but didn't jump right into bed, which was odd, as at that moment in my life I was jumping into bed with anything that moved. Perhaps this could be something more? Janine and I made plans to get together again in Birmingham over Christmas.

I drove back from my last night out at a dive in North Sydney, crossing the Harbour Bridge as the morning rush-hour traffic gathered. I parked the BMW in the underground garage of the apartment building, leaving it for the rental agency to collect. As I slammed the door shut, the fender fell off.

The 'Seven and the Ragged Tiger' world tour kicked off in Canberra on 12 November. From there, we flew back to Sydney, opening up the city's new Entertainment Centre. The decibel level reached by the roar of the crowd as we took the stage was judged to be a record. Our loyal Aussie Duranies made *The Guinness Book of Records*.

David Bowie's 'Serious Moonlight' tour played Sydney that same night, and afterwards both bands partied together in David's hotel suite. On drums with Bowie was Tony Thompson, 'Theodore' from Chic. I told Tony that I would love to work with him one day. Tony nodded sagely. 'I would like that very much, my good man. That would be *smoking*.'

In Melbourne, our old friend and media ally Molly Meldrum threw us a party at his house in the suburb of Richmond; it was filled to the ceiling with Egyptian artefacts and rock and roll memorabilia. On the wall of the kitchen was a signed copy of *The White Album*: 'To Molly, love John and Yoko'. Molly claims to have been the first to break the story of the Beatles splitting up, and that John and Yoko had even told him before the rest of the band.

On the record player was a song that caught our collective ear.

I lifted the disc off the turntable. It was a pre-release copy of INXS's new single, called provocatively 'Original Sin'.

The credits on the label read 'Produced by Nile Rodgers. Engineered by Jason Corsaro'. Now *this* is how I would like to hear our sound moving forward. And we were all equally excited by it, playing it over and over again.

We all felt there was more to be gotten out of 'The Reflex' than the version we had submitted to the album, and that the song had potential to be a big hit.

What if we were to ask Nile to do a remix of 'The Reflex'?

Molly's memory of that night is that we got Nile on the phone in New York right there and then, although we don't remember it quite that way.

By December we were back in the UK.

Having been away for most of the year, we were a little uncertain how we'd be received. We needn't have worried. The December tour was phenomenal. Tickets were like gold dust. We played two gigs at Birmingham's brand new National Exhibition Centre (NEC) Arena – and five nights in Wembley Arena.

Janine Andrews and I did reconnect over the Christmas holidays. We both wanted a romantic experience, having both been through the mill in our own ways – different but similar. Each had a yearning to settle. Again, it wasn't perfect, but it was perfect for right then. After all the cosmopolitan adventure, I appreciated her Brummie accent and attitude. She exuded glamour with her long blonde hair and beloved fur coat, but underneath it all she was a down-to-earth Brummie homegirl.

46 Exploitation Time

1984 was exploitation time. We were the biggest band on the planet. The momentum was powerful, unstoppable, and in the Republic of Durania the focus, as the New Year arrived, was on how we, they, *everybody* could make the most out of our meteoric success.

Even though *Seven and the Ragged Tiger* had not checked all the boxes that *Rio* had checked, and we were not all completely satisfied with it musically, the band was getting bigger and bigger regardless. 'New Moon on Monday' was the current single, but to half the fans, that wasn't relevant, because reissues were now coming out, meaning that new fans who only got turned on to us at the time of *Rio* were going back and getting the debut album.

After a two-day video shoot in Paris for a long-form 12-inch video version of 'New Moon on Monday', the tour started up again in Japan. Freezing cold temperatures, chaotic and often snowbound. It was hard to get around.

The venues on this tour were considerably bigger than on the previous tour and included the Budokan indoor arena in Tokyo, usually home to martial arts championships – the Madison Square Garden of Japan. I knew it from the many live albums that had been recorded there, most famously *Bob Dylan at Budokan*.

That was a big deal.

The shows were nuts. In Fukuoka for a Sunday-afternoon matinee gig, the roadies used brooms to continually sweep the stage, vainly trying to keep it clear of cuddly toys, flowers, bouquets and other gifts that were being showered on us by the crowd.

I had another altercation with an inanimate object on that Japanese tour. Drugs were out in Japan. The penalties for getting caught with any illegal substances were just too severe, so it was all drinking, and that meant things could get violent. I took my room apart after that show in Fukuoka.

Why was I so crazy? As much as anything, it was due to lack of sleep. The daily workload of press interviews, photo sessions and generally being a superstar on four hours' sleep was taking its toll.

One place where the energy level was not lacking was onstage. For those two hours every night, we amped our performances up to the max (even when we were wading through six inches of cuddly toys). It was our way of pushing back against that teeny-bop thing that was threatening to envelop us. Whenever we walked out onto the stage now, we had something to prove: that we were not who they thought we were, that we were louder, angrier, more aggressive and darker than they could possibly allow themselves to imagine.

Seven and the Ragged Tiger is a beautifully textured record, but it didn't hit you viscerally in the way the earlier albums had, so live shows became an opportunity to compensate for that. We were

MB
Key to Fun

**Ages
7 and Up**

Get the most points
by collecting record,
video, and band
member cards.

**For 2 to 4
Players**

**MILTON
BRADLEY
Company**

SPRINGFIELD, MA 01101

4524

D+URA

into the ar

collect record, video, and band me

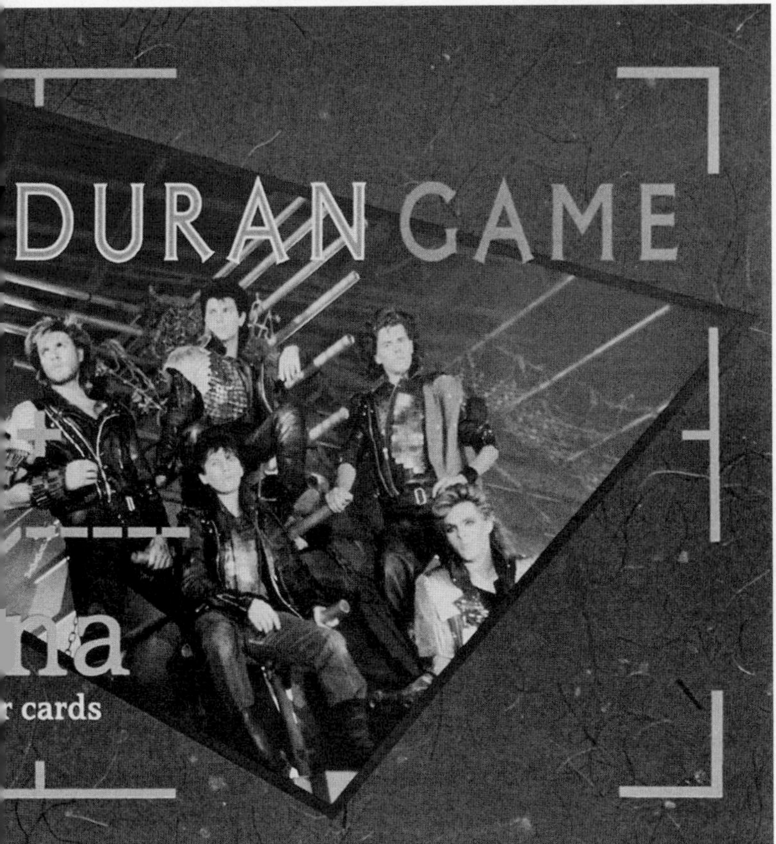
DURAN GAME

playing fantastically well, in spite of the drugs and the hangovers. The guitars got louder. The tempos got faster. I was wearing my bass lower on my hips, fucking the audience hard, harder than the virgins out there would have ever been able to handle.

Offstage, Janine and I were now officially a couple, and she would come out onto the tour whenever she could. The relationship wasn't the calming influence I had hoped it would be, however. It was often tempestuous, and more hotel furniture was smashed. The whole scene was just too fucked-up to try to establish some idea of happy, homespun marital perfection.

That didn't stop us trying. In a rare moment of peace, we got engaged.

That ring would be on her finger for less than three months, which did not feel good.

Next stop was America, where everything had changed since we played MTV's New Year's party at the end of '82. Both *Rio* and the reissued first album had gone platinum, and *Seven and the Ragged Tiger* was on its way up the charts.

We had become superstars.

We made the cover of *Rolling Stone*, with the heading 'The Fab Five', and the night the magazine came out on newsstands we played our first date at the Seattle Center Coliseum. It was our first headlining show in a US basketball arena – not a style of venue we were familiar with, close to British arenas like the NEC and Wembley but much, much bigger. Tiered sides that reached the roof, 110 feet in the air, and a floor in front of the stage reserved for general admission that, every night, was a heaving mass of teenage female bodies. Even before the lights went down, girls were being stretchered away and treated for panic attacks and dehydration.

It was like that date in Brighton in the summer of '81, when we got screamed at for the first time. But this time, it was 18,000 American teenagers, screaming, crying, losing themselves in a Duran-provoked frenzy. It was like somebody had given the entire audience drugs. We couldn't hear the monitors. We couldn't hear ourselves play.

It was awesome, but it was also kind of awful. Scary. We were very, very lucky on that tour not to have any fatalities. Many nights we would have to stop playing, Simon pleading with the kids to move back, to relieve the pressure on the fans at the front who were being pushed up against the wooden barriers that had often been only haphazardly set up. There had been several well-publicised crowd disasters – The Who in Cincinnati, David Cassidy at White City – and we were all well aware of the potential for calamity. We would get extremely angry with management and local security if we felt safety issues weren't being handled appropriately.

Although we had gotten used to the mayhem and the mania that surrounded us twenty-four hours a day, seven days a week, whenever we were on tour, that first date on the US tour in Seattle stunned us all over again.

This was the tour we had been dreaming of back at the Rum Runner office, back when we were telling those record label reps, 'We want to play Madison Square Garden by 1984.' And we did. But it had grown way, way beyond our control. Be careful what you pray for.

The madness was always a micron below the surface, kept at bay only by our shared sense of humour. We all knew to keep any anger, frustration or fears we may have had away from the cameras, the journalists and the microphones. Only Andy would make reference now and again to the sourness that he felt was beginning to creep into the experience, to the fact that we were not in control of our own destinies any more, that we were rats in a gilded cage, subject to the whims and directives of the managers, agents and corporate brand consultants.

We were being sponsored by Coca-Cola.

I crossed a line when I started getting high onstage. I had always remained sober for the duration of the show, as I wanted to give my best and did not want to compromise my talent so publicly. But now I couldn't wait for the performances to end. I wanted to take back control of my life, and getting high felt like that – at least by giving control to the drug, I was taking it away from all these other forces that I felt I was being controlled by. I was anxious to get to the end of the main set, head for the backstage bathrooms and snort up a hundred dollars' worth of coke through a rolled-up hundred-dollar bill. It felt so 'big-time', so 'rock star'. And I would tell myself it gave me the capacity to absorb all the incredible energy that the audience was hurling at me. I WAS A MASTER OF THE UNIVERSE. Or so it seemed.

Once we were done with our encores, I was really ready to let rip. Show me the way to that hotel party suite, and not just after the special shows – weekend shows, big cities – but *every* night, after *every* show. Dallas, Chicago, Atlanta.

When we got to New York, we flew all of our parents out. My mum had never been on a plane before, nor out of the country, and had to get a passport. We put them up in the band's hotel. They went around as if they were a band themselves on that trip. They went up the Empire State Building together. They rented two station wagons and drove to Disney World in Florida together. They went everywhere together.

It was the most profound experience my parents had in their later years. They never stopped talking about it. We were fortunate to be able to give our parents that kind of gift.

We had committed originally to a six-week run across the continent, but the offers just kept pouring in. It's amazing how quickly the novelty of a basketball dressing room will wear off – cold, antiseptic, institutional – but no one could say no. This was the moment of getting rich, and that was part of the plan too.

Was it fun? Sometimes. It was dark and light at the same time. The tragedy of it for me, looking back today, was that by the time we got to the Garden, I had left the room. When that moment hit, instead of really taking it on board and appreciating it for what it really was, I was too busy making sure my roadie was scoring for me.

So what is Madison Square Garden, the apex of fame, the place I had fantasised about in the suburbs of Birmingham, really like?

MSG has the biggest ego of any venue in the world. From the moment we arrived in New York, every driver, every concierge, every shop assistant was referring to it: 'You guys are at the Garden, right?' It was Garden this, Garden that. We had to really try to keep our feet on the ground in the run-up to the performance there.

Selling out two nights at the Garden was an undeniable achievement; the band had come so far in so short a time. The dollars-per-head merchandising sales set a record, unbeaten for over a decade.

On entering the building, we were conducted through a dizzying labyrinth of tunnels and corridors that form the backstage zone, where members of the New York unions slouched against the walls as we rushed past them, conveying a splendidly singular lack of enthusiasm. They couldn't have given a rat's ass.

There was also a curious sense of menace. I never felt more like a pawn in someone else's game than backstage at the Garden that first night, because the music business was there in person, wearing expensive suits and flashing cigars and letting us know that they had a lot of money invested in this and they really couldn't afford for us to fuck it up for them.

I had never been happier for the lights to go down, so I could get out and do my job. Stepping out onto that stage that first time, it was impossible not to be awed by the size. It was the height above all else. The seats were stacked tier upon tier to the height of a skyscraper, accommodating 20,000 fans.

Nile Rodgers joined us onstage for an encore of 'Good Times'. Afterwards, we had a long meet-and-greet line in one of the Garden's many corridors. Nile was keen to introduce us to a girl singer he was working with. She was tiny and didn't seem to give two fucks about me. That was the most vivid impression I had about meeting Madonna.

47 The Remix

I first heard Nile's remix of 'The Reflex' in Roanoke, Virginia, at a hotel dayroom between sound check and show, when Paul Berrow handed me the phone for a listen. He was ecstatic, could barely contain himself. 'We've got ourselves a monster bloody hit here, John. I can feel it in my bones.'

The moment I heard the opening bars, I had to agree. Nile had created something extraordinary, beyond our wildest imaginings.

But our label, Capitol, did not get it at all. They did not want to release it. Paul would have to go and work on them, guns blazing.

I argued that the video should be of our live show. I wanted to put aside all the conceptual filmmaking for a moment and show what a great live band we had become. But with style. With Russell Mulcahy directing.

Any interview we did usually started out, 'So you guys are a video band, right? That's what you do, make videos?'

After months spent writing and recording, months on the road fine-tuning our live set, people outside the organisation thought our priority was the video. The one aspect of what we did that we had not seized complete control of. It was a sign of how big the music video phenomenon was getting, now MTV was coast-to-coast.

And we were getting sick of it.

The one aspect of our video story that we could have capitalised on, but didn't, was the Grammy Awards nominations we received that year. It was the first year the Grammys recognised video, with awards for both short- and long-form videos. We were nominated in both categories. And the night of our Pittsburgh show, we won. Both.

We watched the ceremony on the television in the dressing room, fuming. We should have been there.

A few days later, Russell Mulcahy and his crew flew in to Toronto, where we shot the video for 'The Reflex' over two days on the stage at Maple Leaf Gardens.

Looking at the schedule for the year, I find it extraordinary that within ten days of the US tour staggering to a close at the San Diego Sports Arena, we were back at the good old BBC filming an appearance on *Top of the Pops*.

Mike Berrow was there, and he had been given the unenviable task of raising with me a subject he knew would not be met with a great deal of enthusiasm.

'Obviously, there is going to be no new album this year, we know that John. Everybody understands that. And that is absolutely fine. What they would like, though, is to put out a live album ... with *one* new song. That will get us through 'til Christmas ...'

Boy, and how! The *Arena* project would be the biggest

merchandising vehicle any band had ever undertaken, and our biggest-selling album of all time.

But first, we had to get that one new song cut.

The previous year in Sydney, I had spent a lot of my downtime at Russell's marina-side apartment, which he shared with his boyfriend Gerry, getting high and playing Trivial Pursuit.

Russell, Gerry, and I would meet in the evening at La Strada for an Italian dinner that would inevitably get cut short by a line or two. Then we would take the party back to the harbour flat.

Russell had optioned William Burroughs's book *The Wild Boys* for a potential full-length feature film. I had not read the book, a homosexual fantasy about the 'Wild Boys', who 'continued the human race by artificial insemination and gave birth to a whole generation ... that had never seen a woman's face nor heard a woman's voice'.

Quite anti-Oedipus, and not my style at all. But I liked the sound of a Burroughsian project, and Simon felt the same way. One particularly convivial evening, we both got excited and insisted to Russell that we should be allowed to compose the title song for his movie.

Talking to Russell in Toronto, it was clear he had invested a lot of time and energy in *The Wild Boys* project. Apart from the script, he had developed the visual ideas and special effects. He was dying to get started. But the film had failed to get off the ground.

That was no reason we couldn't write the song.

It made perfect sense to invite Nile Rodgers to London to help us work on this new project. We met up at Nomis rehearsal studios in west London and started hammering out some ideas. Either the room had gotten smaller or we had gotten bigger, but it was a tight squeeze getting all those egos into the space. Nile, thankfully, was the perfect producer for this moment. None of us had a problem with him being in charge, as we all had equal respect for him, and he was up to the task.

We wrote the basics of two songs in two days. The first was called 'Don't Look Back', the second, 'Wild Boys'. There was no doubt in Nile's mind which was the song with the most potential, so we moved over to Maison Rouge studios in Fulham to lay down the basic tracks.

'Wild Boys' was as potent and driving a track as we had come up with yet. Once again, Nile was working his Synclavier magic, editing the groove, retuning Simon's vocals to create something otherworldly, taking the song we had written to another level.

It felt like a big boys' song.

It's not easy producing a band like Duran, all strong musical personalities with something to say. Our best producers (Nile, Colin Thurston, Alex Sadkin and, decades later, Mark Ronson) all discovered eventually that each and every one of us needs to be heard if we are to make our songs – three-and-a-half minute pop singles, yes, but also symphonic – really work.

The recording of 'Wild Boys', made in July 1984, is a perfect example. It's possibly a little incongruous, plopped on the end of side one of the *Arena* live album, but it does advance the band's sound, the British pop dance style we had developed over the first three albums.

'Wild Boys' had to be more than just a hit. It had to be an event. We already had a concert film in the can, shot mostly in Oakland, and Paul's newest obsession was to turn it into a feature-length movie that could be shown in theatres. I'm not sure why, but it seems as though there comes a point in every great music-manager's career when he begins to dream of Hollywood. It had happened to Brian Epstein, Colonel Tom and Malcolm McLaren, and now it was happening to Paul Berrow. We had been shown test footage of the live material one morning at the Odeon Leicester Square. We kind-of-sort-of agreed to call the concert film either *As the Lights Go Down* or *Burning Bright*. We were certain we wanted to call the album *Arena*.

Next would be the ten-minute extended 'Wild Boys' video, which would benefit from all the ideas and fantastical characterisations Russell had developed. With the movie of *The Wild Boys* on ice, Russell wasn't about to waste the work he had done. He just had to find a way to drop in his five pop protégés. I took inspiration for my cameo from Los Angeles artist Chris Burden, who had himself crucified on the back of a Volkswagen in a piece of performance art entitled 'Trans-fixed'. Simon's love of water got him into a lot of trouble when the windmill to which he had been strapped (what's with all this sadomasochism?) got stuck while he was underwater. When the windmill was finally freed, and a gasping Simon was brought to the surface, the cameras were still rolling. It made for scintillating viewing.

The 'Wild Boys' video, which had the largest budget of any music video to date, felt at the time like a massive exercise in self-indulgence, as if the organisation – and management in particular for approving such a crazy expenditure – had gotten way out of control. But today, I do actually think it was justified. 'Wild Boys' was more than just a video, it was an amalgamation of musical, music video and cutting-edge remix, with a production design that rivalled any Hollywood movie. And besides, we had to fight back against one man who was chasing our tails and was hungry to take the video-king crown off us: Michael Jackson.

But it was way out of control and spoke volumes about where the Duran Duran organisation – and I personally – was going.

48 Megalomania at the Wheel

On 27 July 1984, Roger and his girlfriend of three years, Giovanna Cantone, got married.

Roger chartered a 727 jet and flew band, crew and parents down to southern Italy for the wedding.

We were that tight. A happily dysfunctional family.

After the ceremony at the Capodimonte basilica – a photo op if ever there was one – we embarked on a celebratory boat ride around the Bay of Naples. My dad got violently ill on the salmon mousse.

While Roger and Giovanna honeymooned on the Nile, the rest of the guys wisely took a holiday. But I had become so addicted to the ride that the last thing I wanted was time off. The party had become the work and the work had become the party. They were totally indistinguishable, and it was a formula that was working for me.

I had gotten used to travelling at a stratospheric pace, being at

the centre of this tremendous energy, and far from wanting to escape it, even for a moment, I never wanted it to end. I had no idea what to do with free time. Sitting in the living room of my newly purchased Knightsbridge house and 'watching the telly' or 'having friends over for dinner' was too banal a reality for me to contemplate. Plus, there was a twenty-four-hour fan encampment outside the house, so whatever time I got home at night or, worse, in the early hours of the morning, I would be greeted by excitable fans squealing and snapping their cameras.

Whatever time I woke up, the first thing I would hear would be the chatter of the fans outside. I would crawl stealthily to the window and peek through the curtains, trying to get a sense of how many there were and what I was in for, without them seeing that I was up.

If they didn't know I was awake yet, I might at least be able to run a bath and get dressed without having to hear 'Save a Prayer for me now, John' drifting up from the street. Was this their idea of a Romeo and Juliet moment?

Fans were coming from all over the world, so the noise from the cobblestone street was a multilingual one. Numbers ranged from six to thirty at any given time. Some of the kids I was on first-name terms with. For some, it might be their first time at the house.

When that was the case, there was a strange ritualistic moment that would play out when the other fans, the familiars, would offer the new girl forward to me as if she was a sacrificial virgin.

'It's her first time, John. Be gentle with her! Can she have a photograph? Sign her album for her, she's too shy to ask.'

At which point the virgin might say, 'Is true! I am shy. But I love you, John!'

For the most part, they were great kids, and I am still in touch with some of them now. But I didn't like it when one of them had gone through my trash and come out with some journalling, some writing that I had been doing in an attempt to process my feelings. This girl then became obsessively worried about my state of mind. I was more concerned about hers.

It was a truce though, generally. The fans would try to contain their excitement before midday, especially if I had been witnessed coming home around dawn. As the day went on, the excitement and the noise would grow, and I knew that sooner or later I would have to make an appearance, whether I had plans to leave the house or not.

Similar scenes were taking place across London: in Little Venice, chez Taylor; in Chelsea, chez Rhodes; and in Putney, chez Le Bon. My situation was not unique.

I went with Janine to a party Michael Caine was having at Langan's in honour of that year's Wimbledon tennis final, and I recognised Cubby Broccoli, the producer of the James Bond films, sitting at a table.

Janine introduced me and we got to chatting.

I said, 'When are you going to have a decent theme song again?'

He said, 'Well, do you want to write the next one?'

I said, 'Absolutely.'

When I got home, I called the guys, told them, 'I think we have a crack at the next Bond film.'

I went to Cubby's office on South Audley Street in Mayfair the following afternoon. From behind a huge desk, Cubby called John Barry, the composer who wrote the James Bond scores, at his home in Oyster Bay, Long Island.

John Barry was an idol of mine and I was excited to talk to

him. He had a deep, drawling Yorkshire accent. 'Hello, Cubby.'

Cubby said, 'John, I want you to meet John Taylor from Duran Duran; he's here in the room with me.'

'Hello, John.'

'Hi.'

'John, I want you to work with Duran on this new film.'

'Uh-huh. All right . . . '

John didn't sound particularly overjoyed, but Cubby was firm about it. 'I want you to make this work, John.'

John and I made a tentative date to meet the following week in Manhattan.

But it still wasn't enough. I wanted more. Megalomania was at the wheel.

I had wanted to do a side project since Bebe Buell was going to sing 'Get It On'. Nick had had tremendous success with Kajagoogoo, and Andy and I now started talking seriously about forming a breakaway faction, another band. Something 'funkier and more organic' than Duran. Louder guitars.

In Paris for a press and promo trip, we booked some studio time on the Sunday to get things going. But Saturday turned into a hard-core all-nighter.

I felt like I was his best man all over again when Andy woke me at 6.00 p.m.

'What you doing, man? You got to get up. We've got this fucking studio time booked!'

'Oh God, do we have to?'

'You started this thing, now come on, man, get your fucking arse down to the studio. I'm waiting.'

Why did I say I'd do this? What was I thinking?

But, as usual, once we started making music, things fell into place, making sense. We came out of the studio at 4.00 in the morning with a cassette and two ideas, one of them the main groove of what would become the first Power Station single, 'Some Like It Hot'.

49 Shelter and Control on West Fifty-Third Street

In July, a pink envelope arrived in the post at my parents' home, with a return address delicately embossed in silver deco type: 'Mr and Mrs William Friedman Jr., Woodland Avenue, Des Moines, Iowa.'

Inside, on a pink-and-silver card, Mr and Mrs Friedman requested the presence of my parents at the wedding reception of their daughter Julie Anne and Mr Nick Rhodes.

Holy shit! Now Nick was getting married? I thought *we* were married!

Since having met Nick out on the water the day after our Greek Theatre gig in Los Angeles, Julie Anne had rarely left his side.

Their wedding, at the Savoy, was one of the defining pop culture moments of the 1980s, perhaps the most divinely decadent event of a divinely decadent decade.

The press had a field day.

Groom wears more make-up than bride!

Live pink flamingos!

Exclusive photos by Norman Parkinson!

It was a fantastic night.

Marriages and honeymoons do presume a certain hiatus, but not for me. I followed the master-tape trail to New York and the Power Station studio, where Jason Corsaro, Nile's engineer on 'The Reflex', was sorting through the live recordings made on the US tour that would become *Arena*. My justification for being there was that at least one band member should be at the desk, making sure that the mix was right.

And the bass was loud enough.

The Power Station, after which Andy and I would name our new band, was a disused Con Edison plant in Hell's Kitchen on West Fifty-third Street that had been turned into a recording studio. I was soon spending all my waking hours there, completely bewitched by the scene. Chic had made all of their records there. Bruce Springsteen recorded *Born in the USA* there. The Power Station was where it was at, the absolute acme of the recording industry in 1984.

Dylan was down the hall, but I never saw him. Mick Jagger was much more approachable, working on his first solo album away from the Rolling Stones. He would come up and check us out, and he was happy for me to go into his studio to listen to what he was doing.

Bryan Ferry was mixing his *Boys and Girls* album there, but I hadn't seen him because we were working different shifts. I bumped into him as I came out of the lift at the Carlyle Hotel one evening around seven. I was heading out as he was coming in.

I loved the giant speakers recording studios had back then, which could be cranked up so loud that any listener would be pinned to the wall. I have always enjoyed making music at fuck-off levels of volume and have not appreciated the move into the era of the workstation, where recording studios use Yamaha NS10s not much bigger than an iPhone. I get cranky about it today in our studio: 'Can't we get it any louder? I can listen to it this loud at home!'

The Power Station had the best sound system of all. Urei speakers, monsters the size of a double bed.

Plus, I'd never seen more drugs in my life. The access to cocaine was unlimited.

It wasn't like the recording of *Rio* or *Ragged Tiger* or the first album, where I had been out of the picture for weeks while Nick and Andy pondered their next overdubs. This time, it was me at the desk, and I relished that. There was nowhere I would rather be than in the safety and security of the studio, poised between shelter and control, totally coked out of my brain.

I didn't actually listen to the finished album all the way through until twenty-five years later, in 2011. Whenever we finish an album, I do not want to listen to it. I can't. I need time to get perspective on it – although, even by my standards, twenty-five years is excessive.

What struck me about it when I did finally listen to it is how low in the mix the audience is, considering how loud they were. There is a sense of detachment between the band and the audience. It's almost like we are in different dimensions. The band sounds really tight, terrific in fact, and you can tell that there is an audience, a big audience, but they are way, way over *there*. On some live albums, you can hear an audience member going, 'Nick!' or 'Play "The Chauffeur"!' but there's nothing like that on *Arena*. It's distant. There's a sense of us wanting to play down the teeny, screamy thing. We're trying to be grown-ups.

Was the bass loud enough? Definitely.

50 Nouveau Nous

The only way any of us can clearly remember the date and day we began work on 'A View to a Kill' with John Barry is because it was Beaujolais Nouveau Day, which always falls on the third Thursday in November.

The plan was to work on the top floor of my Ennismore Mews house, where I had installed a white grand piano à la Lennon. We met at the pub at the end of the street at lunchtime and drank the fresh French grapes.

By 5 o'clock, we were all quite satisfied that we had the beginnings of a song. At least the first verse. The rest of the track would be built at Maison Rouge, now under siege, as every fan in the country knew we were working there.

It wasn't an easy song to write.

Nick and John Barry didn't click. They found it hard just being in the same room. They were both stubborn and had very specific visions of how things should get done. I was caught in the

crossfire: friend to Nick, adjutant to John. Many times I received late-night phone calls from John, admonishing me to 'sort out this bloody bullshit'. It was a negotiation, and I did what was required in order to get my dream realised. I did not want the Bond collaboration to fall apart.

But how could I keep both Nick and John on the field?

The answer came in the form of Bernard Edwards.

Bernard (Pronounced B'nard, or just 'Nard' to his friends) was Nile's partner in Chic, and it was his playing on the bass guitar that had inspired me to play bass in the first place. Tony Thompson, who was now on board with Andy and me in the Power Station, insisted that he was the man who should produce the project. Meeting him at Le Parker Méridien in New York City was a trip; the man was such an influence, an icon, but he was never grandiose.

We knew enough about Bernard to know that he could bring the Duran/Bond project together (Nile had a previous commitment that kept him from doing the job, a missed opportunity he regrets to this day). Bernard was a firm hand at the tiller, which we needed because the weather was rough.

We got the band's parts recorded eventually. The tapes went back to New York for mixing, along with John Barry's orchestral arrangements, recorded in London, which were then layered on top to create the rich, sumptuous textures that were obligatory for a James Bond title song.

I could not have been happier with the end result. I thought it was our best record so far, on every level.

51 Guilt Edge

In November, Simon got a call from Bob Geldof: 'Have you seen this shite about Ethiopia? We've got to do something.'

When Simon relayed Bob's idea back to us, I wasn't sure at first, but then I hadn't had Bob's voice ranting in my ear like Simon had. Simon had no doubt that the Band Aid project was something we had to be involved in.

It was Saturday night in Dortmund, and we were doing some schlocky TV show, lip-synching to 'Wild Boys'. Spandau Ballet were there, so was Billy Idol and the Thompson Twins, and we were all on the same plane back to London the next day, having all been up all night, again, of course.

At the airport, the Spands were like, 'Oh yeah, we've got to do that thing of Geldof's too.'

We came off the plane and got driven straight to the studio.

It was a mob scene; kids, film cameras, journalists everywhere.

Suddenly it was like, 'Oh, wow, this is big,' and of course, it was. The biggest deal in a year of very big deals.

Who was there? Everyone. Sting. U2. Phil Collins. Boy George. George Michael. Paul Young. Status Quo and Kool and the Gang. A real hotchpotch of talent.

Sting and I both played bass.

Trevor Horn, the mastermind behind Frankie Goes to Hollywood, was in charge. It was his studio. But it was Bob running around with the lyrics to the song he had written with Midge Ure, called 'Do They Know It's Christmas?' saying, 'Okay, Charlie,' – to Simon – 'we are going to need you for this line, and George! George, we are going to need you for this one.'

After Bono had nailed his line, Trevor flicked the studio intercom on and said, 'That one's for the stadiums.'

We all knew the song would go to number 1.

What we didn't know was how profoundly that song would affect the rest of the decade.

People talk about the eighties as being a decadent, glamorous, fashion-conscious time, and in 1984, it certainly seemed that way. There was no reason to think the party couldn't go on for ever.

But the eighties was a decade of two halves. Things that you could get away with in 1984, you could not get away with twelve months later. There was about to be an immense sea change in the culture, and the shift was started by Bob Geldof that cold December day.

Christmas for Duran fans worldwide came by way of a tremendous assault on their pocket money, thanks to the myriad deals Paul and Michael had made with merchandising companies. In addition to the autumn releases of musical product – the *Arena* album, the 'Wild Boys' single in five different picture sleeves (one for each band member) and a video EP – there was also a full-length documentary video of the US tour and three books: *Duran Duran: The Book of Words*, *Arena: The Book* and the *Sing Blue Silver* tour book with photos by Denis O'Regan.

There was also a plethora of T-shirts – again, one for each band member – sweatshirts, scarves, headbands, group posters, individual band member posters, seven different packs of colour photos, postcards, an attaché case, a board game, make-up bags, shower bags, batteries, notebooks, writing paper, ring binders, pencil cases, schoolbags, shopping bags – and even Christmas cards.

I always looked forward to seeing the folks at Christmas. I never got over how Christmas felt at Simon Road. It was a chance to connect with the family privately. But I was under a lot of stress, and the idea of driving up to Birmingham, alone, was not all that appealing. For once, I wasn't sure if I wanted to step out of the fame bubble, if I really wanted the reality check that an old-style family Christmas would inevitably give me.

But by the time Christmas Day itself actually rolled around, I was looking forward to taking some time out from my Duran persona.

Mum and Dad were so excited to see me, of course, but what had really blown their minds, and what they wanted to show me the moment I stepped out of the car, was four giant sacks of mail that the Post Office had delivered on Christmas Eve.

Fan mail. Love letters. Pleading. Begging. Some weird. Some sexy. Who knew? Where could I begin?

It was exhausting. I was struck by the idea that 10,000 people wanted to have a relationship with me and I could barely have a relationship with myself.

And who were these two guardians of the mail sacks? They

looked very like Mum and Dad. But they sounded like two fans who had somehow found their way into the house and inhabited my parents' shells. Invasion of the Parent Snatchers! Help!

The mayhem, the drugs, the guilt.

I just couldn't take it.

I short-circuited.

I emptied all the sacks in a rageful frenzy, dumping the contents violently on the floor, scattering the letters and cards all over the garage, frothing at the mouth, tearing up the envelopes unopened.

My parents watched the rampage, their mouths agape.

'Don't you get it, you two? I don't fucking care about any of this!'

Confused.

Crazy.

Got to move.

Got to get out.

After a rather fretful turkey dinner, I drove off back to London and booked a plane ticket to New York for the next day.

Hotel. Room service. Cocktail. A line or two.

That's better. That's normal.

Charlie was in New York too. On New Year's Eve, at that year's MTV ball, we jump onstage with a new band from Liverpool, Frankie Goes to Hollywood, and sing along with one of the year's biggest anthems, 'Relax'.

Relax? What a concept.

52 The Wheel World

In the autumn of '84 I found myself on a plane with Robert Palmer. We never knew when we were next going to run into each other, or on what continent it might be, but whenever we did, we always connected.

I told him about the Power Station project Andy and I were working on with Tony and Bernard from Chic.

'We're looking for different singers to front the songs,' I said.

At that moment, the plan was for us to provide a 'house band' like Motown's Funk Brothers or the Stax house band, the MGs, to support a revolving cast of singers; men and women, young and old.

Robert was enthusiastic and wanted to hear what we had been working on. I gave him a cassette tape of one of the songs we had just recorded at Maison Rouge. He popped it into his Walkman there and then, and after four or five listens, as the announcement to buckle up for landing played through the intercom, he handed

me a tatty piece of paper, on which he had scribbled a rough lyric about our relationship:

Airmail, cassettes, postcards, telex
Drop me a line, be my grapevine
I'm always trying to reach you
Can't get through
Our communication
Depends on me and you
Got to stay in touch
Even though we're on the move
Keep your lines open
Say, what's new?

I loved it.

We got Robert over to the Power Station for our next scheduled recording session. Tony vaguely knew who Robert was, but was sceptical. Bernard had even less of an idea. Robert wasn't from their musical universe.

What Robert was, of course, was one of the greatest blue-eyed soul singers of all time. When he stepped up to the mic, his manner altered perceptibly. He took on a different persona, changing from a slightly fey, ironically minded English gent who clearly thought about and spent too much on bespoke clothing and personal grooming products into an all-business vocalist.

Robert nailed the vocal part in minutes. Bernard and Tony were impressed.

'What about that T. Rex cover? Are you still doing that?' asked Robert.

Bernard motioned to engineer Jason to unreel the multitrack tape that had the recording of 'Get It On'.

Robert tore into it. A man possessed by a spirit of Yorkshire juju, he took Marc Bolan's song out of the London suburbs, whisked it across the Atlantic and deposited it somewhere in the Louisiana swamplands. As Robert was gathering up his cigarettes and whisky to leave, Bernard turned to Andy, Tony and me and said, 'Stop looking. You've got your singer.'

A few days later, I flew down to Nassau in the Bahamas, where Robert lived, taking with me the tape that Andy and I had worked on in Paris. Robert met me at the airport.

Twenty years later, at a hotel restaurant in Tokyo, Robert told Annette, his long-time girlfriend, his favourite anecdote about me. On our drive from Nassau airport to his house, I had screamed at the driver to pull over, jumped out of the car and fallen to my knees, praying. In front of me was a tyre outlet called 'The Wheel World'.

'Here it is,' I shouted. 'All anyone seems to say to me is, "You don't live in the real world," and I don't know what that is! So this is it!'

He was still chuckling about that.

Robert had been living on the beach at Chris Blackwell's Compass Point studio compound. After lunch, I played him the track I had on cassette, and when I told him the working title was 'Some Like It Hot', Robert gave me his inscrutable look and fired back without missing a beat, 'And some sweat when the heat is on.'

I liked that too.

The Power Station project was intended, as much as anything, as a way for Andy and me to pay homage to Tony Thompson and, hopefully, put him in the spotlight we felt he deserved.

Tony was one of the greatest instrumentalists of the eighties, and his parts on 'I'm Coming Out', 'Good Times', and 'Let's

Dance' were among our favourite musical moments of all time. Andy and I arranged 'Some Like It Hot' to allow for Tony to deliver his ultimate performance.

Playing with Tony was an entirely different proposition from playing with Roger. They were both funky, groove-oriented rock drummers, but their energies were very different. Roger was consistency personified, who never wavered, and I always knew what to expect from him. Tony was the opposite. He had the heaviest foot in the business, and the power and volume that came off him when he was playing was immense. It was a widely held truth that only Bernard could keep him steady. When Bernard was producing or playing bass with Tony, there was no better drummer. But on the road as a rhythm section with me, neither of us were able to achieve quite the same chemistry as we had with our older playing partners.

The other sonic component that would be significant in this new entity would be the sound of the studio itself. The Power Station was famous for its massive reverb, created by harnessing the sounds that would be generated by playing music down the building's disused lift shaft. No one knew how to capture that effect better than Jason Corsaro.

So, we had another team of amazingly talented individuals around us. Before Andy and I even played a note on 'Some Like It Hot', the combination of Tony's drumming and Jason's reverb wizardry would announce to the world the arrival of something pretty fucking cool.

The record label couldn't believe it when we invited them to the studio to hear what we had been spending their money on. They couldn't believe their luck. They had been thinking, 'We're not going to get anything from Duran this year' and instead, they get a funk rock supergroup who had written a hit album.

In a significant act of sedition, Andy and I chose not to involve the Berrows in the Power Station. We were just too dissatisfied with the direction they had been taking with Duran. Paul's desire to become a Hollywood player cost an outrageous fortune, as far as I was concerned, and now their sponsorship of and involvement with Simon in the Whitbread Round the World yacht race seemed to be their focus. Duran Duran as an entity was still linked to the Berrows, but Andy and I had been feeling for a while that Mike and Paul no longer had our best interests at heart. The relationship was too far gone, too many conflicts of interest. It was irreparable. We voted with our feet. What to do when Duran went back to work? We would deal with that when the time came.

Some crazy idea
for Penthouse magazine

Tony -
the most dipper chic

Closer than before -
on the Notorious Tour

The extraordinary Warren

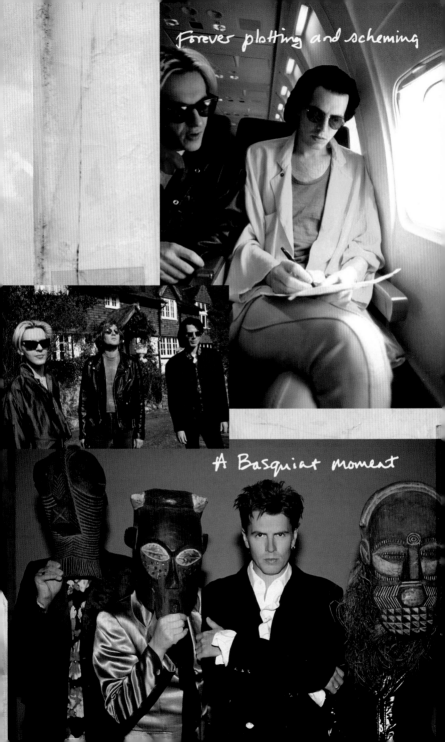

Forever plotting and scheming

A Basquiat moment

Eighth note therapy -
with Sonesy, Slash + Duff

My funky
little playmate -
Atlanta Bean

With Gela + Yazzy LB

Travis Nash –
King of the
Wild Frontier

Instant Sisters –
with Zoe & Atlanta

Queen of my universe – Gela

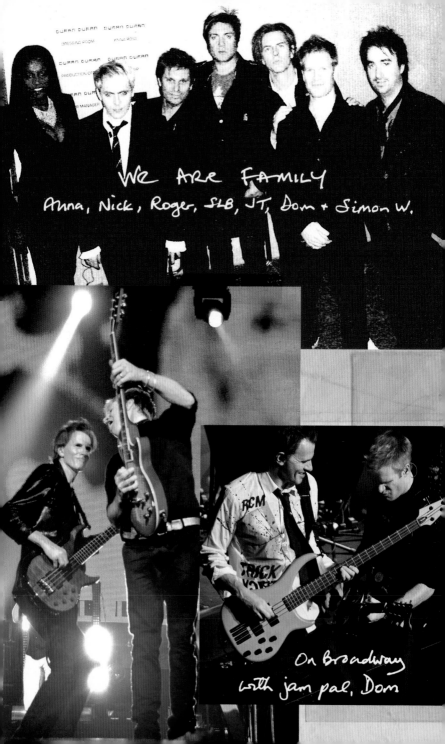

WE ARE FAMILY
Anna, Nick, Roger, SLB, JT, Dom + Simon W.

On Broadway
with jam pal, Dom

This is the real JT

Just play the fucking bass, John!

53 The Model

On Valentine's night, 14 February, I was at the Limelight nightclub in New York at a birthday party Billy Idol was throwing for his girlfriend Perri. The Limelight was a desanctified church on Sixth Avenue and had become one of my favourite hangouts. They had a very efficient velvet rope system in place that allowed me to behave in much the same way as I had back at the Rum Runner. In other words, I had the run of the place. I could take what I wanted, where I wanted, and with whomever I wanted.

Andy and I had been rehearsing with Steve Stevens, Billy's guitarist, and Mick Ronson. We had one extraordinary jam session, but Mick could only complain that Andy and Steve were both playing too loud. Mick stepped away from any future collaboration but Steve, Andy and I agreed to back up Billy for a few songs that night at the Limelight. We played 'Dancing with Myself', 'White Wedding' and 'Mony Mony'.

I was seeing a Swedish model named Chris, whom I h
on New Year's Eve. I took Chris and her friend BJ with m
Limelight.

After the performance, I was sitting on the floor of th
lounge with Chris and some other friends when another girl
over to me. She had a schoolgirl look about her, something
was really young and sweet – too sweet for the Limelight – an
was wearing a tweed blazer and jeans. She asked me if I woul
with her to meet her roommate who was 'in love' with
Would I please come and say hello?

I had been getting quite a lot of that kind of attention, an
had become a bit of a drag. Besides, I was comfortable sitting
the carpet with Chris.

Rather rudely, I said, 'Oh please, not now. Can't you see I'
with someone?' Something unpleasant like that.

The girl was like, 'Asshole!' She turned her nose up at me, spun
on her heel and stomped off.

I didn't think any more about it until a few hours later, back in
my suite at the Carlyle hotel, where Andy and I were staying,
when BJ turned to Chris and said, 'Wow, John must really be into
you! Did you see what he said to Renée Simonsen?'

I said, 'What are you talking about?'

She said, 'You know, that girl that came over to you. The one
that wanted you to meet her friend? That was Renée Simonsen.'

'Was it?'

I made an excuse and went into the bedroom. I had to check
something out. I had a feeling that Renée Simonsen was on the
cover of *Vogue* that very month, and there she was, on my bedside
table.

Wow! She looked incredible. The most beautiful girl in the
world? Possibly.

I was perplexed. How could I have missed her? Renée Simonsen, from Denmark, was the face of Ford Models. She had won an international contest to become Ford's 'Face of the 80s'.

Stunned, I sat on the bed with the magazine weighing heavily in my hands, two thoughts going through my head simultaneously:

1. 'Was that the same girl?'
2. 'Did I really just blow that opportunity?'

I went to bed discomfited that night. I liked Chris, she was great, a good girl, she was lovely but ... well, she wasn't Renée Simonsen.

The next day, Robert Palmer and I were doing a photo session with Eric Boman, and I asked Robert's hairdresser, Harry, a well-connected member of the New York fashion elite, if he knew Renée, and could he get me her number?

He said, 'Let me see what I can do.'

I had to leave New York for a few days, but the moment I got back, I called Harry from a public telephone at JFK and asked eagerly, 'Any luck?'

He said, 'You didn't get it from me, but here it is.'

I scribbled the number down on my cigarette packet and called her right away. When I announced myself, I could hear the sneer.

She said, 'Oh you! The asshole!'

I did some pretty fast dance moves. 'I am so, so sorry, I don't know what was the matter with me. Someone must have put something in one of my drinks. I was just ... you need to let me apologise. In person.'

Reluctantly, she agreed to meet that Saturday night. I wrote down her address and said I would pick her up around 8.00.

This time, I was not going to be so stupid. I left nothing to chance. I rented a limousine and picked her up from her apartment on Fifth Avenue. Took her roses and out to dinner. And on to the Limelight.

Without a hint of irony.

Turns out Renée is not just beautiful, she's a smart girl, funny, sweet. We had a great night. It seemed no effort for either of us. We talked about New York living, the amount of travel we both did, photographers we had worked with, books.

Maybe I got a little high, but I wasn't out of control. And by the time I dropped her off back on Fifth Avenue, the morning light was up. In the background, Gershwin could be heard. Maybe *this* could be the real thing? It was one of those first dates – we've all had them – where you get home to your single bed and think to yourself, 'Maybe this could be the one.'

Despite the rather cynical way in which I had gone about setting up the date, we were actually a good fit.

It would certainly be worth investing some honesty in Renée.

54 Burnout

The bills at the Carlyle were killing my accountant, so I bought an apartment in the Park Belvedere, a new building on the Upper West Side.

I saw the architect's drawings in the Sunday edition of *The New York Times*. The location was perfect for the studio – ten minutes by cab – and it was less than a five-minute walk to Central Park.

There were three apartments on each floor. I chose a two-bedroom north-facing space with panoramic views across the park. When my parents came out to visit me in early spring, I took them to the construction site. It was the highest they ever got with me.

We all put on hard hats, rode the site lift to the twenty-seventh floor and walked out onto the skeleton floorboards; no windows yet in place, the wind whistling around us, shades of *Scarface* or *The Last Tycoon*.

My parents were jet-lagged, bemused and filled with wonder.

Was this the same boy who three months ago had been tearing up sacks full of Christmas fan mail, now leading them out onto the concrete beams above the abyss?

At dinner that night, I introduced them to Renée, who could not have been more charming. She gave them some comfort that their son now had a little normality in his daily diet of madness. They must have spent a lot of time around about now reassuring each other that I was okay, or that I was going to be okay, that whatever trip I was on, I would be safe.

In March, Capitol in the US and EMI in London released 'Some Like It Hot' as the Power Station's first single. *Smash Hits* gave it a cover story, announcing it as 'The New Duran Duran'. In the article, Andy is quoted as saying, 'It's healthy that we're doing these solo things at the moment, it's getting back to basics and hopefully will result in us making better Duran records ... I'm going to get old one day and I won't be able to do this any more so now I've got the chance I might as well milk it and burn myself out.'

We celebrated the release of the Power Station album with an appearance on *Saturday Night Live*. Pamela Sue Martin, Fallon on TV's *Dynasty*, hosted along with Spinal Tap's Nigel Tufnel (aka Christopher Guest). Andy and I loved that. The appearance on *SNL* was the only time Robert would sing with us live, choosing to finish his next solo album, now with Bernard producing, instead of continuing his walk-on part with the John and Andy show. That album was to be the natural follow-up to the Power Station, and the single 'Addicted to Love' put Robert in the superstar bracket.

Nick, Simon and Roger had moved to Paris, where they set up their own alternative project, to be named Arcadia, with Alex Sadkin producing.

I could hardly complain. It would be some time before I got to hear what they were cooking up, so for now I could only imagine. I knew they had a string of guest artists making appearances on the record; it sounded big. Whereas Andy and I were managing ourselves, Nick and Simon stayed with Paul and Michael, who would be thinking that Arcadia was their ticket to the future. That's where their energy would be going, but I could hardly complain about that either.

The rift was everything by now, to such an extent that flying to Paris to film the 'View to a Kill' video felt like making a sortie into enemy territory.

This was my first trip away from Renée, and I was determined not to cheat on her, so I made plans to have dinner with Barbara Broccoli, Cubby's daughter, with whom I had developed a friendship. I hoped a quiet dinner with the producer's daughter would make sure I got into bed on time, because it was an early call the following day at the Eiffel Tower.

I got back to the hotel and made my first mistake. I thought I would look up Andy. Where's my man Andy? He's gone to EMI studios to see the Rolling Stones! That's my boy! Right, let's go!

Knocking on the glass door of EMI's Pathé Marconi Studios, I see Keith Richards at the reception desk.

I call through the glass, 'Is Andy in there?'

He gestures to the security guard to let me in.

I knew Mick from the Power Station, and I had met Ronnie Wood a couple of times, but I had not met Keith before.

Andy had already left, but I stayed and hung out. Woody was the friendliest to me, not caught up in the weirdness between Keith and Mick. Charlie Watts was there too, but Bill Wyman wasn't present, so I got to pick up his bass and jam a little Jamaican boogie with them.

Anita Pallenberg was there. Whoa! She was obsessed, pointing her finger at me accusingly: 'You stole my name! You stole my name!'

I am thinking, 'What is she talking about?'

She had a supporting role in the film *Barbarella* but we hadn't taken *her* character's name.

In an effort to placate her, I offered to teach her how to play bass. She softened at that and said she wanted lessons.

I said, 'Great. I promise. I'll get you a bass and I'll teach you how to play it. Just don't be mean to me!'

I have no idea what time I left, but shortly after daybreak Charlie Watts asked if I would like to have breakfast.

'I've got to go and do a video, Charlie.'

Should I have had that early night? Of course.

But, I ask you, what would you have done?

The filming was tough. It was the worst fucking day. Not surprising, given my complete lack of sleep. But in addition to that, all the band members were on different planets, in different universes. All the video filming was individual shots – Simon does this here, Nick does this there. The directors, Godley & Creme, who had directed *Girls on Film* so many years ago, had been smart enough to realise they were not about to get a band ensemble performance on this one. Not this time.

We were too big to get in one frame.

The on-set photographer, Cindy Palmano, managed to get us together for one group shot in the late afternoon.

How many times had we lined up together for a band shot over the last five years? We were all naturals. We always had been. We instinctively knew how to ebb and flow with each other, give each other room, set each other off, accentuate the positive. We'd done it in Birmingham, in London, in New York, in Sri Lanka and Montserrat. Everywhere the sun shines.

But today felt different. There was a distinct lack of ease. It was as if we couldn't be friends any more, as if the pressures of what we had achieved had set us against each other. As if the competition between us, which had fired us and inspired us, was about to bring us down.

'I just need one band shot, guys, one shot. It'll take five minutes.'

The five minutes that we were standing together felt like an hour. It was painful. The moment it was over, we scattered to the four winds.

55 Is This the End, My Friend?

Despite the tensions in Paris, we were all present and correct on 12 June when *A View to a Kill* opened with a charity premiere at the Odeon Leicester Square. The Prince and Princess of Wales were present, and we lined up in our tuxedos to greet them again. None of us were going to miss that.

I look a mess. The booze is starting to show. I'm overweight and unkempt.

But as we took our seats and the lights went down, the iconic James Bond title sequence, designed by Maurice Binder and set to our music, flooded the theatre. It made all the difficulties in the recording studio and in Paris worthwhile.

It was also a top night for Jack and Jean, who came away with Roger Moore's autograph.

Andy and I decided to tour the United States that summer with the Power Station but, after taking part in the on-air announcement of the tour on New York's Z100 radio station, Robert did an about-face and bailed.

Tickets were already on sale, and there was no way my summer plans were going to be spoiled by Robert pulling out. We put out an all-points bulletin for a replacement singer, and Michael Des Barres walked into my life.

Michael was friends with *Miami Vice* star Don Johnson and was spending time with him on set in Shreveport, Louisiana. It was our US agent Wayne Forte's idea to call him. MDB was on the next plane to New York, in time for a launch party at Area, which had superseded Limelight as *the* New York *club de nuit*. Renée made her own plans for the summer, believing she needed a break from the New York modelling world. In what I thought to be a rather strange decision, she decided to fly to Israel and sign up for a kibbutz all summer. She hennaed her hair and let her freak flag fly. It was going to be a long, hot, solo summer.

The magnificent success of Bob Geldof's Band Aid charity had inspired a team of like-minded American artists, led by Michael Jackson and Lionel Richie, to record their own fundraising anthem, 'We Are the World'. That in turn inspired Bob and promoters Harvey Goldsmith in London and Bill Graham in San Francisco to mount the greatest concert event of the twentieth century: Live Aid.

Bob announced plans for two concerts to take place simultaneously on Saturday 13 July, one at Wembley Stadium in London, the other at JFK Stadium in Philadelphia.

Duran Duran would be one of the main attractions.

Whatever infighting was going on, there was never any question that all five of us wanted to appear at Live Aid together. As a generous concession to the Power Station, Bob offered Andy and me a spot in the Philadelphia show in addition to Duran

Duran. The American bill featured Madonna, Bob Dylan, a reunited Led Zeppelin, Tina Turner and Mick and Keith.

Andy and I met up with Simon, Nick and Roger at our hotel in Philadelphia two days before the event. We had some rehearsing to do, never having played 'A View to a Kill' live onstage before. There was a nervousness in both camps; our relationships had not gotten any better since Paris. If anything, things had gotten worse. And yet, in that ugly, stinking downtown rehearsal room, away from the media and the bright lights, the girls and all the wedges that had come between us, the tensions melted away.

Playing with Duran was fun. I had forgotten how much.

More fun than the Power Station.

Had I come to that realisation too late?

On the day, there were faces everywhere. In our dressing room, Rupert Everett babysat Jade Jagger. As Led Zeppelin took the stage, with my friend Tony Thompson on drums, I made my way stage-side, passing Jack Nicholson on the way. I had never seen Zeppelin before and would never forget them. Their opening song, 'Rock and Roll', was the highlight of the event for me. Mick and Tina created showbiz magic, perhaps the glitziest ten minutes of the day, then it was Crosby, Stills, Nash and Young, introduced by Jack, then Dylan, who played a seriously ramshackle set with Keith Richards and Ronnie Wood.

Following that: Duran Duran.

Before we took to the stage, we posed for one more photograph with Ken Regan, then we were rushed out onto the boards at prime time, opening our set with the number 1 song in America that week, 'A View to a Kill'.

Onstage, we played as hard as we knew how, but when the curtain fell on our performance – twenty minutes and how many million TV viewers later – none of us had any idea that the curtain was falling on the first act of our career, and our lives together.

It would be eighteen years until the five of us would take the stage together again.

As the lights went down on the biggest event in the history of live music, and the trucks rolled away from Philadelphia, Andy, Tony, Michael Des Barres and I rejoined the Power Station tour, which continued to rumble on, rather painfully, for the rest of the summer.

Live Aid had been a moment of transcendence, and for all the pains and process that being in Duran Duran required, the Power Station US tour was now revealed to me for exactly what it was – a vanity exercise that had run out of steam. Despite the great songs we'd recorded, I couldn't wait for it to end.

However, I was soon reminded just how unmanageable the Duran machine had become. A week before the Power Station's final gig, in Massachusetts, Simon's yacht, *Drum*, capsized off the coast of Cornwall during the Fastnet Race, a rehearsal for the Whitbread Round the World race.

The keel of the boat sheared off and the boat flipped. Simon was trapped underwater in the cabin with several of his crewmates, the water gradually rising. They were there for over an hour before frogmen got in and freed them.

Simon and I were completely out of touch with each other at the time of the *Drum* accident. Nobody called Andy or me to say 'Something terrible has happened'. The news first came to us as a rumour, one that gathered in tempo and credibility. But we didn't truly appreciate the enormity of the accident – and how close Simon had come to dying – until we read about it in *People* magazine a week after it happened.

How fucked-up is that?

Andy never had a problem expressing anger, and for him, this was the final nail in the coffin of his relationship with the Berrows. He blamed them for encouraging the whole sailing adventure.

Nick was angry about it too, but he didn't express it as directly as Andy did. He was still working with the Berrows – the Arcadia project, as it was now named, was being managed by them – so officially, they were still a team.

The boat's keel got fixed, and *Drum* went on to complete the Round the World race, with Simon on board. Knowing Simon as I know him now, he was there because he wanted to be there, not because anyone had talked him into it.

But Andy was right about one thing – that was the end of the Berrows managing Duran Duran.

PART 3
DIGITAL TRUTH

56 Dead Day Ahead

The evening started innocently enough with an offer of dinner at a fashionable restaurant in uptown Manhattan. Renée was out of town on a modelling assignment, so I gladly accepted.

My friend Jonathan Elias was seated already, waiting for me at a table right in the middle of the room. At another table, Sabrina Guinness was chatting to Michelle Pfeiffer and the actress Lois Chiles.

I stopped at the table and spoke to Sabrina, who introduced me to her friends, before making my way over to Jonathan. He was grinning broadly.

'I thought you were going to bring them over,' he said.

'Even I know my limitations, Jonny Boy,' I replied.

I sat down and we both pretended to be interested in the menu. This was supposed to be one of the best restaurants in New York, but I don't know how anyone could tell. It was 1985, and nobody ate that year.

Michael Des Barres had turned me on to a super-hot film project, *9½ Weeks*, when we had been on the road in the summer. I had drafted in Jonathan – a producer, programmer and composer who had worked with us on 'A View to a Kill' – to help Michael and me realise what would become the theme tune to *9½ Weeks*: 'I Do What I Do'.

We had gone out to California together looking for more film work. At Universal, we met with one of the music supervisors.

'You know what? Maybe you guys could help us with this other film. We're struggling with it. It's great, but there's something wrong with it. Let me arrange a screening for you.'

We returned that night and watched *Brazil*, unfinished and uncredited, at the Alfred Hitchcock Theater on the Universal lot.

Within minutes, my heart was pounding. What I was watching was a masterpiece. I had no idea what the hell it was, but I wanted in.

When the last reel ended, I was ready to say anything to get a chance to contribute.

Jonathan and I threw some ideas at the executive, who reacted warmly and suggested we should go into the studio and make some musical notes. When I got back to my hotel, I called Russell Mulcahy.

'Don't touch it! That's Terry Gilliam's film. He's in dispute with Universal over control of it.'

I was utterly deflated. There was no way I would want to side with the studio over the artist. However, even though that experience led nowhere, it was encouraging in that it showed us what might be possible for a young British pop musician in Hollywood.

I got two tapes of the film in the mail a few days later. It was such a gorgeous-looking work of art, I kept it on my TV for weeks on freeze-frame.

Jonathan and I had an unlikely friendship; I had my self-taught background in British pop, he was a Juilliard scholar with a breathtaking expertise in classical music, a polymath who also just happened to run one of the city's most successful advertising firms. We had wildly opposing tastes in almost everything.

After not eating dinner at the hip uptown eatery, we thought we might go to a club, or maybe someone was having a party – but we decided first to go up to my apartment in the Park Belvedere, which was not too many blocks away, up on Seventy-Ninth and Columbus, right behind the Museum of Natural History. I lived in apartment 27a with Renée. Boy George had moved in down the hallway, into 27c.

It was hard to tell which apartment partied harder, although we didn't party together. One morning, Renée opened the front door to find a silver tray piled high with white powder outside our door. It was sugar, a Georgian joke about my lifestyle, but Renée was not amused.

She believed there was more interplay between George and me than there was. Although George and I had known each other way back, in Birmingham, before either of our bands had record deals, our stories had differed wildly since then. Right now, we had nothing in common and would not have dreamed of hanging out together.

The views from the apartment, now safely behind tinted glass windows, were truly spectacular, especially at night, when the twinkling city would wrap itself around the living area. It was easy to sit on my black leather sofa and think I was the centre of the universe.

Jonathan sat down and rolled a joint, and I went and mixed us drinks. Let me see, 1985 ... Planter's Punch? And cocaine of course.

I took the drinks back to the table and chopped out a few lines.

Outside, a storm was gathering. Rain slammed against the windows. Visibility across the park was low. It was enough to make us turn on the TV news channels to get more information. What was going on out there?

The wind grew wilder. On the streets below, trees were whipping in the rain, and we could see people running for shelter. It was starting to feel safer to stay indoors.

Let's have a little more.

Music?

Under Jonathan's tutelage, I was becoming passionate about classical music. Jonathan was convinced that the most important cultural event of the twentieth century had been the premiere of Stravinsky's *Rite of Spring*. This was news to me. I wasn't sure I agreed but I was interested in the conversation. And the cocaine was helping the conversation. Lightning lit the sky across the park.

It felt like the weather was spurring us on to do something, something creative. I had a black upright Steinway piano – I still have it – and Jonathan sat down and started playing. He knew all the intricacies of harmony and counterpoint and had technique for days. I was the opposite. My knowledge of music theory was non-existent, but my instincts were good.

I have no doubt, looking back to that night, that there was madness present. I felt that, together with Jonathan, I was on the verge of some extraordinary breakthrough that would change music for ever. But messed up as I was, it was like trying to gather dust particles wearing boxing gloves.

Then it was 4.00 a.m., then 5.00, and music had not been changed for ever, although the building was still rocking. Jonathan remembered that he had a 9.00 a.m. session, and left.

Me.

Alone.

Which I was never very good at, particularly when I was wired to the back teeth.

Why didn't I call Renée? Because she would have had no sympathy for me in the state I had gotten myself into. I didn't need to hear from her, 'You just need to go to bed.'

I needed someone or something to engage with on a profound level. I couldn't perform the pyrotechnics that Jonathan could at the piano, but I stayed at that keyboard for at least another three hours, and an idea began to germinate in my addled mind: what I needed was *spiritual* salvation. A talk with God. Maybe I could have that conversation through music.

Jonathan had introduced me to the term *chorale* – a simple but emotionally charged style of composition made for performance in church, created and offered up by the composer as a gift to God.

St Jude's filled my mind, filled my imagination. I had to write a chorale for Father Cassidy!

The idea crept up on me as the dawn rose. The storm had passed. Was that the sun rising on my new life? It rose like a livid orange scar over JFK, up, up across the park, lighting the living room, tinting it with an autumnal glow. Did the colours have a mildly accusatory aspect? Or was I being paranoid?

On the table, among the unfinished drinks and overflowing ashtrays, were scatterings of powdery cocaine crumbles.

It was a circular chain-link fence; cigarettes, drink, drugs, each causing me to crave the others. Once I had started on the one, the system took over, clamped me in its jaws.

It had been a few years now since I had been able to control my using. One line and I was gone, off to the races. I was no longer managing the chaos.

Take this day that was dawning. At some point, I would remember that I had made plans – a studio date perhaps, or a photo session. Whatever it was, it would have to go. The day ahead was dead.

What was left of last night's supply waited in its crisply folded white envelope, red on the inside, like a warning.

I could measure how a night had left to run by how much powder was inside those envelopes. There wasn't long.

I had to speak to Father Cassidy immediately. I picked up the phone and called my mum.

'4742163.'

'Mum. It's me.'

'Hello, John, where are you?'

'New York, Mum, at the apartment.'

'That's nice. Your father's gone to get the paper.'

'Mum, I need Father Cassidy's number.'

'What for?'

'I need to talk to him.'

'Is everything all right?'

'Yes, Mum, everything is fine. I want to write a piece of music for the church.'

'Do you think that's a good idea?'

'Yes, it's a great idea. I want to perform it at the church.'

It was daylight now. The morning news was on. It was another day. There's always something a bit sobering about daylight.

I sighed into the phone. 'Look, Mum, it's late here. Can you just give me the number?'

She gave it to me.

'Your dad's just walked in. Do you want to say hello?'

'No, Mum, not now, I'll call you back later.'

I had just enough coke left to get me through this next call.

57 In the Dark

Father Cassidy didn't pick up, thanks be to God.

A few weeks later, Nick came to New York to visit, bringing Julie Anne with him. Together with Renée, the four of us had dinner.

Afterwards, we retired to the apartment. There would be no cocaine that night.

We didn't talk about the past. We rarely do anyway, but in 1985 it would have been completely *verboten*. Nick wasn't happy about the *Drum* disaster, and the issue of new management would have to be addressed in due course, but his priority at the moment was not getting hung up on details. It was all about how to move the band forward, if that was what we both chose to do.

Nick brought me a belated birthday present, a beautiful Matisse monograph, on which he inscribed, 'Let's just mix . . . cocktails.' I proudly played him the video I had just directed, albeit simplistically and with plenty of assistance, for 'I Do What I Do'.

'That's great, Johnny,' said Nick. 'But we can do so much more together, don't you think?'

Getting the band back together? Maybe it wasn't a conversation with God that I needed after all. Maybe I just needed to hang out with the boys in the band and make another fucking brilliant album.

Maybe that could fix me.

'In Paris?' I enquired.

'Paris, London. We could come here, if you really want.'

Nick and Simon really wanted this. Would Andy and Roger be in the mix? Andy was in LA. Roger had taken to the country life.

'We'll see,' said Nick.

'I'll go and see Rog over Christmas, see what's going on with him,' I said.

Renée said she would be happy to move to Paris. She could get plenty of work if we chose to go and live there. She decided then and there to take French lessons. But first I made a promise to meet Nick in London.

The 'I Do What I Do' solo John Taylor single was released and did well in both the US and the UK. I did a lot of promotion for the song and learned a lot about myself. I wasn't a solo act. I could not carry the weight of the entire operation on my shoulders. I just didn't want it badly enough. I made a particularly embarrassing appearance on Saturday morning TV after an all-nighter hanging out with Freddie Mercury and Queen in their studio (another of those nights when I had a morning call and should have been a good boy). I showed up a complete mess, slurring my words and clearly out of it, and I managed to insult the entire population of Birmingham when a caller asked me sweetly if I had gone back there lately and I replied, 'Have *you* been there lately?'

My head just wasn't screwed on right.

Backstage in the green room, Bryan Adams suggested I needed help.

'Hey, man, are you okay?'

'Yeah, yeah, I just got in from New York. Jet lag.'

'You need to look after yourself, John.'

The concern was so sincere. I hated him for it.

Back at Mum and Dad's for Christmas Eve, I got a call from Simon. He and Yasmin were to be married in three days' time in Oxford. I was invited, but attendance was not compulsory, he stressed. Yasmin. Yasmin Le Bon, née Parveneh. A few years back, Simon had been leafing through some models' cards, looking for someone who might look good on his arm at a film premiere he had been invited to. Yazzy got the call. Another cynical beginning, but they have been together ever since. Their romance has proved to be extremely resilient. Simon was just nuts over Yasmin, and she, who is simply one of the loveliest girls you could ever hope to meet, loved him right back. She had been his rock during the sailing scare, and they had found a tempo that they have since shared. They were very good for each other and had decided now was the time to put a ring on it. They would become the couple I was closest to. Simon and Yasmin would shelter me in many hours and days of single lonely-heartedness, inviting me to join them on family holiday, and I would spend many a night in the guest quarters at their London town house. But I did not make the wedding. Strange choices were being made.

One right choice I made was to get back on board with Duran. It would be as creative as anything I could do alone or with any other collaborators, and a whole lot safer. In the New Year, I drove down to Gloucestershire, to Moreton-in-Marsh, the village to which Roger had relocated. We had a drink at the local pub.

He was enjoying the calm of life there with Giovanna and their young family, riding horses and working his farm. He seemed happy with the change of pace. I must have come at him like a freight train, assuming he would jump at the opportunity to play with Simon and Nick and me again, especially given the renewed enthusiasm the three of us had for getting back in the game together.

But Roger wasn't up for it. He was apologetic but there was no turning him. We drank up and parted ways.

Walking across the pub car park, I found it almost impossible to imagine Duran without Rog; playing those songs without him on the drums. I had never connected with another drummer the way I had with him. The trust that came with the endless hours of eyeballing, the musical structure that he and I had built together, had come out of our friendship first.

But as I hit the London road, I saw there was no place for emotion. I went into survival mode. Having made my decision to go back to the band, I had no intention of letting my plans be derailed by anyone else, even Roger.

I couldn't charm him, I couldn't change his mind, and Simon, Nick, Andy and I were just going to have to deal with it.

We needed a new drummer.

I had met an amazing drummer at the Power Station, an Englishman from Brighton named Steve Ferrone, who had been in the Average White Band and had become one of the great New York session drummers. Steve's favourite joke about his band name was, 'They're white and I'm average.'

I used to joke that he was like Tony Thompson with time; he had the same big sound that I loved, but was much more disciplined. Also there was more jazz in Steve's playing. I ran the idea past Simon and Nick, and we agreed to invite him to London to play with us as we started laying down the tracks that would form the basis for a new album.

Once again I was going to have to alter my bass-playing style in order to work with a drummer who wasn't Roger. From a creative point of view, that was no bad thing. Playing with Tony Thompson had prepared me for anything. The parts I wrote for the *Notorious* sessions, jamming with Nick and Steve, or working off electronic loops that we had programmed, were not at all what I would have written with Roger. I did miss the easy chemistry with Roger, but without him I was forced to think differently, and that made me grow as a musician.

Duran have often been often applauded for 'not making the same album twice', but we could not have done so had we tried. All the albums that were made after Roger and Andy left had a different flavour, and most often the reason was down to the different personnel involved in the making of them.

At the first *Notorious* sessions it was just Nick, Steve and I. Simon would be joining us soon enough – he had committed to the new album – but it was becoming clear to us that Andy was playing a more elusive game. For now, I played a little guitar, like in the beginning, and my friend Gerry Laffy, Russell's boyfriend from Sydney, played a little too. Nick and I, ever the cineastes, began naming these instrumental pieces after Hitchcock movies: 'Rope', 'Vertigo', 'Notorious'.

We had put it off as long as we could, but the management issue now had to be addressed, so we invited Mike Berrow to come to the studio. He put on a face of confidence, pretending to assume that business would go on as usual. I am sure he and his brother wanted things to go back to the way they had been, but that was never going to happen. There was too much resentment, bad feeling, unprocessed anger. It wouldn't be long before a hard-line decision was made, and what we had all known for some time would soon be formalised in black ink. Our relationship with the Berrows was terminated.

Now my thoughts turned to the missing guitarist. I knew Andy was in LA somewhere, and set myself the task of bringing him back into the fold. I tracked him down in Malibu, and he arranged to meet me at LAX.

On the kerb, Andy's driver took my bag and wordlessly gestured to the open car door, where Andy sat, deep in the back of the limousine, shades on, wreathed in cigarette smoke. It was like being picked up by Phil Spector.

'Hey mon,' he said, a wry grin appearing under the Ray-Bans.

He never failed to put a smile on my face, that guy. The Whitley Bay fucker. He'd done all right for himself.

'Dude.' 'Cos he was.

Before we even got to his house, I was so coked up I could barely speak in words of more than one syllable.

I tried to make my case. 'Andy, Andy, this album is going to be different.'

I'd said exactly the same things to him at the studio in Sydney, and that had led to *The Power Station*, a Top-10 album around the world.

'Trust me one more time, dude,' I said, chopping out another huge line of coke.

Andy watched me laying out the drugs. Andy's habit was not as heavy as mine. He did not see a man who inspired confidence. Not this time.

It was dawn by the time I got around to playing him the tapes.

'Listen to this drum sound, man. Come on, it needs you!'

I went back to London under the impression I had reeled Andy in. I told Simon and Nick that Andy would be showing up. We continued to work as a trio with Steve Ferrone, writing new songs. Nile Rodgers agreed to produce, so even if Andy didn't appear for a bit, we still had a blinding fill-in guitar player available in the shape of our producer.

We were in AIR Studios, working on *Notorious*, happy to be allowed back in the door at our favourite London studio after the arguments in Montserrat. We got a call from guitarist Warren Cuccurullo.

The studio receptionist took the call.

'Tell them it's their new guitar player,' said the voice on the phone. 'Tell Duran I'm the perfect guitar player for them. Have them call me.'

When the receptionist told us what the voice on the phone had said, we all cracked up.

'Cheeky fuck, we've got a guitar player,' I said.

'He's just not very good at returning phone calls,' Simon added.

But the receptionist had more to report. 'Well, apparently, you don't. This guy Warren says Andy has formed a band with his rhythm section.'

Turns out, the little bastard *had* formed another band, out in LA, with the rhythm section of Warren's band Missing Persons and Steve Jones, ex of the Sex Pistols. Andy had effectively broken up Warren's band and was playing around the LA area looking for a recording deal.

Can you imagine that happening now and not knowing about it? I would be getting video clips on Twitter before Andy had finished playing his first number. And yet, back in those dark ages, we really were in the dark.

Simon, Nick and I became closer than we had ever been

before. Our relationship moved to a whole new level, because now we were just three, fighting to survive. Like one of those football teams down to ten men – stronger, more determined, more focused. Less can be more. That was the silver lining.

In 1984, you would never have imagined that the three of us could have gotten as close as we did in 1986.

58 Notorious

The new slimline Duran family – John and Renée, Simon and Yasmin, Nick and Julie Anne, along with Steve Ferrone and his girlfriend Jackie – moved to Paris. Steve and I rented an apartment just off the Place Victor-Hugo. We moved the band gear into Studio 1 at Studios Davout near the Porte de Montreuil in the east end of the city. We continued to write, still not knowing for sure if Andy was in or out. But we were determined the show would go on, and according to our timetable, not Andy's.

We were able to add vocals to the Hitchcock titles – songs now – as Simon was in the house, writing lyrics as quickly as we could write the music.

Musically, change was in the air again. Guns N' Roses, Jane's Addiction and the Red Hot Chili Peppers were the bands breaking out; music seemed to be getting darker and harder. The big albums of '86 were all by veterans who had found a way back into the zeitgeist: Peter Gabriel, Steve Winwood, Robert Palmer;

mature work by mature artists. Would we be able to reflect that level of maturity ourselves?

There was self-doubt, of course. Sometimes it seemed like the whole world was against us. Anthony Burgess, of all people, the author of *A Clockwork Orange*, wrote an incredibly mean op-ed piece in the *Sun* about the cheek of pop stars who expect more than their five minutes of fame. It was actually about Boy George, who had just been arrested, but he used it to take a dig at us. I took it personally.

The second half of the eighties, from a pop-culture standpoint, was characterised by two defining ideas; the first, brought about by Bob Geldof and the Live Aid phenomenon, was that a conscience was now required of everyone in pop. It was no longer enough just to be able to write fun or romantic songs that made people want to dance or escape – you had to take a position. Pop became political.

I went to the Amnesty International concert in Paris in 1988 and watched Bruce Springsteen get an education in political correctness from Sting and Peter Gabriel, who both delivered sets that spoke of global awareness. Their music was inherently political; both of them had managed to metamorphose out of the first act of their musical careers into second acts as spokespeople for Third World nations and rainforests.

When Bruce took the stage, he looked out-of-date in his denims and lumberjack shirt.

The other transformative aspect of late eighties culture lay in sobriety. Arguably the two greatest artists of the moment, Prince and Madonna, made it quite clear that they were not users or abusers. They both famously ran clean tours. If you wanted to work for Prince or Madonna, you couldn't use, period.

The seventies were most definitely over.

We went back to London to finish off the new album, when Nile arrived and immediately raised the ante.

He began working on the tracks that we had laid down so far, funking them up, bringing a new energy to the sound.

When Prince came to London for a run of shows at Wembley, we all trotted along to see him. Afterwards, he gave an impromptu performance at the Roof Gardens in Kensington, and one of his roadies asked me if I would like to join him onstage.

I knew better. 'Not tonight, thanks.'

Eric Clapton took the bait. Watching Eric on the tiny stage, the Purple One behind him, now on drums, now on keyboards, now on guitar, I was glad I had resisted. Eric didn't know what was going on. It was Prince's room.

We all got caught up in Prince fever that week. Nick asked Nile for a lesson in minor sevenths, the funk chords made famous by James Brown and now being reinvented by Prince. The lesson was most fruitful, with the two of them building the basis for the song 'Notorious'.

Simon responded with a lyric about why we were doing this again. Going for it again. Chasing the fame monster.

Nile applied more magic with the Synclavier – a most fantastic sampling device that enabled him to perform tricks with the music, to cut and paste sounds the way you can cut and paste text on a word processor – as he had on the 'Reflex' remix and 'Wild Boys', and when we heard it booming out of those massive studio speakers – 'No-No Notorious' – we knew we had something special.

Because of the physical restrictions of the building, Studio 2 – located over Topshop, high above Oxford Street – had low windows that rose from the floor to knee height. From a standing position, they gave a perfect view down onto Oxford Circus.

There was something romantic and exciting about working in that room in the early hours of the morning. Music never sounded better. To hear something you had written pumping out of those speakers while you looked down on the city below made you feel not just like a master of the universe but also like a master of your trade.

The music we were making with Nile felt like the right music for our time. Nile wanted to mix the record in New York and as there was still quite a bit of singing for Simon to do, the two of them went to work in Skyline Studios in Midtown Manhattan.

It had been decided that Andy Taylor would make a contribution to the album as part of the divorce settlement. It was official. He wanted out. In New York, we met up with Warren Cuccurullo and invited him to take part in the album also. Strangely enough, I know which solos Warren contributed to the album, and I know which parts Nile contributed, but although Andy is credited beneath Steve Ferrone, I am damned if I can pick out where he is playing. I think we felt that the sooner we learned to live without Andy, the better, so we buried his parts. Warren was the new guitar player.

59 Surfing Apoplectic

'Notorious' was a hit. The numbers were not as big as they had been in 1984, but we justified that to ourselves by saying, 'Well, there's only three of us now.'

Three-fifths of the success. We conditioned ourselves to that idea. But 'Notorious' was certainly big enough to support another massive world tour.

Would someone please explain
The reason for this strange behaviour
In exploitation's name
We must be working for the skin trade.

The 'Notorious' world tour of 1987, named the 'Strange Behaviour' tour, brought us for the first time in front of live audiences in Italy. We had been there before as a five, but only for TV appearances and press. Now we would play seven concerts there:

Palermo in Sicily, Bari on the heel of Italy, Cava de' Tirreni near Naples, Rome, Modena, Milan (at the San Siro stadium) and Florence.

In the late eighties, Italy became 'fame rehab' for us. There could be no denying, no ignoring the waning of Duranmania as a phenomenon in the markets that had been most supportive to us. We still saw healthy ticket sales, and *Notorious* would achieve platinum disc sales in the United States and Great Britain (for 1,000,000 and 100,000 respectively), but the madness and the mayhem had most definitely abated.

One would think we might have been grateful. For the first time in years, we could take regular walks outside of our hotels, go shopping or visit museums, without a mob scene developing. We were now shown to the guest lifts, and we could exit through the lobby like civilised folk instead of using the stinky kitchen exits. And we *were* grateful, for the most part, to have these freedoms restored. We certainly kept telling ourselves that.

However, I had a nagging fear that this was only the beginning of what could be the end. Who knew how low things could go? A total and all-out end to sales of any kind? Surely not, not with the decent catalogue of hits we had already written.

But then, Italy arose like a knight to defend the honour of the virgin princess! It would protect us. It drew us to its heart, held us tightly and would not let go. The audiences and media there warmed to us even more as a trio than they had to the five, maybe because the super-Catholic Italians related to us more easily as a (holy) trinity?

Ciao Italia!

It was beautiful, *bellissimo*, the support our Italian fans gave us in the late eighties. They took us to their bosom, and we surrendered to them.

Our visits there were characterised by a manifold craziness that relished its exclusivity. The Italian fans realised how important they had become to us, and they were proud of that. A weekend in Rome, ostensibly for a Sunday afternoon TV playback appearance – hardly work at all, in my view – was in fact a forty-eight-hour piece of living theatre in four acts: ARRIVAL, STRUGGLE, SURRENDER and RETREAT.

It was all of that Tokyo madness, turned up to eleven: taxicabs loaded with flash-snapping, screaming, teary-eyed teens; dozens of scooter-riding mercenaries known as paparazzi, weaving in and out of our motorcade, engaging in madcap rides around the city like it was the national pastime. It would leave us breathless and barmy. How did no one get hurt?

Italy was only just becoming a legitimate stopover on the international touring circuit. In the seventies and early eighties, it had been the Wild West. British and American bands toured Italy at their peril. Violence and riots were rife wherever crowds gathered and you could lose your shirt, your truck and most definitely your amplifiers if you were not careful or ran afoul of the corrupt officialdom in place there. Just ask Genesis or Van der Graaf Generator. When Lou Reed played Italy, the building was fire-bombed.

Promoter David Zard approached us with promises of propriety, honest book-keeping, tip-top security and a lot of fun. We signed on for the seven-date tour of football stadia. The potential for chaos was high. 'It was the tour they said could not be done,' Simon would tell the end-of-year fan-club magazine.

In order to announce the dates, we arrived in Rome, from where we drove to the coast and boarded a private motor yacht that took us to the Isle of Capri. The level of security was intense, mean eyes beneath mean peaked caps following us as we walked up the hill from the dock to the hotel. In black leather boots and armed with guns, the guards were quite rough – we could see that – with the kids who had lined up to welcome us. We gratefully sought the sanctuary of our rooms, checking in just before midnight.

The following morning there was to be a press conference. Italy had a variation on the standard press-conference rules: whereas in every other country the press would act out the roles they had seen played by the press in films of Beatles press conferences, in Italy we all acted out the press-conference scene from *La Dolce Vita*, which takes place in Anita Ekberg's hotel suite. Of course, there were variations; unlike Anita Ekberg, we would rarely answer a question about what we most liked in life with, 'Love, love and more love,' but I'm sure we did it once or twice.

'How do you find Italy?'

'Which do you like better, English or Italian girls?'

One has to be diplomatic answering questions such as that one, particularly when one is a guest in the country.

More work for the interpreter, who seemed to have his translations prepared in advance. How do they do that? Perhaps it was the work of Mr Zard.

After the formal Q and A session ended, we were led outside to a garden that looked out over the Mediterranean. On a giant half-shell sculpture, evoking the beauty of Botticelli's *Birth of Venus*, sat the great Italian actress Sandra Milo. 'She knew Fellini, she was Fellini's *greatest* creation,' we were told.

Miss Milo had indeed been a Fellini muse and starred in *8½*. Miss Milo, who barely spoke English, seemed to have been held suspended in the thrall of her character in that movie, which she had filmed over twenty years before.

The lady we were introduced to on the half-shell was no mere actress. 'I am the great star, the muse of the greatest, Signor Fellini,' she managed.

'Ah, yes,' we murmured. 'We love Fellini.'

'I was his greatest star.' She echoed *Sunset Boulevard*, stretching like a cat and reaching out her head on an impossibly long neck, out towards the horizon.

'It's so beautiful out here,' said I, in a dumb attempt at conversation. She merely struck poses as the cameras flashed, the photographers hypnotised by her, proud of the home-grown grandeur that she exhibited against the relative plaintiveness of these young British upstarts. What did we know!

I wish I had appreciated her message at the time. Nick got it, but I laughed the whole episode off. I can see now how it is possible to get fixated on some moment, some past performance, how one can get stuck but also feel safe, living and functioning only in a nostalgic reverie, when your career highlights happen before your thirtieth birthday. The temptation to return and remain, frozen in lost time, is powerful.

The tour opened on 28 May in Palermo, the concert nicely timed to coincide with some high-profile Mafia trials that were going on there. Off the plane, we were herded into an armoured police bus and set off for the hotel, where we were to wait out the afternoon before going to the venue shortly before show time. We were accompanied by a half-dozen motorcycle outriders and a handful of police cars, all flashing lights and honking horns. God forbid a farm truck or a bicycle race should get in our way. Above us hovered a police helicopter, the noise terrific. No chances were being taken with our bony white asses!

The van we were in could not have been less comfortable. As we rattled along, bouncing up and down at the mercy of Sicilian potholes, we held on for dear life, teeth clenched, both petrified and highly amused. It was certainly exhilarating.

'A View to a Kill' made a great show opener on the 'Strange Behaviour' tour, followed by 'Notorious'. We played both 'Election Day' and 'Some Like It Hot', honouring both the side projects that had been so divisive three years earlier. 'Skin Trade' was a winner on that tour and, of course, we played all the big guns from the first three albums, beefed up with a three-piece horn section and a three-part backing-vocal section. We would record the vibe of the show with a live 'bootleg' release recorded in Holland, *Duran go Dutch*. It felt as though we were winning and could recapture whatever it was that might have been lost.

The clenched teeth remained set for the next few days. In Bari, the concert had become a symbol of the struggle between the incumbent and incoming local governments, who were fighting for control of the locality. The concert had been called off by one bureaucrat, restored by another, off again, and then finally reinstated by the mayor of Bari himself, succumbing to the demands of his daughter, who insisted the concert *would* go ahead, in the city's 40,000-seat football stadium.

The mayor's only caveat was that no ticket holders were to be allowed onto the pitch. This meant, with our stage set up at one end of the ground, the fans had to stand a long way from the action, behind the opposite goal. We would be playing to an empty stretch of grass. It was a Sunday, and it began raining torrentially at midday.

By show time, the fans were in their places, happy, singing and chanting despite the absurd efforts of their local representatives to ruin their experience entirely. And the empty football field was getting filled too, by every police officer and carabiniere in the province – uniformed, locked and loaded, their girlfriends on their unarmed arms barely able to contain their excitement and sense of entitlement.

Ronnie Wood arrived backstage. 'What the hell are you doing here?' We were so happy to see his smiling face. 'What a scene you've got going on out there,' he said, pulling a face. 'Not very nice.'

Woody was moonlighting with an Italian TV company and was there to interview us. Another surreal lesson in the possibilities ahead for us. 'Don't give up your day job, Woody!' Thankfully, he didn't. We hoped he might join us for a watery 'Miss You', but the rain and intimidation sent him back to Rome.

The longer the show ground on, the more excited did the WAGs get, and the more frustrated and fierce their old men became. I purposely backed off, as did SLB, from our usual repertoire of teasy moves. I thought for sure something was about to go off; they were surfing apoplectic out there, eyes popping out of their heads. Thank God for the rain, which does have a habit of dampening the most violent of spirits. We played the shortest encore of the year, which was a shame for the crowd who, despite having the worst sightlines of the tour, never lost their enthusiasm, and then we got the hell out of Dodge.

In Florence, we played the Stadio Comunale, a cool slab of Art Deco architecture.

I relate this next story with my head low in shame. On arrival at the Florence hotel, I spotted a delightful eighteenth-century banquette with typically Florentine candy-striped cushioning that I thought would fit perfectly in the lobby of my London house. I decided to try my luck and see just how much power my fame had here. I approached the hotel manager. 'Would it be possible to buy the chair?' I asked, slyly. 'It's so beautiful.'

'Signor Taylor,' my hotel manager and new friend beamed, 'it would be our honour for you to take a small part of our humble hotel back to your home in London. Where should we have it delivered?'

The fame thing wasn't all downhill. My delicate ego was satisfied, for now.

Milan was the best show of the year. Fifty thousand happy hooligans in a June heat wave. They had to be hosed down every ten minutes and loved it.

And Italy has never stopped gifting us. We have had some of our best times there. If you aren't in the mood for the fuss and nonsense, it can be a real drag. And who is in the mood for that always? Even bass players have off days. But while international fame faltered, we found a new friend in Italy, who went a long way to convincing us that we were every bit as valid as a threesome as we had been as a quintet.

We had a future.

60 Chasing the Wave

Outside Italy, however, there would not be a second hit on the *Notorious* album, and it was getting hard to dodge the sense that music had moved on, leaving me behind. The wave – the zeitgeist – that I had been riding my entire career, from before 'Planet Earth' through to the summer of 1985, seemed to be over *there* now. I was not surfing it any longer. Instead, I was swimming as hard as I could, trying to catch it.

With our next album, *Big Thing*, and the tour that would accompany it, I felt this even more; the empty seats and relative lack of interest from the media really started to hit home.

There is one bona fide hit on that album, 'I Don't Want Your Love', which reached number 14 in the UK and number 4 in the US (as well as being number 1 in Italy for six weeks, thank you!).

But it felt like a follower.

By the end of that tour in April '89, things, far from going to plan, seemed to be getting worse. We were not making up ground, we were not getting closer to the wave; if anything, it felt to me we were getting dragged farther away from it.

Expectations were a big part of the problem. With the enormous sales of the first four albums, plus *The Power Station* and Arcadia's *So Red the Rose* – both platinum albums in their own right – everything we touched had turned a very satisfying shade of yellow.

But now the Midas touch seemed to have deserted us.

I started to think that we needed to do an about-face, that Duran Duran had to go back to being a quintet, not a trio. As much as we had pushed the boat out with *Notorious*, presenting to the world the all-new Simon-Nick-and-John three-headed Duran, it didn't seem to me as if it was working. And most importantly, the three of us could not just walk out onto a stage and play a song as a trio. We always needed augmentation.

It was looking as if Warren Cuccurullo would be coming on board as the full-time guitar player. But what about a drummer? It was one thing to be augmented by a horn section or by a couple of back-up singers, but to be augmented by a drummer? The drummer should be full-time.

The drummer playing on the *Big Thing* tour was Sterling Campbell, a kid from New York who had stepped in at the last minute when Steve Ferrone went to work with Eric Clapton. Could Sterling be the fifth band member? I thought so. As the tour wound down, I went to work on him.

I told him I wanted him to be a part of the songwriting process, that we needed to find a way back to the way we had worked before, that I believed we were becoming too reliant on computers and drum machines. I thought I knew what was needed to fix Duran, that if we could just get back to our previous style of writing and recording – five guys in a room jamming, exchanging

musical ideas, fighting, firing energy off each other – then everything would fall back into place.

Sterling was an up-and-comer, a talented musician who had
graduated from LaGuardia High School, the 'Fame' Academy on
New York's Upper West Side, where you had to be gifted to survive. He agreed to come on board as a full-time band member,
and as a deal sweetener, I offered to let him move in with me, in
my house in Ennismore Mews.

Bad idea.

There was plenty of space there now, for in an utterly perverse
act of self-sabotage, I had broken up with Renée, telling her I
needed to be single again.

It wasn't because I wanted to return to the field of play, but
rather because I had become obsessed with the idea that Duran's
success, and my particular appeal, had been down to female fans
perceiving me as single and available.

Renée had been ready to have a baby. She was broody. She had
covered the fridge door with children's names. I pretended not to
notice. All I could think about was how to get the damned band
back on top.

Simon and Nick both had considerable emotional investments
in family, they both had wives and children who naturally occupied their time and thoughts. I didn't. I could only think of myself
as 'John from Duran Duran'; my net worth as a person was determined entirely by what the band's net worth was. And it was
going down.

So I could not get my mind on baby-making or family-making;
it was solely focused on 'How do we get this band back to the top
of the charts?'

I became terrified that she would get pregnant. I projected dis-
astrous futures for Renée and me in that eventuality: the inevitable

divorce, Renée moving back to Denmark, the kid raised in Denmark – because I obviously couldn't raise a kid – where he would speak Danish as his principal language.

How horrible would that be? I'd go and visit the two of them and they'd just be talking about me in Danish together behind my back and I wouldn't know what they were saying.

Paranoia the destroyer.

I took a lot of long baths and escaped into books. I was reading *The Lives of John Lennon* by Albert Goldman. John had always been one of my totems, but this book was a day-by-day analysis of John's life, and the myth was totally unable to bear up to that scrutiny. Any magic that you might have felt about Lennon the writer, the performer and legend was gone, and sitting in the bath one day, reading it, I threw the book down on the floor and just broke down crying.

I was crying for John, but also for myself.

What chance do I have?

Getting the band back together clearly hadn't been the mental panacea I had hoped for. There was just too much wrong with me. I was so addicted to so many things – to fame, booze, cars, drugs.

And a sense of doom was ever present.

I was depressed for the first time in my life. I still felt the world revolved around me, but I also felt like a piece of shit.

I was yet to understand that it takes more than a career to make a life. I genuinely believed that if I could just concentrate on music-making, I could play my way through.

61 Tabloid Fodder

Moving Renée out and Sterling in was a disaster from Day One.

The last thing I needed to be doing was giving over my home life to a kid from New York who was just getting going. I needed to take it easy, start having a few nights in, learn my way around the TV remote. But dude here, he wants to party! He wants to sit up all night playing the rough mixes, analysing the snare sounds!

And he wants to run the band too. He is telling me exactly what Simon should be doing, what Nick should be doing. He can't help himself. That's how much energy he has, and it is all being funnelled through me.

I quickly realised I had made a catastrophic mistake.

So what did I do? I drank over it. Got high over it. Tried to obliterate it.

The writing sessions for the new album, which we would call

Liberty, mostly took place at Stambridge Farm in Sussex. MTV sent a film crew to document our work there.

We could not believe who we met working with their crew: Les McKeown, the singer of the Bay City Rollers.

We would see Les again, riding the front seat of a London bus one afternoon, from the privileged position of our tour coach, as we drove north on the Edgware Road to a concert in Birmingham. What cosmic trick had been played on the lead Roller to bring him to this place?

There but for the grace of God went I.

EMI approached us saying that the time was right to release a greatest hits album, which they proposed to call *Decade*. Apparently, 'tests' had shown it could sell several million copies around the world, and as they were careful to point out, the last couple of albums hadn't really been doing the business.

None of us really wanted to consider a retrospective release. We were in the process of trying to reinvent ourselves, always writing new material, but we weren't really in a position to argue with EMI either.

We were at least able to take creative control of the project. We brought in clothing designer Stephen Sprouse to create the cover and had fun building a 'Decadance' remix, using elements from many of the hits for a track we called 'Burning the Ground'. The album was in the stores for Christmas 1989, and the three of us went to New York to promote it.

Simon and I were doing an interview with CNN at the Capitol Records office building. The cameras were set up in the boardroom, and on the wall facing us there was an Absolut Vodka ad, a poster on the wall that blended the Capitol Records Tower in Los Angeles with the Absolut bottle. It said *Absolut Conviction*. As the CNN interview started rolling, I totally tuned out, focusing all my attention on this poster on the wall.

The interview started. 'Simon, John, this is your greatest hits album and it's time to look back over an extraordinary career. What are some of the highlights for you, John?'

I swear I could not think of one highlight. I couldn't think of one positive thing that had happened over the past ten years. I was reduced to monosyllables. For so many years I'd been so glib. I could turn it on in interviews so easily, do them standing on my head.

And now? Nothing. I didn't want to look back on the last ten years, there was too much confusion.

Get me out of this room, get me out of this town, and get me back home.

Anywhere but here.

But before we left town, the universe had another trick up its sleeve. I was getting out of our car to go into a radio station on Broadway, in among those Midtown glass towers, when a film crew and a journalist with a rather sad-looking girl in tow pounced on me before I even had a chance to put both feet on the sidewalk.

'John, do you know this girl? Do you know this girl? She says she's having your baby.'

'What? What are you talking about?'

Simon and Nick hustled me into the lobby of the building, leaving the guy behind calling after me, 'John! John! She's having your baby! Would you like to comment?'

I didn't know what the hell this was about, and I had no recognition of the quiet, supposedly pregnant girl standing in the shadows, but there had been so many episodes over the last six or seven years that I couldn't help but worry. Was there something to it?

The girl had taken her story to the *People*, a trashy British Sunday tabloid, saying, 'I'm having John Taylor's baby. He and I are really close and we're going to be married. Look at the photographs.'

Apparently the parents got on the phone and substantiated it; they said I'd been to their home for Sunday lunch.

The truth of it came out over time. The girl had completely invented the story. She had altered the photographs to make it look like we were together.

I will never know what the parents' story was. The *People*, in classic tabloid fashion, turned it around, with the headline, DURAN STAR VICTIM OF PATERNITY HOAX. They took all of their responsibility out of it and still got a story.

As the drama of the paternity hoax was unfolding, I was grateful to have the support of a new girlfriend, Amanda de Cadenet, one of the most media-savvy individuals I have ever known.

Aged nineteen, Amanda was already infamous for being a wild child. She had been to Princess Anne's private boarding school Benenden, and her father, Alain, had been a successful racing car driver. Amanda's infamy began the day her dad contacted a friend of his at Scotland Yard and arranged an intervention to have Amanda arrested and taken from the home of some dubious individual she had moved in with. The story was a tabloid sensation.

Seeing a picture of her at a gallery opening, I thought to myself, 'This is exactly who I need in my life!'

We met at a play Julie Anne Rhodes was starring in at an alternative theatre on the King's Road in Chelsea. Amanda had blonde hair and blue eyes, looked like an angel. That night, she was wearing a red riding jacket. Tally-ho! It should have been a warning to run a mile, but later on, over dinner after the show, Nick said to me, 'I like Amanda, I like the way her mind works.' 'Right,' I thought. 'Exactly. *I like the way her mind works . . .* '

We started dating right away.

On our first date she took me to Portobello Market on a Saturday. I had never been there. I loved it.

I had been living in my ivory tower, and the idea of mixing it on the street at a Saturday market would never have occurred to me, mainly as a result of the years when doing something that normal without getting chased around the block was just not a possibility.

But that was now some time ago. It was safe to go outside again. Amanda opened that reality up to me. She let me out of the cage.

Within a few months, Amanda and I learned that she was pregnant. Given that I had been so hostile to that idea less than a year ago, I was surprised how good it was to hear the news. Any thoughts about breaking up, that this relationship might not be 'the one', were instantly dispelled. We both went to work right away. This pregnancy would be perfect! There was not a moment of doubt in either of us that we should have the baby, which put us immediately on the same page. In fact, I was thrilled: a baby sounded great! I would allow myself this rounded life experience, and maybe it would help my art as well.

What had changed? During a tough twelve months, I had come to realise that the sacrifices I misguidedly thought had been necessary in order to have a career were unwarranted.

We both embraced the news, which gave me impetus to make some changes. Amanda and I decided to give up drinking altogether, and we put the party schedule on hold. What better motivation can there be than the knowledge there is a baby growing into the relationship. Staying sober for nine months was easy.

With Amanda's help, I confronted the financial mess that my life had gotten into. I sold the house in Knightsbridge, the New York apartment and the house in Paris I had bought when the band relocated there to record *Notorious*. I had taken great pride in that perfume-bottle real estate thing I had going – *John Taylor of London, Paris & New York* – but now was the time for stock-taking. I had to let go of that idea. I paid off my enormous credit card debt and the mortgage with Crédit Lyonnais. I bought a house on Ossington Street at the unfashionable end of Notting Hill Gate, and we moved in together.

When we first met, Amanda had just begun a job as a presenter on the burgeoning BSkyB cable TV channel. After a few months, she took an audition and got a better job presenting a late-night music and culture show to be called *The Word*. The series began as Amanda's bump began to show, and Amanda would dress to show it off. The bump became a little star in itself.

The bump had given me a higher purpose. It wasn't all about me any more, and I liked that. I was happy.

62 Wedding Spaghetti

On Christmas Eve 1991, Amanda and I married at Chelsea Registry Office on the King's Road.

'A shotgun wedding!' said John Jones, our co-producer, gleefully. I didn't like him for saying that – although Amanda and I were both traditional enough to want to tie the knot before our child was born – so I named one of the instrumental tracks we were working on 'Shotgun', as if to say, 'And proud of it, you fucker.' That indirectly led to us naming the album *The Wedding Album* and to Nick's inspired sleeve concept, which featured the wedding-day photos of all our parents.

I call that creative revenge.

The wedding party was last-minute and small, not a cultural event like Nick's had been. Neither Amanda nor I had a desire to be extravagant. I was still reluctant to shout my non-availability from the rooftops, and by this time 'the bump' was getting in the way of her style.

There was a certain street cool in getting married at Chelsea Registry Office on the King's Road. Nick was out of the country for the holidays, but Simon and Yasmin were present. Mum and Dad were there, with cousin Eddie and his wife, Liz. On the bride's side, her dad Alain, her mother Anna, and her brother Bruiser were all in attendance. From the registry office, we walked to photographer Bob Carlos Clarke's studio on Flood Street, where we posed for the wedding pictures. Our baby's arrival was less than four months away, and Amanda was not happy having to squeeze into any kind of wedding outfit. She opted for a pink Chanel suit.

From the studio, we went to an Italian restaurant – Leonardo's on the King's Road – for a low-key plate of wedding spaghetti. Just as everyone was loosening up and starting to relax, Bob appeared at the table. Something was wrong with the pics he had taken, and he needed us all back at the studio right away for a reshoot. Doing it all again was a real drag.

We were not fans of those pictures. Neither of us kept copies of them.

Afterwards, at the house on Ossington Street, my poor mum made the mistake of welcoming Amanda to the family. Amanda, who wasn't crazy about being a member of her own family, let alone mine, freaked out.

'I can't handle this,' she told me that night. 'I have to get away.'

So she did. To Barbados.

If she hadn't gone with two gay friends of ours, I might have been a lot more put out than I was, but by now, I knew Amanda well enough to know that when she needed a time-out, I'd best let her have it.

Besides, there was work to do. The band was working on new music, which always kept me in good mental humour, so I went back to the studio.

Although *Liberty* had been a flop – our first – EMI were standing by us. We had made a lot of money for them over the years, but they told us they were going to tighten the financial reins. Instead of handing over the usual six-figure advance, Nick Gatfield, EMI's new A&R head (who had once been the trombonist in Dexys Midnight Runners), said he would review our songwriting on a monthly basis, and if he was happy with what he heard, he would dispense the next month's stipend.

Warren had moved into a terraced house on Octavia Street in Battersea that Simon and Yasmin had occupied while construction work was being carried out on their Chelsea abode. Now they were back in their own house, and Warren took over the Battersea lease.

He offered to install a studio in the back room that we could use to write and record new material. It would be cheap and effective. How we got away with it, I do not know. I'm not aware of receiving any complaints from the neighbours for the entire duration of those recording sessions. Warren could certainly charm those south Londoners.

He also agreed to be the interface with Nick Gatfield, go over the bills and play him the fruits of our labours. I was grateful to him for taking on that role.

Sterling was now out of the mix and out of my house. For the first time in my life, I was delighted to use drum machines.

After a fun but unfruitful period of being managed by ex-Rolling Stones manager Peter Rudge, we were now basically managing ourselves. We had a meeting at Manchester Square with EMI Records president Rupert Perry, with whom we had a good relationship. We voiced some of our concerns about the band's status and where we were at.

'Just take your time,' said Rupert. 'There's no rush. Just make the right album.'

Well, on the one hand, he was right, we did need to take our time, and *The Wedding Album* did become the right album. I would laughingly refer to the album we were working on as 'The Right Album' – referencing the Beatles' *White Album* – and tried to convince the rest of the band that we should name it just that.

But I missed having deadlines. Maybe we could have done an even better job if he had said, 'We need it in eight weeks, better get your skates on, guys.'

Artists don't do well with time on their hands; that is my experience. All creative projects have their own energy, which is not infinite. Deadlines are what I need, otherwise I get lazy and start taking days off and loafing around on South Molton Street.

Amanda got back from Barbados in late January.

On 30 March, she went into labour, checking in to the Wellington Humana Hospital in the late afternoon. Everything went smoothly. Mozart and Stevie Wonder tapes were playing – we'd done the research and read the books, so we knew what to expect.

Having said that, there is nothing that can quite prepare you for the incredible experience that is the arrival of new life into the world. We had made a choice not to know in advance whether we were having a boy or a girl, so the arrival of a baby daughter came as a complete surprise. It was the most joyful moment of my life. Fantastic!

I had not had a lot of experience with infants or babies, but holding that serene and tiny bundle of flesh and bone felt beautiful. It felt like all good things had come. For once, I was not thinking about myself, about how this was going to impact me. I was thinking about us.

Amanda came from a long line of As, so giving her child an A name was a priority. I was okay with that, but it would have to be an A name with a difference. I liked the sound of 'Atlanta'; it reminded me of something from the past – Atlantis or Atalanta, princess of Arcadia. It would turn out to be a most appropriate name for my daughter, born in London but to be raised across the Atlantic in California.

63 Take Me to LA

John Lennon once advised that songs should always be written in one sitting. A pretty tall order if you ask me. More often than not, I have found, a song develops over time. After the energy of the initial idea, the arrangement and subject matter, melody and harmonies need time to develop. Now Simon, Nick and I all had families, the rush to finish had started to slow. We were cool with a slow-cook approach. None of us wanted to be 'all work, all the time', as we had been in our twenties.

It is rarely the case that everyone likes an idea equally, so songs need champions. There might be one idea that Nick really believes in and won't let go, keeps in the spotlight. Or it might be me, or Simon. Warren took 'Ordinary World' under his wing, nurturing it and tending to the fragile chords.

It had begun life on his acoustic guitar and was not typical band material. At one point, Simon was singing 'Ordinary Girl' but then developed the words in a different direction.

A couple of years previously, during the sessions for *Big Thing*, Simon had lost a very good friend of his, David Miles, to depression and suicide. It was a massive blow. Simon wanted to address his feelings about David in song. He knew it was not the kind of subject Duran usually employed, but it was a good thing for us to do, and it yielded the song that would have the biggest impact on that album, 'Do You Believe in Shame?'.

When introducing 'Ordinary World' onstage, Simon often refers to losing David and how it took him writing three songs about the experience before he could truly get over it. 'Ordinary World' was the second of them, and I don't know which song was the third; he has never said, and I have never been able to figure it out.

I was never a fan of the song, particularly – it had no bassline to speak of, didn't rock or groove – but everyone who heard it fell in love with it.

When Nick Gatfield heard it, he was happy. His happiness triggered the release of money, which made us happy. It was a bit like a game show.

As the album took shape, we hired a Los Angeles-based firm, Allen Kovac's Left Bank Management, to manage us. Allen was among the new school of music-business entrepreneurs who made a science of getting their artists onto US radio stations. After he listened to our finished album, he got on the phone to us. We took the call in Warren's kitchen.

'I need six months to set this up,' he said. '"Ordinary World" is a hit song but I need time.'

This was a new concept to us, and a taste of things to come. Up until then, EMI had always wanted new songs as fast as we could produce them, and they would schedule releases as soon as material was complete, sometimes even before. Now we were being told to chill out and wait while the organs of power ground out their (hopefully) green notes.

I went back to Ossington Street, to Amanda and Atlanta, now a delightful three months old, and told Amanda we had been gifted some free time, as the album we had been expecting to release in the autumn had been put back to the following year.

Right away, Amanda said, 'Then I want to go to Los Angeles.'

She wanted to get into the film business, and I was okay with that. I didn't have a great sense of LA, had not spent much time there other than being there for tour dates. I really only knew the hotels and the main strips: Sunset Boulevard, Melrose Avenue, Rodeo Drive.

I said I would be happy to play a supporting role in Amanda's dream.

When we got there, I found to my surprise that I liked it. A lot.

I liked the light and the heat. The ocean. And the food was healthier than it was in London. I even overcame my allergy to pot and took to the California grass.

'Ordinary World' was released in January 1993 and went into the Top 10 in the US and the UK. We were back on the radio and back on television. On 13 January, I was picked up by a rather large and incongruous RV and driven to film *Top of the Pops* at Elstree Studios (not Shepherd's Bush any more).

As the vehicle turned left onto Bayswater Road, the song came on the radio. There it was, the sound of my bass guitar! It may not have been a funky bassline, but it was on the radio, and not on an oldies show.

Thank you, God!

We had a hit song in a second decade, and thanks to 'Come Undone' (a song I missed out on the writing of, as I was unwilling to come back from Los Angeles to work on 'one last track', a decision I will always regret), but Duran Duran were back.

The tour behind *The Wedding Album* began in South Africa, our first time there and my first time on the road as a dad. South Africa was a great place to take a one-year-old, who got to go on safari and play with lion cubs. After a few weeks of the touring life, however, Amanda wanted to go back to Los Angeles and get on with her career. We started spending a lot of time apart, and I experienced the absolute torture of driving away from home to resume the tour's next leg to the sound of a screaming daughter.

'Daddy!'

It took her a while to get used to the idea that I wasn't leaving for good.

Amanda was a natural networker. Born to it. Her career plans seemed to my jaded eye to involve going to a lot of parties or having intimate dinners for two with movie stars at their Mulholland lairs. I didn't feel good about that, and I felt even worse about it when, coming home after a particularly rough few weeks on the road, I heard Amanda announce that she was going out. I was feeling my age.

64 Paranoid on Lake Shore Drive

The tour just kept growing. That's the sign of a successful album. You keep going, adding new countries and returning to others to play bigger venues a second or even a third time around.

My obsessive desire to get the band back on top had been realised. I should have been happy about that: the tours, the sales, the TV, the flashbulbs. It was like 1985 all over again.

I *should* have been happy.

But was I? What do you think?

Why wasn't I satisfied?

When I was living the family life, I wanted to be a rock star, and when I was being a rock star, I wanted to be at home living the quiet life.

We rolled into Chicago just after midnight and checked into Le Méridien hotel for a few days. We had learned to 'hub' in major cities and fly in and out for gigs in the area. That way we

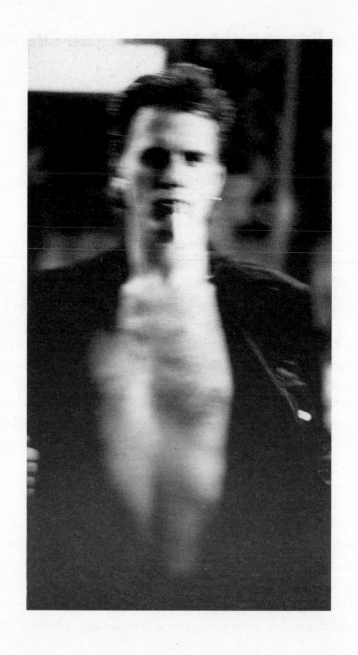

could cut down on the number of hotel rooms we had to check into and out of.

I had a huge duplex overlooking the city, which I attempted to fill with the contents of two Samsonite suitcases stuffed with clothes, books and music, the crap that keeps my identity sewn on when I'm away from home for extended periods of time. But this time it wasn't working. Opening my cases on arrival, I thought, 'I could empty both these cases out of the window right now and not give a shit. I don't care about one thing in either of these cases.'

So I guess I wasn't in the best place, overall.

The following day, Allen Kovac and his brother Lewis flew in for a meeting. It was ugly. We were all exhausted and ready to go home. Nick was furious. Simon was missing his family. However, Allen and Lewis still managed to leave the meeting having gotten their agenda passed; we agreed to extend the tour dates still further.

Warren was a full-on member of the band as regards songwriting and imaging – his parents featured on the cover of *The Wedding Album* next to mine – but band business was still decided by Nick, Simon and me. We have never let a non-founding member into that area of concern. That may change in the future, but it hasn't happened yet; there is just too much history.

I watched Allen and Lewis run off to the lift, thinking, 'They're going back to LA, back to their homes and families, and here we are, out of our minds and fit to drop.'

In an angry daze, I went back to my room and smoked a joint, as if I wasn't paranoid enough already.

And I called Amanda. Big mistake. She wasn't going to be able to fix this. Damn the phone.

I called Simon, who was in the room next to mine, and asked him if we could talk. He came by right away.

I poured my heart out.

'I've got to go home, Charlie. My family is falling apart. I'm not going to make it.'

We stared at the walls for a while. Empathetically. We were both depressed.

'Why don't we take a walk, Johnny?'

We walked down to Lake Shore Drive and along the 'concrete beach' as Chicagoans call it, that circles the lake, where two years ago we had been inspired by the idea that became 'The Edge of America', the song that closed the *Big Thing* album.

This time we spoke silently, as men often do.

Everywhere I looked, I saw coded messages, signifiers, on billboards and licence plates. A green jeep drove past us as we stood on the sidewalk waiting to cross. It was our family's jeep. What was it doing here?

Fuck, I was losing it.

I was at the epicentre of my own emotional drama.

The following morning, I got an extraordinary call from our tour manager. Simon had gotten sick and could not sing. The next few weeks of dates were to be cancelled, and we were all going home that very day.

65 A Million Tiny Seductions

Although I had often been extremely depressed and despondent because of the state I had got myself into as a result of not being able to control my intake of drugs and alcohol, I wasn't ready to accept that many of my 'problems' were intimately tied up with mood-altering substances.

I just thought the problem was that I was so fucking unhappy.

I was difficult to be around. I felt hemmed in. I would go from one situation to another, but whether I was in the studio or at home with Amanda, wherever I was, I just didn't want to be *there*.

And I should have been happy.

What was the matter with me? I'd actually bang my head against the wall and moan, like the character in the Monty Python series, '*What is wrong with me? Why is it all so difficult?*'

No life skills.

I must have missed those classes at school.

I did have my daughter, and I was determined that she would

be a music lover, so I was particular about her musical diet. I could sing Bob Marley songs to her any time of day, and our one-hour 'Kool and the Gang Dance Class' was compulsory. But when I look at photographs of myself from that time, I see someone who is clearly in pain, is suffering from some undiagnosed disease of the heart.

The struggle was not with little Atlanta. She was a funky play-mate who you could take anywhere, but her mother and I both had issues and they were rearing their heads, unresolved. Surrendering to family life was not easy for either of us.

I found myself resenting those who looked from the outside to have a regular family life. I would pull up at traffic lights and look into the SUV stopped next to me, look at the family on their way to a ball game, kids and parents having fun together, and I would hate them.

I was angry because I just couldn't seem to make that side of my life work. Simon had been diligent about his family. There was never any doubt in his mind about the importance of having a strong family structure, and his three daughters were thriving. He had a family that loved spending time in each other's company.

Yes, I now had my own daughter, but her mother and I could not settle down. Once the novelty of playing house had worn off, we both reverted to our old ways, looking outward in very dif-ferent directions. Our needs could not have been more different.

Amanda was a decade younger than I, and she was just getting into the big schmooze, the million tiny seductions required to make her famous. When I came home, I wanted to chill, and she would be off out. We were not on the same planet. All we had in common was Atlanta.

What was the price of a normal life? Another deal with the devil? Maybe it was time to start talking to the guy in white. God?

In 1994, with the strain on our marriage becoming increasingly apparent, we started going to therapy.

The sessions lasted an hour, three or four times a week. One of us would go in first while the other waited outside in the car. At the end of the week, we would do a session together and see if what either of us had learned independently could be applied to practical use as a couple. I was not sure we were really getting anywhere, but at least we were still together.

I had done therapy before and was a pretty competent manipulator of therapists. There was power and comfort in knowing I could get my way. But this time it was different, and pretty soon, it felt like my psyche was being held together by these sessions.

I had to go to London to work with the band, and I said to the therapist, 'You have got to find me somebody. I need somebody in London that I can talk to when I get off the plane.' I didn't think I could go straight to see the band. I needed somebody in between.

So I got off the plane at Heathrow and went directly to visit a therapist in Earls Court. I talked to him for twenty minutes or so, until he stopped me and said, 'I am not the person for you. Go and talk to Lois Evans at the healing centre in St John's Wood.'

So I called her and gave her my sixty-second pitch: 'I need to see you. I need this, I need that, me, me, me.'

'I think I can fit you in – how about seven thirty?'

I went up there and fed her the same old lines I'd been giving every therapist I had ever seen: 'Poor me.'

And she saw right through it. I'll never forget what she said.

'If you can get sober, you could really be somebody.'

It was the most extraordinary line, and it made absolutely perfect sense.

After everything that had happened in the eighties, part of me

wanted to say, 'But don't you know – do you know who I *am?*'
But another part of me knew exactly what she meant.

She said, 'John, you need to get sober. If I am going to treat
you, I need you to be clear and consistent. And while you are
drinking and taking drugs, however frequently or infrequently, I
cannot get at you. I recommend you get into a thirty-day rehab.
Take the time off work, you can afford it. The best ones are in
America. I will give you the names and numbers of a few places
and I suggest you go and call them right now, because if you can
get sober, then we can get at what the trouble is.'

I made a call to the Sierra Tucson centre in Arizona, and they
said, 'We will send you a package right away.'

Then I called Nick.

'I just met this woman and she thinks I need to go into treatment. She thinks I am one of those Betty Ford types.'

'No. Really? Do you think you have got that kind of a problem?'

'I don't know, man.'

A few days later, the package arrived.

It was a video.

I put it on. Images of people holding hands and saying prayers
filled the screen.

I couldn't believe it. What the fuck was this? For a day or two
I had been relieved, buoyed by the thought that maybe there was
a solution, but this couldn't possibly be it.

What did I need with holding the hands of strangers reciting
prayers? I had done that back at St Jude's. I needed something
more specialised, more sophisticated.

A few nights later, I went out with my brother-in-law Bruiser.
We went to the Coliseum to see *Tristan and Isolde*. It was long and
difficult, and when we got out I was thirsty. We went for sushi and

one drink, and the next thing I know, we are at the Chelsea Arts Club ordering shots at the bar. Then I'm back in the West End, alone, after midnight, scoring blow, and then, later – much later – at some stranger's house, telling people that the key to success lay in the Buzzcocks, talking a load of fucking nonsense.

So confused. Don't know the way forward, don't know the way back.

Some impulse got me on my feet and out of the door. It was way past dawn. I had no idea where I was.

I needed to piss, I needed to shit, I needed to vomit. I needed a cab. Was it a cab or was it a winged horse? Whatever it was, it got me back to Ossington Street. It must have been ten in the morning. Amanda answered the door with Atlanta at her side. Atlanta had so much to tell me. Important news about bears and horses.

I couldn't tune in to her frequency. I was letting everybody down. Badly.

There was a wisp of a thought that maybe Sierra Tucson *was* the way to go.

I had a day of work ahead of me, but that wasn't going to happen. Another dead day ahead.

Amanda took control. She told me to go to bed. She would call the office.

66 Tucson

When I woke up, it was already evening, and I just *knew.* I was going to have to go through with the rehab. Call the damn place, pay the price, and deal with the praying and hand-holding when I got there.

Rehab. What a loser. Was there a more blatant, obvious acknowledgement that I had totally fucked up my life? As I lay in bed with last night's booze and drugs oozing out of my pores, I was haunted by the familiar wave of regrets: the opportunities I had wasted in the eighties, the bad choices I had made, over and over, again and again. What an asshole I was! 'I could have been a contender.'

Et cetera ad infinitum.

Was it really alcohol and drugs that had washed me up on this beach of disillusionment at the age of thirty-three? Disillusioned is exactly what I was. The illusions had all long gone.

I had been in London for less than a month. Perhaps two or

three weeks had passed since I had been told I could 'really be someone' if I could stop using drink and drugs.

I flew out to LA on the Thursday, giving myself a long weekend to acclimatise, maybe one last party, and booked myself a flight to Tucson for the Monday morning. Atlanta and Amanda stayed on in London, Atlanta assuming Daddy was off to work again. The band supported this trip of mine into the unknown.

Monday morning, I was driven to the airport by my assistant, Bev Raff, who had been working for me for some months. I was in turmoil, didn't want to go, trying to talk myself out of it, looking for an escape route. Out loud I said, 'This is pointless, ridiculous. It's just going to be a waste of time.'

Thank God she wasn't a yes-man. If it had been an episode of *Entourage*, Bev would have said, 'You're right, JT, fuck it. Let's go to Vegas instead!' But she didn't; she kept on driving. After a moment or two, she said, 'You never know, John, you might make some new friends.'

'Fuck you!'

LAX loomed like prison gates. There was no turning around. The rehab centre was several miles outside the city of Tucson, set deep in the heart of nowhere. Hot. Dry. The facility building looked a little like a seventies motel, the rooms set around a swimming pool area. I had stayed in worse.

Except if you needed to leave this place, you had a long, hard walk back to civilisation. I suppose you could have arranged to have your wife meet you outside the gates with the getaway car, like a prison break, but as far as I could tell, contact with the outside world was to be extremely limited.

On arrival, I was processed by the duty doctor. I signed the papers and put my life into the hands of the medics. It was an act of faith, the first faith I had in years. I didn't see it like that in the moment, though; in the moment it was terrifying. I was paranoid and filled with suspicion this might be a conspiracy – by bandmates, wife, assistant, whoever – to get me out of the way, get me sectioned, committed to an asylum. I was so in my head, so sure that I had become such a useless piece of meat, that they would all be better off without me, would like to see the back of me for good, that I thought this might be my *One Flew Over the Cuckoo's Nest* moment. Lock me up, put me on meds and throw away the key.

The first two nights, they don't let you into the main house, not until they know that whatever you've got in your system is out. Sometimes it's longer. After forty-eight hours, I was given a small double room, which I shared with an Aussie guy who worked in TV. Two single beds, simple but clean.

The philosophy at this particular rehab was to empty your body of all toxins, so there were no processed sugars allowed, no processed food of any kind, no soft drinks, and no stimulants like caffeine. Cigarettes were allowed in designated outdoor areas, but I was really only ever a smoker when I had a drink in my hand or a coke rush going on.

As I was coming down to my natural state, all vulnerable and exposed, the therapists started to zap me with huge amounts of information – philosophical, biological, psychological: this is what happened and why you got into such a mess, and this is what you can do about it.

It was all about *us*, as a species, but it was also very much about *me*. Apparently some of us are more likely to succumb to addiction than others.

I was one of those in the 'more likely' category.

Why else would I be here?

I was introduced to a new idea in rehab: that it wasn't

necessarily my fault that I had not been able to control my drink and drug use, that I had something not dissimilar to having a defective gene that was unable to process alcohol and drugs in the way that others could.

I had never talked about my drug and alcohol problems with the guys, and certainly not with my parents. It's not the English way, and I had way too much shame about it. But here it was talked about all the time; it was all anyone talked about! I took to rehab, to the work and the analysing, and to the psychology.

It was unavoidable that I would be somewhat of a celebrity. There were too many videos on MTV for me to be incognito. Everyone knew who I was, eventually. But what could I do? Grow a moustache?

I wasn't given any special treatment, though. I was just another addict among addicts. After all the time I had spent in isolation, absorbed by my uniqueness, I liked the feeling of camaraderie there, the problem-sharing.

Not everyone had the same enthusiasm as me. A lot of them were there because the boss had ordered them to do something about their drug use if they wanted to keep their jobs, or their wives had said something similar about the marriage, or a parent had told the off-the-rails offspring, 'You won't get another penny out of your mum and me if you don't get a hold of yourself and stop drinking.'

I had always thought my problems were down to the bad choices I had made and because I had been a stupid, bad person. The idea that this might not be so was a revelation. Rehab was not judgemental. I was told, essentially, that I belonged to the branch of Homo sapiens that could not process alcohol properly, which meant that all that lack of control had not been my fault.

It was no one's fault.

One unexpected benefit that would come from accepting that I had a disease I had been born with would be the dissipation of all blame, towards everyone and everything – myself included. That would in turn point me in the direction of love, learning to love myself and those around me in a way I had not ever been able to do before, nor had I thought it would ever be possible.

Unfortunately, that doesn't mean you stop apportioning blame overnight.

And who are you going to blame when you feel like shit and your life is falling apart around you? Someone who is very close to you, someone you have at one time loved very much and who most likely loves you right back. When you are angry and lash out, it's those closest that get sideswiped.

I expressed a lot of anger towards my parents. They were at the top of my blame list. Recently, I had gotten quite mean with them. We had stopped having conversations, per se; I just punished them any chance I got, wanting them to know how much pain I was in and how I was struggling at the game of life. The poor things, they just could not understand where I was coming from but, then again, neither could I. Not until now.

Third week at rehab was family week, and the patients were all encouraged to invite their most intimate and significant family members for a week of fun, games and inward-looking group therapy that would prove to be useful and insightful to all.

I called Mum and Dad.

'4742163.'

'Hey, Dad, I'm in Arizona, at this hospital-type place. It's good, good. I'm learning a lot about myself.'

'Really, John? I'm happy to hear it. Your mother and I have been worried. Where is Atlanta?'

'At home in London. Dad, they have a family thing here; it's a week where all the relatives are invited to come and take part. Do you and Mum want to come out?'

'Oh John, I don't think so. It's a long way, isn't it? I don't think your mum and I are really up for that. Thank you, though.'

'Okay, all right. Fine.'

I hung up.

Typical.

Family week would turn out to be an extraordinarily powerful event, even without Mum and Dad. They would have most likely spent the week in a state of daze and confusion anyway, just getting over the travel, and the jet lag would have been challenging for them. This would be work I would have to do without them, but perhaps it would not be too late for them to benefit. Amanda came out with Atlanta who, at two-and-a-half, assumed she was at a resort.

Family week works because it is not just about your own family, you get to see how other families deal with their issues, and everyone takes part in everyone else's process.

Again, not very English, not at all. There were fifty or more of us in rehab at the time I was there, broken down into five groups of ten or so. Everyone in my group took part in our family therapy, and we took part in theirs. It was mind-expanding, beautiful. I wish everyone could have an experience like that, and I will be forever grateful for it.

I was ready. We saw a lot of pain, and equally, a lot of healing.

67 Day 31

After thirty days in rehab, reality TV has no interest for you. Too much real life and too many real tears, all that pain and vulnerability.

I had never been exposed to so much feeling, nor had I ever been encouraged to talk so openly about my own feelings. In rehab, I understood how easy it could be to love someone I had known only for a few days, having been exposed to their heart and soul.

Loving in a new way.

We talked a lot about honesty and authenticity, a word and a value I have since become obsessed with. It's about not acting, being who you are, being prepared to honestly present yourself to the world.

On the last day, our group therapist chose a song that she felt was representative of each person, and everybody held hands while she played this song.

Just like in the video.

For me, she chose the Foreigner song, 'I Want to Know What Love Is'. It's one of my favourite love songs of all time. My friend Mick Jones wrote it for his wife Ann, Mark Ronson's mum. Everybody was bawling by the end of that.

The people I met at rehab formed the first sober group that I had around me. I exchanged a lot of phone numbers and stayed in touch, and when I was playing dates in cities around the United States, I'd look up the guys from rehab.

But one by one, they almost all fell away. They would say, 'I don't really do those meetings any more,' 'I'm not getting anything out of it,' or, 'I think I can drink.'

But I didn't feel like that at all. I knew I couldn't drink, and I felt better. The fog, the existential fuddle, the paranoia and self-hatred that were in me when I went in, it all cleared quite quickly.

I saw being diagnosed as an alcoholic as similar to being diagnosed as a diabetic. The bad news is, you've got this disease; but the good news is that you can treat it. Just follow these instructions: stay close to a lot of other recovering alcoholics, meet up with them a few times each week, don't take the first drink, and everything will be okay.

I got that.

I came out of rehab on 15 December 1994.

Browsing through the magazine rack at Tucson airport, I noticed a cover story on Michael Douglas in *Vanity Fair*. 'Michael's Full Disclosure: Michael Douglas Confronts Addiction, Sex and Kirk's Legacy'.

Turns out Michael is an alumnus of the same rehab centre as me. And here he is talking freely about it in the pages of *Vanity Fair*.

Maybe I could have a career and stay sober.

That was a revolutionary concept. The *NME* had done a thorough job on me, programming me to believe I had to be wasted to do what I did well, but here was Michael Douglas saying something entirely different. Just because I had given up drinking and drugging didn't mean I couldn't have a public career in the entertainment business. Maybe the best was still to come. Maybe it could be even better.

Being back in LA ten days before Christmas was a shock after thirty days of meditation, group therapy and life classes. It was like hitting a crowded freeway filled with speeding cars after going out for a drive on a Sunday afternoon on an English country lane.

I hadn't gone to rehab with the intention of making my marriage work. I had already written it off. I imagined the gap between Amanda and me to be too great and our problems insurmountable. I was too used to wanting an easy way of dealing with things, and if they couldn't be dealt with easily, then I wouldn't deal with them at all.

So my marriage to Amanda never got the benefit of my sobriety, although our separation did. I moved into a one-room loft space in Venice Beach, next to Gold's Gym. I chose that neighbourhood because I had no history there, not having thrown up on any of the sidewalks or left anyone's house at dawn.

Neurotic Outsiders

Matt Sorum   Steve Jones
Duff McKagan   John Taylor

68 A Fine Bromance

You could put me on a desert island and I would form a band. I just can't help myself; *TONIGHT, AT THE PALM, IT'S JT AND FRIDAY.*

Ultimately, if I have time on my hands, I'm always going to get together with other musicians and start playing. It's still my preferred method of communication.

Spending more and more time in Los Angeles, I become close to Steve Jones, the 'Guitar Hero' of the Sex Pistols, the man responsible for the fountain of four-letter words on daytime TV that started a revolution in the UK in 1976.

Steve is really something else. He is as close as England has produced to a Chuck Berry or a Jerry Lee – 100 per cent rock and roll – and he's a comedian to boot. Max Wall, Jerry Lewis, underwear over the head, that sort of thing. Steve had been in Andy Taylor's first band out of Duran, but that was a long time ago now. Working with Steve is almost all laughter. Which comes as a surprise to people who don't know him. He puts on quite a tough-guy bravura.

Steve has been living in LA for years and he is clean, too. And he loves to play his guitar.

One day, Matt Sorum, the drummer from Guns N' Roses, called both Steve and me and said, 'You guys wanna play a few songs at this fund-raiser I am organising for Cubby Selby at the Viper Room next Monday? Three songs, maybe four?'

Why the hell not.

Matt brought Guns N' Roses bassist Duff McKagan along. The four of us together were an unusual combo, but we jelled. We played a couple of Sex Pistols songs and Bowie's 'Suffragette City'.

It was great. The audience loved it, we loved it.

Afterwards, Sal, who ran the Viper Room on behalf of owner Johnny Depp, said, 'You guys should come back, do Mondays.'

Another residency.

We needed a name. I remembered that *Guardian* article about the *NME* in the seventies. Matt and Duff didn't like 'Boy', though, they thought it was too precious, so we named the band Neurotic Outsiders. Then, each Monday we were all in town together, we would hit the stage at midnight, usually opening with 'Planet Earth', which I would sing, then blazing into 'Bodies' from *Never Mind the Bollocks*. Duff would sing 'New Rose', the Damned song that Guns N' Roses had recorded, and we would invite guests to join us onstage to add further to the chaos; Iggy Pop, Billy Idol, Brian Setzer, Simon, whoever was in town.

We even went on the road, to New York and Boston, along with Slash and Billy Idol. Those shows were some of the most exciting I have ever participated in. We started getting really good.

I had never been into playing 'cover versions', but where I was at, right now, it was fun and easy to follow Steve's driving eighth notes, playing the songs I had loved when I was a teenager. Kind of a Holiday in the Sun.

Then Guy Oseary, who ran Madonna's record label, offered us a deal, and it got a little serious.

Instead of releasing the live album we had recorded at the Viper Room (to be titled *The Story of My Life*) we chose to write all new songs. Jerry Harrison from the Talking Heads was drafted in to produce. I was happy with one song Steve and I wrote together, an introspective ballad, 'Better Way':

Set up the mission, unfurl the flag
It's time to lay roots down, take my head out of the bag
Make me a baby, take me a wife
With these things, maybe I'll be alright
There's a better way
I know there's a better way
When I need it, and I need it for sure everyday.

'Better Way' was a testament to our sober lives, and it was not the song I would have envisaged writing with the co-author of 'Pretty Vacant'.

But the Neurotics had been conceived as an antidote to the day job, not to *become* the day job. When it became a career, it lost its mojo, but along the way I learned a lot about having fun with a musical instrument in my hand. It was an important part of my re-education.

Eighteen months into a sober life, I met Gela Nash, designer and co-founder of Juicy Couture.

69 Gela

Gela with a hard G. Born in Corning, New York, daughter of Sara and 'Steady' Ed Jacobson, whose family moved every two to three years, to wherever Ed's business acumen was required. The opportunity this provided for constant reinvention is how Gela developed her eccentric sense of style and fierce independence. She told me to say that!

After graduation from Pittsburgh's prestigious Carnegie Mellon University (where Andy Warhol had held up the art department in the late forties), Gela moved to New York and got a job on Broadway, dancing her way through *Zoot Suit* with Edward James Olmos.

California had a strong allure for her.

We met at a party in the Hollywood Hills, at the house of producer Mimi Polk and her husband Richard Gitlin. Gela and I exchanged glances across the room.

'Who is that gorgeous woman?' I asked my friend Nancy,

just as Gela was asking her friend Tracy, 'Who is *he*?'

'*He* is married to *her*,' said the friend, indicating Amanda, who was also present, across the room, although we had been separated for some time now and had not arrived together.

Before I left the party Gela and I were formally introduced. I got a frisson of excitement on touching her hand. She was quite exquisite. I wanted to see her again. On the way out I chattered excitedly to my mate Cassian about her, who could not believe we had not met before.

'Oh my God,' he said. 'You two are perfect for each other,' and proceeded to give me the Gela Nash story as far as he knew it.

By the time I met G, she had been married once and given birth to two amazing kids, Travis and Zoe. And Juicy Couture was already, like, a phenomenon. When I mentioned to female friends that Gela and I were dating, they would swoon, 'Oh, I luuuurve my Juicy,' as if it was the Beatles. I would witness the California phenomenon that was Juicy replicating itself around the world.

A few days after that party, Nancy called to invite me to another party – this one at Gela's house. I would be the last to leave.

Our second date lasted seven days, by the end of which we'd become inseparable.

Don't ever stop going to parties, I tell my single, mid-life friends.

Gela was not like any woman I had ever met before. I fell deeply in love with her. And she with me.

And I really loved her for her complete lack of a musical education. It would matter not what song was on the radio; if I asked her what it was, she would pause for a few seconds before replying, 'Genesis?'

Bizarre for someone like me, who is such a music guy, but

somehow this reassured me we were together for the right reasons.

Gela is the queen of the musical malaprop. Third Eye Blind becomes Three Blind Mice, the composer of 'Mood Indigo', Duke Elliot.

She once said to Sony CEO Don Ienner; 'Now Donny, I understand you work with Bruce Springfield?'

Strange looks all around.

'Sorry, Rick Springsteen?'

I loved her even more for that.

So you can imagine Gela had little idea about Duran Duran. Back then, one of our songs could have come on the radio and she would have thought that was Genesis too.

She's a fan now, though.

I fell hard for Gela, and I liked the idea of 'blending' our families. Atlanta would become the youngest of three, Travis the eldest, and Zoe now the older sister. So now we are five, and a new quintet is born. My only wish is someone had handed me a self-help book along the lines of *What to Expect When You're Blending*, but I'm not sure it exists.

Pulling it off takes more stamina and tenacity than getting a hit record. I always thought *blend* was such a gentle word, evoking images of banana smoothies and health. I forgot that at the bottom there are those shredding blades cutting everything to pieces. It can be difficult.

In Gela's and my family, I found something that was now more important than writing another hit song, and I figured I could not do both. If I was going to lay down some new roots and make this family work, I had to stop travelling for a while.

After a year or two more of commuting back to Duran's London HQ, I began to tire of it and made the massive decision to leave the band.

I called Nick, then Simon, and finally, Warren.

They were scary calls to make, filled with existential fear. Would I disappear after leaving, would I cease to be? Would I never again get a return call from anyone in the music business? My entire adult life I had been 'John from Duran Duran'. Who would I be now?

I would be John.

I would be Dad.

I would devote myself to the Nash–Taylor family.

I started doing the PTA meetings and coaching Little League soccer.

The Neurotic Outsiders experience had given me confidence to start writing songs for myself and singing. I got my own band together, and we went up and down the California coast playing live. I spent weeks mastering how to play 'Rio' and sing it at the same time.

Once, I sat outside a Venice Beach art gallery and gave an impromptu acoustic performance. Fans sat on the sidewalk; none of them could believe what I was doing.

I had read an interview with Dave Grohl who said he formed Foo Fighters after Nirvana split because he wanted to know what *he* was capable of. I felt the same. The lines between Duran and me had become so blurred that I didn't know what I was capable of alone.

I stripped away all the artifice, the lights and the projections, even the PA system, to see if I could connect with people on the most basic level. Well, I'm still John from Duran Duran, aren't I? Always will be. There can be no rewriting of that history. But it felt honest and real. Authentic.

I went off on a tour around the States with my band, playing to audiences that were not on the scale of Duran Duran, and that's putting it mildly. I remember playing a club in Miami during a terrifying storm, to eight people.

You were there? Wow.

Eight people.

That's when you find out if you are the real thing or not. If you've got it in the blood. Anyone can walk out onstage in front of 30,000 people who all have the records and know all the words and are having a good time. But if you can walk onstage in front of eight and enjoy yourself, then maybe you've got something. I realised I could have a crappy gig in front of thousands but an amazing time in front of a few.

The size of the crowd didn't matter, because so much of performing is actually an inside job. I learned to approach every gig as the most important gig I will ever play.

Which it is.

It's a fantastic formula.

70 A Different Kind of Profound

In 1998, Mum died.

Mum's death was one of the first times I truly appreciated the gift of sobriety. I was able to be present for her last days, really be there in mind and body, for her, for myself and for my dad.

Up until Mum's passing, the most important moment in my life had been the birth of Atlanta, the one time I had seen the awakening into life of another human being. But seeing Mum die, actually expire before my eyes, that was a different kind of profound.

The doctors had been increasing the morphine supply to ease her pain, and she had not been conscious enough to acknowledge Dad or me for hours. Dad was confused; he had not seen this moment coming, not at all. Mum's illness had lasted only a few weeks, thankfully, and although she had been in and out of Selly Oak Hospital several times, Dad saw no reason why she wouldn't be out and back home again soon.

Poor man, sitting there on the edge of her bed, imploring the doctor, 'There must be something you can do?'

But as the words come out of his mouth I see Mum's eyes filling up with blood, and that, I know, is the end.

'Dad,' I say as gently as I can, 'it's over. She's gone.'

'Oh dear, oh no. Oh dear, dear me.'

He took a deep breath.

At that moment, he was the saddest man in the world.

I had a fantasy as a kid, awful to admit, especially now, that I wanted Mum to go first, because I fancied having Dad to myself, even if it was only for a short while. I was looking forward to getting to know him better, finding out more about who *he* was, and I imagined that would only be possible with Mum out of the picture.

I always thought that Dad was in possession of some extraordinary male lore, some secrets of higher purpose that he had somehow forgotten to pass on to me, or that he had been too busy or self-involved to remember, and that I had to get out of him, one way or another, before *he* died.

Mum was always such a talker, always so busy and in our faces, cooking, ironing, *do*ing, that I just couldn't get to Dad, nor he to me.

At least, that was how it seemed.

Mum gave so much of herself to me. She gave up work and her community of friends when she set up house with Dad and moved to the suburbs. After she gave birth, she devoted herself to raising me. But there was something of the hungry ghost, the little girl lost, in Mum, something that was a little needy, wanting for something.

Behind the noise and constant chatter, there was always a quiet sadness. I don't think she had any idea what it was. Mum had lain

in her mother's womb with an identical twin who had died at birth. I think Mum was still grieving that loss right up to her own death. How lucky are we of the therapy generation, oversharers perhaps, but at least it's not considered 'bad form' any more to want to discuss your most personal problems with others.

Both Mum and Dad would take all their issues with them to the grave.

Mum instilled in me a remarkable desire for recognition, and she never even knew it. She did it almost by telepathy. She certainly could not have articulated it in English.

She was a simple person living in complex times. Mum on sex and birth control: 'Be careful you don't get compromised' (her only words to me on the subject). And on plastic surgery: 'Don't go under the surgeon's knife unless it's life or death' (not worth much in Los Angeles).

Almost painfully shy, she could not bear to be the subject of attention. And she valued niceness above almost all else. My mother had not a bad bone in her body; it just was not in her nature.

She was not unhappy with her lot, and had there been any lack in her life with Jack, in later years she found great compensation in being my mum. She took pleasure in being the biggest Duran Duran fan, an experience that took her way beyond any ambition she might have ever allowed for herself.

She was the humblest of Harts.

Dad would never fully recover from the loss of Jean. His life would go on for another ten years or so in an increasing vortex of isolation. He was not the same man he had been with her alive. He had never developed much in the way of social skills and most certainly was not a joiner, having always relied on Mum to get him by, to be the social grease for them both.

He would have cancelled Christmas if it had been up to him; not that he was a miser, he just didn't like the fuss. He was a workaholic and could cope in the world of working men, but he was now long retired and all he had wanted was to be able to spend his remaining days in the company of two: Jack and his Jean.

His world would start to shrink the moment she passed away.

I got some of that father/son bonding time I had hoped for as a boy, but it was not quite what I had in mind. Our first joint project was making the arrangements for her funeral.

If Mum's death had happened ten years earlier, I would not have been able to be there for him. I would not have been able to get my head around all that pain. Instead, I would have escaped into a bottle and a gram. I was far too self-absorbed in the eighties to have been able to cope as a man and a son, and to have been there for them.

But in 1998, with a few years of clarity and consistency of feeling under my belt, I was exactly where I needed to be, where the universe wanted me. Dad had earned that, at least. I could be a strong son for him, be there for his needs. I was so glad not to have been on tour, glad not to be having to record *Top of the Pops* that week. I needed to be at my dad's side. I could only feel great gratitude at having reached such a state of mind.

Gela had come to Birmingham with me to see Mum and to say goodbye, then stayed on to support Dad and me. After the funeral we returned to Los Angeles.

I felt such deep appreciation towards her and for having her in my life. I wanted to become whole with her, I wanted her to be my wife.

We made plans to marry.

71 The Reunion of the Snake

In March, Gela and I married in Las Vegas. Travis, Zoe and Atlanta accompanied us, and Gela's sister Anita acted as witness. It wasn't an Elvis wedding; there was nothing particularly Vegas about it, but it was a short flight from home and easy to organise. Neither of us wanted anything extravagant or flash. What we really wanted was a private moment with our kids. There were five unions that afternoon.

2000. A new millennium. We all survived Y2K. What a load of nonsense that was.

Late summer, and Gela and I are enjoying a latte at Barneys top-floor restaurant in Beverly Hills, when I spot a familiar face.

'Oh my God, Gela, that's Simon over there!'

They had yet to meet. I got up from the table and slyly sidled over to my sexy ex-bandmate, surprising him with my presence.

We hugged. He was in town with Nick and Warren, playing a series of shows to support their *Pop Trash* album release. There had been one other album before that, *Medazzaland*, which I had participated in the writing of, although I had left before it was completed. *Pop Trash* was the first Duran album I had played no part in. I led him back to the table to meet Gela, who could not contain her excitement at meeting him.

Of course they clicked. Why wouldn't they?

'You have to come back to our house, Simon, come and hang out by the pool!' said Gela, who would not have accepted an answer in the negative.

He came over a few hours later.

Simon is not good at hiding his feelings, especially when they are strong; he wears his heart on his sleeve. That is one reason he is such a good lyricist. Our private reunion at my home was filled with sentiment, both of us feeling a sense of nostalgia as we traded our war stories. We were both still working hard, playing live a lot, and music was still the ruling passion in our lives. He played me *Pop Trash*. I was knocked out by the single, 'Someone Else Not Me'. It was crazy beautiful, and I felt a twinge at not being a part of it.

It was a little overwhelming. We had been so close for so long, gone through so many experiences together, yet since the day I bowed out of Duran, we had not had even a phone conversation. Is that the English way?

Perhaps. There was a lot to process.

Gela could see something in our friendship that needed further drawing out. Out of the blue, she asked Simon if he would come to New York for a party Juicy was throwing to launch their menswear line. A party I was playing at with my band.

'You guys should sing a song together!'

'Come on, Gee, that's the last thing Simon would want to do!'

'I'd love to,' Simon said.

A few days later, he and Nick came over to the house for lunch. The idea of a reunion of the original band line-up was floated over the *penne arrabbiata*. Nick had reservations, but by the time we were sipping on our espressos, we had Roger on the phone.

Roger had played with us a few years ago on the sessions for the *Thank You* album. He had played on 'Perfect Day', our version of the Lou Reed song, and 'Watching the Detectives'. He had appeared in the video for 'Perfect Day' and had spent most of the day complaining about the waiting around and time spent between takes. I wasn't sure if Roger would want this badly enough.

However, his response to our suggestion of putting the original band back together was an immediate and enthusiastic yes.

Now it was time to call Andy, and Nick, Simon, and I held our collective breath when he picked up the phone. But guess what? Andy was cool and happy to hear from us too. His response to the proposition was equally positive.

There was the question of Warren, and whether there would be a part for him to play in the reunion, but that was put off for now. As it happened, his participation didn't make sense to anyone involved, and Warren bowed gracefully out of the reunion project once it got rolling.

Simon came to New York and joined me onstage for the Juicy launch. It was ten of the best minutes I have ever had under the lights. The audience went through the roof, pandemonium breaking out all over us again. It was exhilarating. After that, there was no doubt in either of us that a band reunion was what we wanted more than anything. Whatever the effort, it would be worth it if we could create more moments like that around the world.

It was one thing to have the idea, but the execution was something else.

The Reunion of the Snake, as I like to call it, turned out to be an immensely challenging undertaking, not least because we had been out of touch with each other for so long, especially in the case of Andy and Roger. Nick and I had work to do on our relationship too, which had been damaged not inconsiderably by my decision to leave. I didn't realise quite how badly.

All of us underestimated how difficult it would be to just pick up where we had left off. *Unfinished business* was the term we used to describe our reasoning why, after so many years away from each other, we now decided to kiss and make up.

The reunion was not so much about the money as it was about the creative opportunity a reunion would afford us to prove how we always had more to say than we got a chance to, and to show that the whole 'Too Much, Too Soon' thing, all the fame and adulation and business stuff we had to deal with as young men, had actually stifled our creativity rather than furthered it.

Thinking we could just slip back into each other's lives turned out to be somewhat naïve. Nick insisted we record an album of new music before taking it on the stage.

That was not what I wanted to do. I draw my energy from the stage and wanted to give the re-formed band the injection of confidence that going out in front of live audiences, hungry to see the five of us back together, would give, before rising to the far more formidable challenge of writing new hit songs and revamping the old band sound for the modern world: post hip-hop, click-hop, DJ culture, rap rock, boy bands and electropop. Andy agreed with Nick, and the argument was won, but it would be a tall order.

Nick's idea to begin the songwriting process in Saint-Tropez helped soften the blow. We spent a week there in a rented house, no WAGs allowed, sleeping under the same roof, eating meals together, then playing through the afternoons and evenings before spending time out on the town.

It was a crash course in the pros and cons of band reunions.

By the time I got home from those sessions, I realised I was going to need every skill, every tool, every bit of clarity and courage my sobriety had given me to get through it with my sanity intact.

I'm sorry if I'm being a tease, but it's not my place to go into all the issues and problems we had. My friendships with all of my bandmates, future and past, are my highest priority. Suffice to say there had been a lot of water under the bridge, and none of us were great swimmers.

It would be almost a year later, after another half-dozen such writing sessions, three short but turbulent relationships with possible managers and dozens of meetings with A&R people, label heads and lawyers that an offer came in for us to play a series of concerts in Japan.

Specifically, the Budokan in Tokyo.

We had played the Budokan at the peak of our eighties run, when we had been showered with soft toys. There was something symbolic about us returning to the live stage at that venue, with or without an accompanying album of new music.

We had settled on a manager, Wendy Laister, whom we all respected and who had the ear of each band member. Wendy set a conference call to discuss the offer. She was in New York, I was in LA, the rest of the guys were on GMT in England.

It was do-or-die time as far as I was concerned. I had been committed to the reunion but was just about out of gas and belief. I needed some of that live love.

I took a walk and picked fistfuls of wildflowers, bringing them back to my office desk. I laid them out in a pagan offering to the gods. Said a prayer, lit a candle and waited for the call to come through.

72 Osaka Time

My prayers were answered. We were headed to Tokyo, but first, Osaka.

The night before opening night, there was so much tension in the air, so much vying for control, and I'm the worst in that area.

My stress levels were reaching upward towards an all-time high. Less than twenty-four hours to go to show time and there was still a risk this whole thing would blow up in our faces.

My recovery was under siege. I needed a drink. I could not remember being this thirsty since rehab. For the first time in years, a drink was looking really good. Necessary.

Whenever I had been out of town before, away from LA, I had found it easy to check in with other addicts and alcoholics walking the same walk as me. London, New York, Birmingham; you'd be surprised – we're everywhere.

But Osaka? Zilch. Maybe it was time to call a friend. But it was nine o'clock in Osaka, which meant it was four in the morning in Los Angeles. The phone was ringing off the hook and my head was about to explode.

There was one last call I could make.

Some of you are going to hate me for this.

I had to hit my knees, transcend human help, throw myself at the mercy of the universe. I had to ask a higher power for help.

In rehab, they told me that eventually I would need to relearn how to pray, that I would have to work on changing my ideas about God. After my Catholic upbringing, I was certain that all religion was a load of bollocks. Opium for the masses. Freedom for the weak. But I acknowledged that in my first year sober, I had gone from being a man with no faith in anyone or anything to being someone who had faith in something; a few dozen individuals at first, then some kind of a philosophical ideology.

One idea in particular had been proved to me, I felt, and that was: if I could just stay sober and not use drugs or drink booze any more, everything would turn out okay. I would be able to handle anything the universe might choose to throw at me and the ball of confusion would untangle.

A glass of sake would not be the answer tonight.

So I had been working on a new concept of God, with the intention of creating something that I would feel comfortable praying to, conversing with, *trusting*. That would have seemed heretical to the old Catholic in me, but the truth was, the old ideas had only been able to get me so far. I was a nice enough guy, who knew it was wrong to kill and to steal, but it wasn't enough to get me all the way through life successfully, and it wasn't going to be enough to get me through this night.

The God I now turned to for help was not a God who might blow me up for asking questions or having doubts, would not be a God of judgement, or use thunder and lightning as techniques of intimidation. I chose to turn to a higher power that was filled with the generosity of spirit and unconditional love that my parents always had for me and was as supportive as my family now were, as loving as my wife and as good-hearted as my bandmates.

This God was on my side, had my back and wanted the best for me.

Help take my ego out of this. Help make this a positive experience for everyone involved. Help soften the tensions between us. Help take away my fears of failure.

Next thing I know, I'm waking up from a deep, restful, much needed sleep.

Today is: Showday.

Your name is: John Fucking Taylor.

Walking out onstage that night was the best live experience in a long, long time. Fans had flown in from all points to be there. Flags and banners draped around the hall from the United States, Great Britain, Italy, Australia, Korea.

Wherever Duran Duran music is sold.

It was an amazing sight, encouraging and energising, and it was a great gift.

We still had it, and they still wanted it.

73 Learning to Survive

2003 brought the loss of two of my closest musical colleagues. First there was the sudden death of Robert Palmer at a Paris hotel in September, closely followed by that of drummer Tony Thompson, who lost his battle with cancer in November.

There would be no more music from the Power Station.

Andy Taylor had been a member of Duran Duran for the release of the reunion album, *Astronaut*, when it came out in 2004, but he was no longer in the band by November 2007 when we celebrated our next studio album, *Red Carpet Massacre*, with a run of shows at the Ethel Barrymore Theatre on Broadway.

Why did he leave? Let's not call it 'musical differences' for once; let's call it what it was: differences!

Andy's replacement was Dom Brown, a bluesman from Clapham in south London who is a player of great depth and versatility. We were lucky to find him. I value Dom's friendship highly, not least because we are happy to jam with each other for hours on end.

On the first Friday of the Broadway run, I was in New Jersey for a live drive-time interview with a local radio station. On the way back to Manhattan, I got a call from cousin Eddie back in Redditch. It must be quite late there, I thought, about eleven o'clock. Unusual to be getting a call at this hour.

'Hello, kid, it's me.'

'Hey, Ed, nice surprise to hear your voice. What's going on?'

'Well, not to worry you, but your dad's gone missing. Apparently, he left the house around lunchtime and he hasn't come back yet. You know he likes to take his little drives every day, but he's usually only gone for an hour.'

I breathed in this information.

'I've contacted the local police station and filed a missing persons report. The car was picked up on cameras in Leamington Spa about four o'clock.'

Leamington was fifty miles away from Simon Road and way off Dad's beat.

'What was he doing in Leamington, kid? Any ideas?'

'None whatsoever.'

Dad took a drive every day. Rain or shine, sleet or ice. He lived for it. It gave shape to his day. Generally, he took the same hour-long route: south down the Alcester Road, cutting across country as he would have done with Jean, both of them liking to stop at some favoured country pub – except Dad never stopped at a pub any more, he just drove around until his hour was up, then he would come home.

None of us who loved Jack were happy that he was still driving. I used to ask myself, 'Would I let him drive with Atlanta in the car?' and my answer would always be a resounding no. I wouldn't choose to be a passenger with him myself, either. Last time he had driven me to the chip shop, I had almost had a heart attack.

I had discussed this with his doctor, who told me there really was nothing we could do, so we waited, sure of some bad news to come, sooner or later.

There was no separating him from the tiny A-Class Mercedes I had bought him a few years ago. Just discussing him having to give up his driving rights at some time in the future would get him agitated. He had put so much bloody stock in car ownership over the years, and now those daily drives had become the only interaction he had with anything outside his own home.

I couldn't get him interested in moving into a retirement community either. I'd had hopes that after the initial shock of Mum's passing had faded, he might meet another lady he could spend his later years with. He was still a handsome devil, with the sweetest nature, but when Gela would tell him, 'Jack, you're a good catch!' he had no interest.

'How could anyone possibly follow Jean?' he would say whenever the subject was broached. 'She was perfection.'

Eddie promised to keep me up-to-date on any news of Dad's disappearance. I told him I would be onstage for a couple of hours later that night but was otherwise entirely reachable. I called Gela and told her, but did not mention it to the boys in the band. Throughout the performance, I had some rather horrid thoughts about what could possibly have happened to him, but I played through it.

As I walked off the stage after 'Girls on Film', our manager Wendy Laister took me aside.

'Did you know your dad had gone missing?' I did not pick up on the past tense.

'Yes, I got a call from my cousin before the show.'

'Well he's been found, and he's all right.'

'How do you know?' I asked Wendy.

'I received a call about an hour ago from a gentleman who lives in Nottingham. He and his wife had been in Manchester, and they were on their way home after midnight. As they were exiting the motorway, they saw your dad's car, zig-zagging across the road. They pulled alongside and flagged him down. The window was broken, they said, and he was freezing cold. The man said it looked as if the car had been in an accident.'

She continued, 'This man, Rob, who really is the most extraordinary Good Samaritan in all this, he and his wife took your dad to a Travelodge, which is where he is now. And all your dad kept saying to them was, "My son John, he's in Duran Duran, you know; they're playing in America." Really, that's all the sense they could get out of him. So this man, Rob, when he got home, he went online and tracked us down here and sent me an urgent email for me to call him, which is what I did.'

When Rob and his wife had flagged Dad to pull over, he was ninety miles north of his home in Birmingham, 150 miles from Leamington. We'll never know what happened, exactly – a stroke perhaps? Dad had absolutely no memory of it or, more likely, would not allow himself any memory of it.

Sadly, it only meant more pain for him. He had to give up the car now. And that would be the beginning of the end. Within a year, he stopped leaving the house altogether. He had to be forced to visit relatives, pubs and restaurants.

*

The last time I took him out for a drive and a bite to eat, we settled into a table at the Hare and Hounds, just off the Redditch Road. By now, Dad was moving very slowly, with a cane, which he despised, and conversation was stuck in a rut.

The war years. The very subject that had been so unmentionable for all of my youth was now all he could summon out of the past.

'I was lucky, not smoking. I could trade my cigarettes for an extra potato.'

He had developed a pathological hatred for full plates of food.

'How can I eat all this, John?' he fumed. 'It's so ridiculous. It's all such a waste.'

'Don't worry, Dad,' I would say. 'Just eat what you want, it's not a big deal.'

'But it is, John, it is.'

The waste was symptomatic of a world he couldn't understand any more. There was too much of everything. He would go to the local chip shop and make an order of fish and chips last three days.

When the social services finally got involved, they said to him, 'You can't eat this any more. It's not safe.'

The most important war story was the one that took, oh, only about fifty years for him to get out of his system.

'On the march, there were thousands of us, walking across Poland and then through Germany.

'So many didn't make it. I watched one after another fall at the roadside. At one point, I don't know where we were, I saw a bridge up ahead and thought to myself, "I'm going to die when I get to that bridge." I was in so much pain, you see, I just could not imagine myself making it any further. I said to myself, "They can shoot me, hit me, it doesn't matter. I'm going to fall down when I get to that bridge, and curl up and die."'

His hands were clenched in fists on the pub table as he travelled back in time.

'What happened, Dad?'

'When I got to the bridge, the pain disappeared.'

He had learned to survive.

Nice lesson, Dad, thanks.

(Dad never spoke in any more detail about exactly what happened to him in Germany – I had to find this out for myself. Dad was one of the 12,000 occupants of Stalag 344 involved in the 'Lamsdorf death march' that took place at the end of the war. They were force-marched over 500 miles during the coldest winter months of the twentieth century in Europe, with little in the way of food, clothing, shelter or medical care. Hundreds died from exhaustion and pneumonia, diphtheria, and other diseases. Some who tried to escape or could not go on were shot by guards. As the prisoners reached the Western side of Germany they ran into the advancing British and American armies. Dad was one of those lucky ones. His last PoW diary entry read, 'American troops coming up the road. Kommandant going out with white flag to hand over. Is this the end?'

It was.)

Communication with him went downhill fast. He lost patience with his hearing aid and stopped wearing it.

'Hello.'

'Hello, Dad!'

'Hello, hello, who is this?'

'It's me, Dad, John.'

'I'm sorry, but please stop calling. I cannot hear you.'

'Dad, please. It's JOHN.'

'I'm putting the phone down now. Bye.'

The guilt and concern piled on. I would call Liz and Eddie.

'He's fine. We saw him at the weekend. A little grouchy but you've got to expect that.'

'I just feel so bad.'

'Don't worry, he's got the nurses coming in three times a day now, and you've got to live your life, haven't you?'

'I'll be back in a few weeks.'

'We'll keep an eye on him 'til then, all right?'

'Yeah. All right. Thanks, guys.'

As soon as my flight touched down at Heathrow, I would get on the motorway to Birmingham, let myself in the house with the Yale key I had taken off Mum's key ring, the grooves and indentations worn smooth from fifty years of use. Closing the door behind me, I would get hit by the heat of the central heating on high and the sickly smells of medicines and disinfectants. He would be in the living room. The more time had passed, the more I would notice how his appearance had changed.

He would be as quiet as a mouse, wasting away in his easy chair, which was threatening to overwhelm him completely.

'Hello, Dad.'

'Hello, lad.' Tired, stirring, a glimpse of happiness at seeing me.

'How ya doin', Dad?' A bony hug, me holding back a tear.

'Oh. Not too bad. More importantly, how are you?'

'Good. Good.'

'And where are you staying?'

'At the house, at Wiltshire.'

'Well, don't leave it too late, lad. You don't want to get caught in the traffic.'

And that was how it would go. The memory loss drove me crazy, so I could only imagine what it was doing to him. I would try to engage him on subjects he had always loved, like cars and dogs.

'Remember the Cortina, the bronze one?'

'I don't, John, no.'

'Come on, Dad, you spent half your life working on that car.'

'I'm sorry.'

'Dad. Think about it. You had three Cortinas; the bronze was the first. It was a great car!'

'I don't remember.'

I would have to back off.

His anger was understandable, I can see that now. I thought I was helping, digging into the family photographs; sepia-toned weddings, faded christenings, bleached-out holidays.

'Here's your old dog, Bruce!' Handing him a tiny picture of the bull terrier I used to hear about all the time.

'What's this?' Peering at it over his badly fitting glasses. They had grown like the chair.

'That's Bruce, Dad. Your dog. You would talk about him all the time. You loved that dog.'

'Where was this taken?'

'In the back garden at Nan's, I reckon.'

There was no recognition.

'Oh. I don't know, John.' His voice would trail away. The loss of remembrance was more painful to him than the loss of things past.

I made a book for his Christmas present, 'Jack's Book'. I filled it with cards and photos that told his and Mum's story. His family, her family. The two of them as children, teens, young adults. Dad in the army, Mum at the Austin. Courtship, wedding, honeymoon. Moving in together. The final page was a picture of me.

On the cover I put that picture of Bruce. It was a *Jack and Jill* book, but instead of being a teaching aid to show children the names of people, places and things for the first time, this was to show an old person the names of people, places and things he had forgotten, to stimulate, to stir something up.

But it was too late. I could have filled it up with photographs from anyone's family album.

In late 2009, his elder sister Elsie passed on. Dad responded to that by going on hunger strike, and there was nothing I could do.

I could have bought him anything, taken him anywhere, got him in to see any specialist, but he was not interested. He did not want what I had to offer.

Surely, I asked him, he wanted to see his granddaughter at Christmas? What about the plans I was making for his ninetieth birthday party, which was going to be the biggest gala Simon Road had ever seen?

'John. Please. Just let me die.'

I had no answer to that. As Eddie put it, 'He just didn't want to play any more.'

I wasn't there for Dad's passing. I had gone to New York for a session with Mark Ronson and went on from there to LA, intending to stay only a few days. Gela and I were woken by the telephone, one of those early morning calls we all live in fear of.

'It's me, kid. Sorry if I woke you up.'

'It's okay, Ed.'

'He's gone, kid. Very peacefully.'

At the funeral, Simon sang 'Save a Prayer'. There wasn't a dry eye in the house.

74 Coachella, Indio, California, 17 April 2011

Behind the stage, to the side of the ramp, our band has gathered. We've stepped off the pair of golf carts that have brought us the half-mile from our dressing room in battery-powered silence. The air is warm, an electric blue. We acknowledge each other without words, using nods and smiles, backslaps and other gestures of encouragement.

Instincts surge, every other concern falls away.

Since 1981, we have released our songs on vinyl, cassette tape, CD, digital audio tape, minidisc, ringtones, mp3, streaming and download, for purchase or rental.

I've long since learned to relax and cease worrying about how the music finds its way to your ears.

Just play.

Just write.

As long as I keep those calluses on my fingertips hard and

maintain an enthusiasm for making music, I'll be happy most of the time.

The addictions are still there, and keeping them at bay requires work: therapy, physical exercise, journalling and meeting up with other addicts in recovery many times each week. It's a big commitment and not to be taken lightly.

Red Carpet Massacre was hard. We had massive problems getting the news out that we had a new album. No radio play, no MTV and no interest in writing about the band at *Rolling Stone* or the *NME*.

But by the time we released our most recent album, *All You Need Is Now*, things were different. The industry had learned to love iTunes. In December 2010, we released the album as an exclusive digital download. The album went to number 1 on almost every iTunes chart around the world. It was one of the most thrilling moments I have had in thirty years of being in the music business. I could feel excitement around the band begin to build again. I joined Facebook and Twitter. Social networking put our fans back in touch with us and put them back in touch with each other.

By the time we began the 'All You Need Is Now' tour, which tonight's performance at Coachella is a part of, excitement levels had reached fever pitch.

We have come a long way together to get to this holy place, Coachella, and a lot has changed in the last thirty years. Cell phones. Computers. SUVs. Nose-hair trimmers. Supplements. Propecia. Paperless itineraries. In-room humidifiers. Steam rooms, saunas and gyms. Pre-show massage. Twitter, Spotify and Amazon. Touring with 3,000 songs in my pocket and thirty books on an iPad. Therapy by Skype. Great coffee everywhere.

Another difference is out there, where there are just as many men as women in the audience tonight. At day's end, my job is to be a catalyst for connectivity, to help bring people closer together. Men and women, girls and boys. That's what the music has done for me.

What hasn't changed are the notes that run up and down the neck of the bass, and the feeling that hits you when one note rubs against another in a way that sets the hair up on the back of your neck, and the sound of the crowd and the feeling of adrenaline that charges through my body when I hear it, holding that four-string machine gun onstage, less than six feet away from YOU.

Simon is running through his vocal warm-ups, which we so often rib him about. Nick has a plastic cup in his left hand and is taking sips from it, now reaching his right hand upward to flash a snapshot on his camera. We all fiddle with our in-ear monitors, trying the volume, listening for interference. A photographer from *Spin* magazine wants to take a picture. We assemble reluctantly, everyone just wanting to get on with the show.

It's an outdoor festival, so tour manager Craig will not get to give his usual cue to take the house lights down. Tonight, that is one of God's jobs. And what a job of it he is doing: a glittering bauble of sunlight fights to stay above the horizon; a full moon appears, a late-coming VIP that takes a seat above the lighting gantry at eleven o'clock high. Nature presents for us a better light show than any human could ever have created.

A perfect breeze causes my Buddha scarf to flutter. All the signs are good.

We walk together up the ramp. The stage is set, the electronics are primed, the audience ready. Nick walks on first, in a black net snood borrowed from Lady Gaga. He walks across the stage and onto his riser, puts down his camera and touches the Andromeda synthesizer, from which issues forth a sample of the exact sound he used to begin our first single, 'Planet Earth', written and recorded over thirty years ago.

My heart is pounding. There is no better time than this, when I am about to take the stage and the future belongs to me. This is what the moment feels like as I walk out onto the stage one more time.

Roger's drums kick in. An eight-bar count and I'm in with him, the galloping groove that started it all for me.

Thirty thousand California kids, eyes and teeth smiling, cameras and cell phones popping, a million tiny seductions all at once.

And the music never sounded better.

Acknowledgements

Thank you Tom Sykes, who, with good humour, kept me moving forward. He held the torch steady as we ploughed through three decades of memorabilia from my parents' attic. It wasn't always pretty, but we kept laughing.

His agent, Jonathan Conway, became mine, and we have become friends.

Antonia Hodgson at Little, Brown signed the book and showed me what I could expect from the very best of editors. Jill Schwartzman in New York stepped into the breach and did the same from the American point-of-view. Thank you both for your detailed commentaries that again, kept the show moving forward.

Thanks always to Wendy Laister at Magus Entertainment, Duran's manager and mine on this deal – the best in the business who, thankfully for us all, has a degree in psychotherapy.

Patty Palazzo did a sterling job on the cover art and helped to identify the images that would best accompany the text. Kristin Burns made the cover shoot a fun event.

Patti Pirooz produced the audio-book, helping to ease me through another first, simultaneously editing the final draft.

Thanks to Gela, Atlanta, Zoe and Travis – my sweet inspirations – and of course to the guys: Nick, Simon and Roger, without whom none of you would be reading this line.

Credits

Images

Every effort has been made to contact the rights holders for the photographs used in this book. If notified, the publisher will be pleased to rectify any errors or omissions at the earliest opportunity.

Author Biography: © Kristin Burns

Black and White Photographs
Brighton, 28 July 1981: © Watal Asunama
Part 1 Analogue Youth: Author's personal collection
1 Hey Jude: Author's personal collection
2 Jack, Jean and Nigel: Author's personal collection
3 Sounds for the Suburbs: Author's personal collection
4 The Catholic Caveat: Author's personal collection
5 A Hollywood Education: Author's personal collection
6 In Between and Out of Sight: Author's personal collection
7 Junior Choice: Author's personal collection
8 My Moon Landing: Author's personal collection (Eddie Sears)

36 Down Under and Up Above: Author's personal collection

37 Incongruous on a Yacht: Still from 'Rio' video, © EMI Records

38 Theodore & Theodore: © Jeffery Thomas

39 Coffin Sex: © Denis O'Regan

40 Jacobean: © Robert Hayes

41 Year of the Geographic: © Denis O'Regan

42 A Caribbean Air: © Tom Sheehan

43 Resentments Under Construction: © Popperfoto/Getty Images

44 Unlimited Latitude: © Paul Edmond

45 Anticlimax to Reflex: © Denis O'Regan

46 Exploitation Time: Author's personal collection

47 The Remix: © Denis O'Regan

48 Megalomania at the Wheel: © Denis O'Regan

49 Shelter and Control on West 53rd: Archival

50 Nouveau Nous: © Getty Images (Bernard Edwards)

51 Guilt Edge: © Denis O'Regan

52 The Wheel World: © EMI Records

53 The Model: © Virginia Liberatore

54 Burn Out: © Ken Regan

55 Is This the End My Friend?: © Ken Regan

Part 3 Digital Truth: © Virginia Liberatore

56 Dead Day Ahead: Archival

57 In the Dark: © Virginia Liberatore

58 Notorious: © Denis O'Regan

59 Surfing Apoplectic: © Virginia Liberatore

60 Chasing the Wave: © Denis O'Regan

61 Tabloid Fodder: ©Teajay Smith (fan photo from a Duran Duran fanzine, circa 1989)

62 Wedding Spaghetti: © Bob Carlos Clarke

Colour Photographs

Page 11 Top: © Denis O'Regan; middle: © EMI Records; bottom: © Denis O'Regan

Page 12 Top left: © Nina Rich; top right: © Sofia Coppola; bottom: author's personal collection

Page 13 All images from the author's personal collection

Page 14 Top and bottom left: © Wendy Laister; bottom right: © Patty Palazzo

Page 15 Top left and top right: author's personal collection; bottom left: © Roger Deckker; bottom right: © Kristin Burns

Page 16 © Wendy Laister

Music Credits

'Better Way': John Taylor and Steve Jones
© 1996, Reproduced by Permission of A Thousand Miles Long Music Inc. and Lips Is A Penny (PRS). All Rights Administered by Sony/ATV Music Publishing LLC, 8 Music Square West, Nashville, TN 37203 and Magus Entertainment 40 Wooster Street, New York, NY 10013.

'Communication': Andy Taylor, Derek Bramble, John Taylor and Robert Palmer
© 1985, Reproduced by Permission of Parchi Music, Gloucester Place Music Limited (PRS) and Bungalow Music (ASCAP). All Rights Administered by EMI Music Publishing Ltd, London W8 5SW and Warner Chappell Music Inc.

'Girl Panic': Simon Le Bon, Nick Rhodes, Roger Taylor, John Taylor, Mark Ronson and Dom Brown
© 2010, Reproduced by Permission of Skin Divers (ASCAP). All Rights Administered by BMG Rights Management (US)

LLC, EMI Music Publishing Ltd, London W8 5SW and
Perfect Songs Ltd.

'Night Boat': Roger Taylor, John Taylor, Andy Taylor, Simon
Le Bon and Nick Rhodes
© 1981, Reproduced by Permission of Gloucester Place Music
Limited (PRS). All Rights Administered by EMI Music
Publishing Ltd, London W8 5SW.

'Ordinary World': John Taylor, Simon Le Bon, Nick Rhodes,
and Warren Cuccurrullo
© 1993, Reproduced by Permission of Skintrade Music Ltd
(PRS). All Rights Administered by BMG Rights Management
(US) LLC.

'Rio': Roger Taylor, John Taylor, Andy Taylor, Simon Le Bon
and Nick Rhodes
© 1982, Reproduced by Permission of Gloucester Place Music
Limited (PRS). All Rights Administered by EMI Music
Publishing Ltd, London W8 5SW.

'Skin Trade': John Taylor, Simon Le Bon and Nick Rhodes
© 1986, Reproduced by Permission of Skintrade Music Ltd
(PRS). All Rights Administered by BMG Rights Management
(US) LLC.

'Sound Of Thunder': Roger Taylor, John Taylor, Andy Taylor,
Simon Le Bon and Nick Rhodes
© 1981, Reproduced by Permission of Gloucester Place Music
Limited (PRS). All Rights Administered by EMI Music
Publishing Ltd, London W8 5SW.

sphere

To buy any of our books and to find out
more about Sphere and Little, Brown, our
authors and titles, as well as events and
book clubs, visit our website

www.littlebrown.co.uk

and follow us on Twitter

**@BtweentheSheets
@LittleBrownUK**

To order any Sphere titles p & p free in the UK,
please contact our mail order supplier on:

+ 44 (0)1832 737525

Customers not based in the UK should contact
the same number for appropriate postage
and packing costs.